ROUTLEDGE LIBRARY EDITIONS: TRANSLATION

Volume 1

REDEFINING TRANSLATION

REDEFINING TRANSLATION
The Variational Approach

LANCE HEWSON AND JACKY MARTIN

LONDON AND NEW YORK

First published in 1991 by Routledge

This edition first published in 2019
by Routledge
2 Park Square, Milton Park, Abingdon, Oxon OX14 4RN

and by Routledge
711 Third Avenue, New York, NY 10017

Routledge is an imprint of the Taylor & Francis Group, an informa business

© 1991 Lance Hewson and Jacky Martin

All rights reserved. No part of this book may be reprinted or reproduced or utilised in any form or by any electronic, mechanical, or other means, now known or hereafter invented, including photocopying and recording, or in any information storage or retrieval system, without permission in writing from the publishers.

Trademark notice: Product or corporate names may be trademarks or registered trademarks, and are used only for identification and explanation without intent to infringe.

British Library Cataloguing in Publication Data
A catalogue record for this book is available from the British Library

ISBN: 978-1-138-36785-2 (Set)
ISBN: 978-0-429-42953-8 (Set) (ebk)
ISBN: 978-1-138-36687-9 (Volume 1) (hbk)
ISBN: 978-1-138-36690-9 (Volume 1) (pbk)
ISBN: 978-0-429-43005-3 (Volume 1) (ebk)

Publisher's Note
The publisher has gone to great lengths to ensure the quality of this reprint but points out that some imperfections in the original copies may be apparent.

Disclaimer
The publisher has made every effort to trace copyright holders and would welcome correspondence from those they have been unable to trace.

Redefining Translation
The Variational approach

Lance Hewson and Jacky Martin

London and New York

from JM to Wendy with admiration and love
from LH to Branka with admiration and love

First published 1991
by Routledge
11 New Fetter Lane, London EC4P 4EE

Simultaneously published in the USA and Canada
by Routledge
a division of Routledge, Chapman and Hall, Inc.
29 West 35th Street, New York, NY 10001

© 1991 Lance Hewson and Jacky Martin

Set in 10/12 pt Times by Megaron, Cardiff, Wales
Printed in Great Britain by Biddles of Guildford

All rights reserved. No part of this book may be reprinted or reproduced or utilized in any form or by any electronic, mechanical, or other means, now known or hereafter invented, including photocopying and recording, or in any information storage or retrieval system, without permission in writing from the publishers.

British Library Cataloguing in Publication Data
Hewson, Lance
   Redefining translation: the Variational approach. –
   (Linguistics translation studies)
   1. Languages. Translation
   I. Title II. Martin, Jacky III. Series
   418.02

Library of Congress Cataloging in Publication Data
Hewson, Lance
    Redefining translation: the Variational approach/Lance Hewson and Jacky Martin.
      p.   cm.
    Includes bibliographical references.
    1. Translating and interpreting. I. Martin, Jacky.
II. Title.
P306.H45   1991
418'.02—dc20   90-8451

ISBN 0-415-03787-5

Contents

	Preface	vi
	A note on the text	vii
1	**Introduction**	1
2	**The nature of translation**	14
3	**Building a theory of translation**	34
4	**Interlinguistic homologies**	58
5	**Extrapropositional relationships in homologon definition**	86
6	**The Cultural Equation**	111
7	**The Translation Operator as a Cultural Operator**	133
8	**Socio-cultural parameters and norms**	156
9	**Applications of the Variational model to translations in various fields**	184
10	**Related fields of interest**	208
11	**Conclusion**	229
	Appendix	230
	Notes	241
	Bibliography	253
	Index	258

Preface

This book attempts to present a new approach to Translation Studies. We call this the 'Variational' approach because it is based on a double movement – first generating a wide set of correlated paraphrastic possibilities in two or more languages, then going through a number of selection procedures in order to choose a final Target Text. Much of the research work presented comes out of a postgraduate seminar on Translation Studies at the University of Montpellier III (France). The two major parts of the book correspond to our main areas of research: Jacky Martin has been responsible for the first half of the book dealing with the generation of homologies; Lance Hewson for the second half, where the different parameters governing the selection procedure are examined. The final three chapters have been written by both authors.

It is customary at the beginning of a work of this kind to thank the people who have directly or indirectly helped the authors by their suggestions, remarks, comments, etc. We consequently would like to thank collectively colleagues and students alike for the many remarks made. We would like to thank in particular Sándor Hervey for his extremely penetrating and useful comments when the book was at the first-draft stage and Bertrand Boulfroy for his remarks on the working conditions of the professional translator. We would also like to thank the Fulbright Commission and the Universities of Colorado and Connecticut for the use of library resources and research facilities.

A note on the text

In order to clarify the terminology, 'Translating' will be taken to refer to the process of translation and 'Translation' to the product of the translation process, whereas 'translation' without a capital letter will be used in its common way as referring to one or the other of the preceding concepts.

Frequently used terms have been reduced to the following initials:

DC Dissimilative Competence
LC Language Culture – thus LC1 goes beyond what is called elsewhere the 'Source Language', as it necessarily brings in the indissociable pair of Language and Culture. The same applies to LC2, which replaces 'Target Language'.
SC Source Culture
SL Source Language
SR System of Representation
ST Source Text
TC Target Culture
TI Translation Initiator
TL Target Language
TO Translation Operator
TS Translation Studies
TT Translated Text

1 Introduction

Translation is an ambiguous term. It contains at the same time the idea of translation production and that of translation product. Thus, defining the general objective of this book as a reflection upon translating in relation to the production of translations seems a natural though slightly naive clarification. Yet, none of the terms employed in this declaration of intention can be said to be clear and well defined. Language, so to say, seems to be 'speaking for itself', i.e. according to people's needs and expectations. Definitions normalize our relationship to phenomena; they can in no way be said to improve our perception of them.

This working definition takes for granted three problematic notions: reflection, translating, and translation. Reflection implies an 'object' that is supposed to be reflected, and the possibility of defining and materializing the 'reflection' thereof; more crucial still is the 'perspective' that is going to be projected on the object, the position of the observer and what the finality of his or her observations is going to be. Even a cursory look at the field of Translation Studies is enough to convey the idea that objects have been as various as the representations they have been given. As to the perspectives, paradoxically in a field so directly related to empiric finalities they have been widely divergent, as if the evidence and the ubiquity of the process of translation called for a corresponding pattern of complexity.

As to the process of 'translating', it has never been made quite clear whether that word refers to the actual cognitive operations involved in the production of a Translated Text proposed as the translation of a Source Text (ST), or to some instrumental process meant to achieve the same result, or to a combination of both; and, furthermore, whether the two operations are comparable, complementary, or radically different from each other. Besides, it is not certain that this process can be studied in isolation from the cross-cultural relationships in which it is inscribed. Most of the previous approaches, in various degrees of conceptual perceptiveness, describe one activity while at the same time referring to another, treat all at the same time or resort to a unifying concept that obscures the above-mentioned distinctions.

Moreover, should the 'translating' concept be validated, there is considerable confusion in the literature regarding the extent to which it exclusively involves linguistic and semiotic manipulations or whether it should be considered as a social practice in which the linguistic component is one component among others. This fundamental issue has often been reduced to a very confused controversy between the linguists, who thought that 'translating' should not be left in the hands of the practitioners, and the translators, who tended to consider that the complexity of the act of translation disqualified the linguists' sometimes niggling distinctions. The disagreement on both sides accounts for a great deal of the simplification and also paradoxically of the over-elaboration that prevails in this field.

Finally, most perturbing and superbly ignored among the problems contained in our initial declaration is the definition of what a Translation is supposed to be. Is it an objective product assignable to a systematic process or is it an artefact, a qualitative production that should be studied in itself and for itself? Do normative, comparative, or systematic judgements apply to these productions and under what conditions? Is a Translation the end-product of the translation process or only one aspect in a cross-cultural complex involving both the ST and TT but also the translator and other parameters as well? It is even harder to determine whether the translation process aims at producing through trial and error one and only one Translation or if it gives rise to a range of potentially adequate options susceptible to be adjusted to Target Culture (TC) specifications.

When one looks at the recent developments in Translation Studies, the general impression is that these questions have either been ignored or syncretically treated. The answers are widely diverging or frustratingly empirical. Theoretical reflection appears plethoric, repetitive, and generally unproductive. Besides, it is more than probable that the ever-increasing mass of translations actually produced is no longer affected by, and exceeds in its exigencies, the vastly artificial confines of Translation Studies. To crown it all, a certain commercial success has been extracted from the general confusion by those who tout automatic-translation systems or machines. Are there any specific reasons for this confusion and for the breach between theory and practice?

Among the most determining factors, we should cite the fact that all the studies devoted to translation seem to have been affected by the extent and the complexity of the field that they are supposed to cover. The translation process involves at least two Language Cultures (LCs), a variety of domains of definition and the problematic intervention of a translator. The general tendency has been to annex this sprawling field of enquiry to already well-established sciences such as semiotics and especially linguistics; or, alternatively, to reformulate this problematic question in terms of a cover-all concept such as hermeneutics or functionalism. It is not surprising consequently that those concerned with the actual process have failed to recognize the activity they were practising and so continued to formulate problems from the workplace with as little theoretical distance as possible but also with the greatest measure of expediency.

Another reason can be traced to the ineradicable parasitic effect of ideological images that obtrude between translation itself and our perception of the phenomena involved. Although the same is true of the generality of cultural representations – systematic sciences among them – it seems particularly reinforced when it comes to representing meaning-producing or -reproducing functions, translation among them. Before proceeding to the in-depth analysis of the 'ideological bias' (see Chapter 2), it is necessary at this stage to mention its distorting influence on the definition of some of the systems that we are going to survey. The debate on translation issues has very often been limited to a polemic between ideological stances rather than to a clarification of problems and an assessment of solutions. We do not pretend to eliminate parasitic preconceptions completely – this would be a contradiction of our theoretical basis – we only attempt to control and correct some of their perverse effects.

In addition, some of the confusion and inconsistency that one comes up against is perfectly justifiable when one considers the variety of objectives which have been pursued. As it happens, most of the wide-scale studies on translation have originated in one particular undertaking. Some of these studies are applicative, exploring the consequences of theoretical conceptions; others are derived from accumulated experience; others again clearly hinge on a particular task, such as Bible translating in the case of Nida and Taber (1969) for example or even rationalizing a didactic objective as in the case of Ballard (1980, 1987). When their objectives are considered, there are few systems that could actually be considered incoherent or unproductive. It is consequently difficult to come to equitable conclusions when comparing these systems.

Finally, because of the variety and the immediacy of their objectives each of these theoretical constructions is not situated at the same level of systematic explicitness. Some studies describe the objects they are dealing with in taxonomic classifications, others lay the stress on processes and strategies, others again concentrate on formal construction. They very rarely articulate these different levels of systematic knowledge into one coherent whole and so it is manifestly unfair to compare them according to the same standards of epistemological coherence.

Comparison is nevertheless the main orientation that we have assigned to this chapter, though the practical objective is noticeably different. We do not intend to be exhaustive but rather explorative. To all intents and purposes, the totality of this book would not be sufficient to cover adequately the Translation Studies field.[1] Our main interest is in discovering some of the common problems uniting all these approaches, eliminating, as far as possible, uncharacteristic or unproductive directions.

Moreover, it should be made clear that our objective will not be so much evaluative as heuristic. The presentation of the various systems will be at the same time incomplete and even biased by the search for a widely acceptable basis of exploration. In the pursuit of this objective, we shall simplify, decontextualize, or overemphasize some of the systems. The guiding principle will be whether any given proposition is conducive to the definition of a coherent field independently of its place or justification in its original context.

Finally, our exploration should not be considered as critical, but rather as integrative. We are looking for epistemological coherence, sometimes at the expense of clarity and expediency. Far from cutting ourselves off from the current literature on the subject, we hope to make the continuity manifest. Most of the notions that will be introduced can be traced to previous studies. Our sole merit, if the term can be said to apply in any way, has been to organize, clarify, and systematize these scattered conceptions into a coherent whole.

In accordance with our specific objectives, we have rather bluntly divided the systems into studies of the productive and the counterproductive types. Among the best-documented and the least productive, we have placed Mounin's study (1963), which questions the validity of our initial declaration of intention. According to Mounin's argumentation, there is a fundamental contradiction between the theoretical impossibility of translation and the everyday evidence of its ubiquity. Naturally, the contradiction had to be resolved, and Mounin rather unconvincingly attempts to reconcile theory and practice in linguistic universals. According to this conception, universals would provide a common ground between languages on which equivalences could be established. But, even if we do not take into consideration the fact that universals are far from being proven, it is clear that this common basis only contributes to making the differences between languages more glaring and the problem of their conversion even more daunting. It can scarcely be used to found a theory of translation, since it would amount to generalizing all meaningful content out of it. By contrast, Mounin's epistemological quest points to the inadequacy of the 'equivalence' concept, which it takes for granted and which needs to be reconsidered in the light of the radical incommensurability of languages and cultures.

Others, such as Pergnier (1978), do not deny the possibility of formalizing practice, or rather of the relevance of theory to practice, but think that Translation Studies do not constitute a valid field of study, since they only exist as the intersection between various existing scientific domains:

> Indeed, one can hardly doubt the existence of translation. What is rather more doubtful is its existence as a predefined field susceptible to be treated as one and only one scientific field. It is more probable that this ill-defined object belongs to several scientific approaches at once.[2]

But this conception does not take into account the well-known fact that all sciences are initially 'intersections'. They stake out their fields of exploration by encroaching upon neighbouring sciences and subverting for their own specific purposes the concepts and methods that they find therein. Intersections do not always create a field of research; yet, when these intersections cover activities which cannot be translated without important losses into the language of any of the intersecting sciences, obviously a new domain has to be accounted for.

Among the anti-theoreticians, but for different reasons, we place Cary (1985). He also considered that a global theory of translation was an impossibility because each and every type of translation should be theorized *per se*, since these translation types correspond to radically different discourses. This empiric attitude strongly emphasizes the contextual determination of translation, although it fails to give it full sociocultural treatment. Besides, in its eclecticism, it damagingly undercuts the common pool of operations that unite all these translation types.

The most evidently atheoretical approach is also the most widespread and probably the most damaging to Translation Studies. We will call it the 'practical' approach. It is as if for its exponents – mostly practitioners – theoretical reflection was considered to be not only pointless but also counterproductive. According to them,[3] translation is an art or a craft that can only be justified through practice and it is evident that for them practice does not call for justification, only reproduction. Theory might eventually contribute to disrupting a perfectly natural and spontaneous expertise based on accumulated experience. It is rather like saying that there is no more to breathing and walking than just taking a deep breath or putting your best foot forward.

Though it is easy to caricature this approach, we do not intend to minimize the practical side of translation or the importance of the individual translator's competence. On the contrary, we will make application the ultimate goal of our study and competence the working basis of our systematic construction. But, as in the case of breathing and walking, it is our conviction that the naturalness of the process should not obscure the complexity of the underlying phenomena. When these fundamental functions have to be acquired or re-educated, it is necessary to envisage some simplified but effective simulation strategy. This is the only justification we claim for our translation system, the ability to simulate and supplement practice. Besides, the practical approach – limited as it is to the practitioner's competence – is bound to be highly sensitive to cultural infiltration and irresponsible distortions – as for example in the academic practice of translation – and thus for that reason difficult to generalize.

One point is clear at the end of this first stage in our exploration: reflecting on translation processes is not only licit, it is meaningfully related to the production of translations. It appears besides, as Oseki-Dépré has shrewdly remarked, that the act of translation is never completely dissociated from some form of theoretical conception: 'Whether you like it or not, every act of translation... is already a conscious or unconscious "thought" about translation, either corresponding to an existing option or creating the option that it is setting up.'[4]

Theory and practice are the two complementary aspects of the same reality. Whether one considers them, with Ladmiral (1979: 189), as formalization of practice (praxeology) or, as we intend to do, as theoretical construction opening onto practice, both aspects are bound to be treated together. They jointly constitute our field of research.

Whereas the above-mentioned approaches can be said to indicate tentative steps in the clarification of issues, other conceptions, such as the theory and method expounded by Vinay and Darbelnet (1958), are in direct contradiction with our general orientations.

If we do not take into consideration the reference to the linguistic system of Bailly or the psycho-cultural implications that Vinay and Darbelnet derive from their observations because they do not concern the objective of this survey, the main purpose of their book is to define from their translating practice a set of translation 'techniques' that they thought could be generally reproduced. This perspective is a natural extension of the empiric approach, with the notable difference that empiricists, far from generalizing their practice, rather tend to consider it unique and ineffable. In the case of Vinay and Darbelnet (1958), the existence of translation invariably points to a means, technical or otherwise, to convert an ST into a TT. The problem does not lie so much in identifying what defines ST and TT in themselves or in relation to each other but in finding a conversion strategy between the two.

If we examine one of their most widely accepted conversion strategies, the 'chassé-croisé' or cross-translation (pp. 105ff.), we discover that the same inversion between 'action' and 'modality of action' that is supposed to appear in translations into French is confusingly applied to such linguistically different categories as those commonly described as 'postpositions' and 'prepositions' in 'We jogged *back* in the short winter twilight' and 'Bleriot flew *across* the Channel'. Even if we do not take into consideration the fact that these examples are only minimally contextualized, this technique, with its weak linguistic foundation, is bound to come up against counter-examples. Should we exclude for the first sentence a translation reading: 'Nous partîmes au petit trot sur le chemin du retour' that could be justified for some specific emphasis on modality rather than on action, thus resorting to the obverse of the cross-translation; or, if Bleriot were not the famous pilot that everybody knows (a situational consideration never taken into account by Vinay and Darbelnet) but Mr Everyman, would it not be more advisable to translate this example as: 'M. Tout-le-Monde a pris l'avion pour traverser la Manche'? Would, without more contextual determination, the 'chassé-croisé' solution, 'Il franchit le fossé d'un bond' for 'He jumped over the ditch', be more probable than the process–result order in 'Il sauta par-dessus le fossé' or could not the modality ('d'un bond') be left out altogether in certain contexts? This brief enquiry into the validity of one of Vinay and Darbelnet's translation techniques points to the necessity of considering *options*, the 'chassé-croisé' and its opposite among others, rather than *obligatory* conversions.

It should be clear by now that we think that translation does not involve re-usable techniques to convert an ST into a TT but rather a variety of conversion strategies which are to be assessed in relation to the comparative requirements of LC1 and of LC2. Translation is not an *instrumental* but a *comparative* and *adjustable* process as de Beaugrande (1978: 14) has clearly indicated: 'It is inappropriate that the theory provide a set of patent solutions for every type of translation problem.

8 Redefining Translation

... The theory should rather account for the principles and strategies needed to approach these problems.'

Systematized conversion techniques of even partial validity preclude the comparison between cultural worlds. The same analysis invalidates machine translation which further systematizes the translation operation. There can be no algorithmic representation of the translation process since both input and output are variables placed in interactive positions. The reflection on translating and translation that we propose as the general objective of this book concerns the comparison between sets of meaningful translation options related to identifiable socio-cultural norms. The emphasis is on *comparison*, not on *conversion*.

If we explore the more recent studies in order to discover how this particular formulation of the translation problem has been treated, we discover a number of contributions notable for their concentration on one or several but not all of the constituent factors of the translation situation. They constitute the next epistemological stage in so far as they escape both the trap of self-explanatory praxis and the illusions of instrumental logic.

Prominent among these, Pergnier (1978) and especially Nida (1964) have worked from the evidence that socio-cultural factors are fundamental for the definition of signification, particularly in the Target Language (TL). If meaning is fundamentally culture-bound:

> No two languages exhibit identical systems of organizing symbols into meaningful expression. The basic principles of translation mean that no translation in a receptor language can be the equivalent of the model in the 'source language'. (Nida and Taber, 1969: 27)

Translation – because of the fundamental disparity it reveals between ST and TT – 'will depend in very large measure upon the purpose to be accomplished by the translation in question' (Nida and Taber, 1969: 33). In the case of Nida, the objective was Bible translation, and most of the solutions proposed are clear indicators of the crucial incidence of the 'cultural-adjustment' factor. Consequently, if we try to generalize from the socio-cultural position, we should not be thinking in terms of one single, albeit perfectible, translation for any given ST but of a potential range of translations varying according to the relevant norms induced by the LCs brought together in the act of translation. Adaptation rather than optimization of solutions should be the objective.

The ESIT school of translators[5] – Séleskovitch and Lederer among the most prominent and Delisle in his recent study (1984) have shifted the emphasis on to the 'interpretative' situation in what they sometimes refer to as the 'communicational approach'. These linguists give absolute priority to the functional equivalence established by taking into consideration all the factors contained in textual and situational contexts over the simple transcoding of the linguistic components involved in translation. An extreme formulation, based it is true on the particular case of interpretation, can be found in Séleskovitch (in Brislin, 1976: 93):

> Interpretation focuses on the ideas expressed in live utterances rather than on language itself; it strictly ignores all attempts at finding linguistic equivalents and concentrates on finding the appropriate wording to convey a given meaning at a given point in time and in a given context.

Although we feel that there is a continuity and not a complete hiatus, as communicationalists would have it, between linguistic, textual and contextual meanings, this continuity has to be established according to new modalities giving final importance to global and peripheric factors. This shift in emphasis, clearly reflected in the socio-cultural component of our approach, is a direct consequence of these new developments in Translation Studies.

Starting from a radically different conceptual background – from philosophical rather than practical evidence – one of the major breakthroughs in Translation Studies in recent years (based, it is true, on a long-established concept) has been introduced, along more or less similar lines, by Steiner (1975) and Meschonnic (1973). These two writers consider translation as a particularly consistent example of human consciousness in the process of understanding through hermeneutic exploration. Hermeneutic translation or translation as hermeneutics is the experience of the contradiction between two cultural worlds, which at the same time causes the translator to question his own preconceptions and to assimilate those which he finds to be foreign to himself. Seen from the point of view of the cultures for which the translator acts as a converting operator: 'A culture is a sequence of translations and transformations of constants' (Steiner, 1975: 426). The role of the translator is not simply that of an interpreter but that of a mediator and the consequences of his or her activity, as Meschonnic has clearly shown (1973: 305–16), are cultural changes, be they of the expansive, regressive or conservative type.

When one considers such recent studies as Guillemin-Flescher (1981) and Chuquet and Paillard (1987), which have made their main object of enquiry to account systematically for the translation processes between English and French, a new difficulty is immediately perceivable. Even though translation is now clearly considered to be a proper field of investigation, the results and the procedures utilized raise doubts as to what the object of study can legitimately be, how it is going to be approached, and under what conditions valid conclusions can be drawn about it.

Guillemin-Flescher and, with important qualifications, Chuquet and Paillard consider that translations effectively produced starting from any given ST constitute a justifiable field of research. They proceed to isolate and list a certain number of 'regularities' (recurrent translations between pairs of languages clearly to be distinguished from the conversion 'techniques' of Vinay and Darbelnet) in the translation of a set of linguistically determined problems: 'the linguist can only reflect on the way people translate, in other words on the finished product .... The translated texts evince regularities which cannot be arbitrary.'[6] For example, concerning problems of determination, Guillemin-Flescher notes that: 'clear tendencies can be observed: determination is weakly marked in French, determination marks being often vague or even absent; determination in English is strong thanks to a closely knit determination network.'[7]

These regularities in turn are supposed to represent a set of dominant functions or 'tendencies' characterizing each of the languages under consideration:

> It is not simply a question of stylistic variations but, more fundamentally, of the strategy proper to each language. It is the observance of dominant grammatical patterns at this level, even before the finer lexical or grammatical distinctions, that imparts to the translation its authentic character in the TL.[8]

Yet this approach, rigorous as it may seem to be, does not take into account the inevitable but parasitic effect produced by various parameters indissociable from the situation of translation itself and particularly what Larose calls the translator's 'médiatisation' (idiosyncratic interposition) (Larose, 1987: 217). It takes no account, for example, of what the communicationalists consider as central. Consequently, some of the regularities which are described as characteristic strategies of the TL are for the most part induced by the linguistically very specific conditions of the translation operation. They can hardly be considered as valid results proceeding from observation, since the observation basis has not been sufficiently clarified in the first place. In addition, most of the possible translation alternatives, which in the corpus of observation are not numerically significant, do not qualify as 'relevant' regularities from the point of view of translation research. Yet, it is evident that if these statistically 'deviant' translations were actually produced they must correspond to some identifiable justifications. There is no more point in excluding them from consideration than in overemphasizing the regularities. It is the whole concept, inspired by the experimental-sciences paradigm, of generalizing from corpus observations that needs to be reconsidered in Translation Studies.

The translation theoretician, in order to avoid distorting his or her object of study, should not select and exclude but should concentrate on ranges of variations and study conditions of variation in translation production. These, properly speaking, constitute his or her field of observation. He or she should consequently shift away from the heterogeneous corpus constituted by the translations actually produced and define: (1) the linguistic potentialities that any given ST gives rise to in relation to any TL, i.e. *virtual* as opposed to *actual* translations; and (2) the validating conditions for these various possibilities in the receiving sociocultural context, i.e. the conditions of *insertion* of translations rather than their *justification* in TC.

It is the virtuality of the translation process and its productions that constitute the object of Translation Studies. The actual translations, the regularities and irregularities they evince, can easily be accommodated within this general perspective.

When it comes, finally, to integrating these components of translation within a coherent system, it is necessary to examine some of the previous attempts at finding global coherence. In the majority of cases, this was achieved through reference to some already established field of research. Such was the orientation of Ljudskanov (1969) with semiotics, or the various studies considering translation as an extension of the linguistic science such as those of Catford (1965), Nida (1964), or more recently Garnier (1985), respectively relying on the structuralist, generativist, and psychomechanical systems. These approaches are inevitably reductive in so far as the translation process by far outreaches the narrow confines of the linguistic field. Some, like Meschonnic, even seem to think that the applicative stance is the sure sign of ideological saturation: 'a translation that pretends to be uniquely linguistic is a cultural translation that does not want to recognize itself as such.'[9]

Besides, even if we took for granted that the field of linguistics could be ideally extended to account for the totality of meaningful features contained in any segment of communication, it is not certain that even then the specific problems of translation would be correctly solved. As we will discover later on, in Translation Studies the linguistic question – however central its role may be – must be formulated in a specific way, with considerably less emphasis on structure and more on conditions of variability and comparability between utterances.

Consequently, the next epistemological stage should be an attempt at imparting systematicity to the definition of Translation Studies. This objective has been clearly defined by Lambert and Van Gorp (1985; 50-1): 'It *is* new, however, to stress the need to combine and connect them [all the aspects of the translation problem] systematically, and to insist on their *systematic* nature, both on the *intersystemic* and on the *intra-systemic* level.' To date, only two studies seem to meet these new criteria. Both Wilss (1982) and Toury (1985), after a rigorous and thorough investigation of the translation problems, propose an organic and systemic representation of the translation field of studies. But in each, and for different reasons, the distinction between real object and formally reconstructed object seems to have been only partially completed. Wilss's study (see p. 159, 'Diagram of Applied Translation Studies'), is mainly oriented toward application, and Toury's lays a disproportionate and hypothetically introduced emphasis on the target system: 'DTS [Descriptive Translation Studies] ... should start from the hypothesis that translations are facts of one system only: the target system' (Toury, 1985: 19).

The present study, although different in its concepts and procedures, must be considered as an attempt at continuing in the directions these two researchers have originated. We intend in the process to correct the bias that can still be felt in these recent studies, and particularly to make as clear a distinction as possible between formal representation and its applications or extensions to contiguous fields.

Since the orientations are clear and most of the fields covered by Translation Studies had already been defined, it seemed important to the co-authors of this book to achieve a complete redefinition of the translation operation itself. Besides, at this point in the reflection on Translation Studies, the most urgent necessity did not seem so much exhaustivity, or even perhaps immediate applicability, as internal coherence and external compatibility within the general context of social sciences.

We therefore chose to redefine the constitutive phenomena involved in translation in a series of systematic analyses. In Chapter 2, we try to (1) analyse and control the effects of the parasitic images induced by ideological representations; (2) resituate translation within the general framework of meaning-producing behaviours and justify its specific role in the global process of communication; and finally, (3), specify the constitutive factors of Translation.

Once the process under consideration is clearly isolated, and after considering the comparative merits of the available theoretical constructions, we intend in Chapter 3 to formulate an original body of

Introduction 13

hypothetical concepts capable of accounting for the observed phenomena. Our system will be seen to comprise two complementary fields of description whose coherence and conditions of validity will have to be demonstrated.

The next chapters will be devoted to exploring in detail the defining factors and the characteristic procedures included in each individual field: Chapters 4 and 5 will deal with interlinguistic 'homologies' or the range of potential options definable for any given ST, at the sentential, extrasentential, and textual levels. Chapters 6, 7, and 8 will analyse the various parameters involved in the socio-cultural referencing of translation options. In Chapter 9, we try to demonstrate on a choice of application texts the complementarity and the productivity of the two fields of description in a variety of textual and contextual configurations. Finally, Chapter 10 will trace some of the possible extensions of the present system to two related fields: the teaching of translation and Translation Criticism.

2 The nature of translation

We saw in Chapter 1 that some of the difficulties encountered in giving a correct definition of Translation Studies were due to the parasitic influence of ideological representations. The same holds true when one tries to determine the nature of translation itself. Scientific enquiry is normally based on the questioning of commonly held conceptions and on the definition of new ones more directly adapted to the phenomena under consideration. Yet it appears that the updating process which is the rule for expanding sciences in general cannot be applied with the same facility when reassessing social sciences.

Whereas conventional sciences create conceptual fields completely detached from the common system of representation,[1] thus explicitly invalidating all 'naive' ideas, social sciences have to construct theirs by using the cultural concepts commonly associated with their field of research. Initially, both types of sciences are based on and are determined by common experience. Everybody has some notion of, and can put forward general ideas on, what producing meaning, associating ideas, or translating texts signify. Nearly everyone also has had some experience of what thermodynamics is about when watching milk boil over, for example. But, in the case of this particular physical phenomenon, there is such a conceptual gap between the simple empiric notions of everyday life and the scientific concepts that account for it that there is hardly any risk of their ever being confused. On the other hand, the specialists in social sciences always start from rough and ready conceptions such as, in the case of Translation Studies, convertibility, equivalence, and untranslatability that already map out the field of research to be accounted for. Redefinition does not simply consist in proposing new concepts and procedures but in first eliminating the well-established conceptions and then proposing new and consequently unfamiliar ones. Systematic enquiry is obviously placed at a disadvantage since it comes up against well-rooted preconceptions and will inevitably run the risk of overelaboration in order to account for what are conceived as simple and unproblematical facts of common experience.

This particular complexity justifies the meticulousness of our approach. The process of conceptual reassessment will not be based so much on the definition of a distinctive terminological field as on the *clarification* of available conceptions and on their *verification* in connection with the basic facts of the translation experience.

Our first development (pp. 15–28) will consist in exploring and thus controlling the conceptions of translation within the cultural system. We will outline the evolution of traditional conceptions in time, underlining at each stage the specific causes and effects of their parasitic function. This historical survey will offer a better comprehension of the nature and entanglement of contemporary notions. This will lead us in turn to the reconstruction of not a 'truer' but a more consistent image based on well-defined concepts such as 'signification', 'communication', and 'linguistic expression'.

The second development (pp. 28–33) will be devoted to verifying this redefined conception in relation to empiric evidence: (1) by assimilating translation to the conversion function in language as represented by the different forms of intralinguistic paraphrasing; and (2) by emphasizing the distinctive features of the translation situation, i.e. the interlinguistic factor.

IDEOLOGICAL REPRESENTATIONS OF TRANSLATION

Ideological representations do not replace each other in an orderly process of evolution and complexification. Rather, they tend to accumulate and overlap and replicate themselves in progressively widening cycles. But, if we take a sufficiently wide-ranging historical perspective it seems, nevertheless, possible to present them in chronological order. Besides, since each form of ideological representation that we are going to survey in connection with translation corresponds to a specific function in the cultural system of representation, the chronological dimension gives a good general idea of their progressive enforcement.

1 *Myths* are the most ancient forms of representation of the constants and mutations in man's existence. In fact, the mythical stories that we are going to examine represent both aspects at the same time – some of the permanent factors involved in translation and also indications as to some of the crucial mutations in its cultural perception.

Paradoxically, the original and most persistent myth about translation is precisely that there is no justification for translation. Translation is a falling away from grace. It is something that happens to man in the process of his perverse evolution or as a consequence of his natural degradation. The original or Edenic state of man is one of optimal and unrestricted expression and intercomprehension. That blissful state places him in direct correspondence with the world around him and with the Creative Logos. There is no discontinuity or fundamental difference between conception, perception, and designation – they are merely different facets of the same reality. Translation stands in direct contradiction to that ideal state of harmonious communication; it highlights it without justifying itself in the process. However primitive and naive that conception may look with hindsight, it seems to be ever-present at the back of our conceptions of translation, whether spontaneous or systematic. In that perspective, systematic construction appears as a quasi-fantasmal attempt at recovering a long-lost coherence.

In most myths about language, the pristine harmonious situation is disrupted by man's perversity. The often quoted Tower of Babel myth, quizzical as it may seem to us, particularizes the nature of that perversity. It is not the nature of man's transgression – pride – predictable though that transgression may have been once the concept of a deity had been posited, which will be of interest for the present study; we should, rather, be attentive to the circumstances according to which the curse of speaking in several languages was inflicted upon man. The Tower of Babel builders disrupted the Edenic harmony of signification when they decided to 'make a *name*' for themselves instead of abiding by the Lord's *Word*. They also introduced bilaterality and verticality in discourse by initiating an ascendant interrogation (the unfinished, unfinishable Tower itself), thus *de facto* provoking God's descendant punitive response. The original all-pervasiveness of discourse was consequently destroyed. Thus was also inevitably instituted in the logic of the myth the process of communication and the necessity of translating.

That degenerate predicament seems to have been reflected with less damaging consequences in the Greek world picture. The Pythoness in a state of trance used to interpret the will of the gods as an answer to the perplexed questions of those who had come for consultation to the temple of Apollo. The conversion was accomplished and so the contact re-established with the realm of ultimate truths, although at the cost of explicitness. There was a price to pay for translation which sometimes resulted in the discomfiture, not to mention the death, of the questioner.

These myths and others similar in different cultures mark an important transition in the perception of man's ability to produce meaning: the original rupture with the deity or the loss of ubiquitous meaningfulness and the separation of men by language barriers.[2]

The next stage in myths describes the bridging of the communication gap between men, the necessity of overcoming differences and thus reducing the zone of strangeness that protected and enclosed protohistoric communities. This kind of regeneration seems to be represented in the biblical episode of the Pentecost, in which the Holy Ghost significantly 'descends' (thus redeeming God's curse) upon the Apostles and causes them to speak in tongues. Yet more than an indication of changed socio-economic conditions, this development seems to be the natural extension of the general process of the Redemption originating in the sacrifice of the Son.

The Oedipus myth is more appropriate to our historical perspective. Although the whole story is in some ways relevant to the particular episode we want to isolate, it is Oedipus' ability at solving enigmas that will concern us primarily. The Sphinx is a female composite monster figure, thus highly associated with strangeness as animality, femininity, and anomaly. She is a provider of enigmas or rather of one enigma. She stands guard above the plague-ridden city of Thebes, thus blocking its exit. She is wont to pose a riddle to the travellers entering and issuing from the city and dash them on a precipice if they fail to answer. The riddle consists in a charade representation of man himself. The strangeness, the danger lurking upon the city, the unresolved complexity are thus cryptically associated with man's inherent nature. The very obviousness of the riddle and the repeated absence of perspicacity on the part of the travellers points to man's constitutive inability to become aware of a new challenging reality – the necessity to outgrow the limits of the city and face the unknown that lurks beyond. Oedipus, despite or because of his ambiguous past, is able to decode the riddle and overcome the strangeness and eventually liberate the city from the 'sickness' that kept it fenced in.

The same myth, though apparently situated at a later stage in man's new discovery of the necessity of breaking through the narrow confines of the self-sufficient *polis*, can be found in the encounter between David and the Queen of Sheba. Clearly again, the myth transposes the pressure of the developing commercial enterprises of Israel in relation to southwest Arabia. Yet, the positions have been radically changed. The city represented by its king, far from being threatened from the outside is now placed in a position of power. The Queen of Sheba (with only the very slightest suspicion of devilry about her connected to femininity, foreignness and such curious features as 'hairy legs' and 'ass's hooves') attempts to trick the king of Israel but is easily defeated by his perspicacity and in due time associated by marriage to his people. This later variation on the reduction of the unknown through decoding riddles seals the end of mythical representations. The union of David and the Queen of Sheba instigates a new period in ideological representation. The necessity to account for foreignness that the myths transposed in terms of an inside/outside relationship is converted into the conflict between antithetic, though inevitably complementary, ethnic or national entities.

With the rise of organized states, myths ceased to play their uniformizing function in cultural representations. The contradictions revealed by the advent of modern times are so flagrant that they can no longer be homogenized in a discourse of plausibility. They have to be recognized and conceived as such.

2   This is the beginning of what we call *polemic ideological conceptions*, a period which spans the historical space of time between the beginning of the Middle Ages and the Renaissance. During that period two necessities seem to have governed the perception of exocentric relationships comprising difference, strangeness, and foreign idioms. On the one side, for political, religious, or economic reasons, European states experienced the necessity to discover, expand, and exchange surplus merchandise. It was then felt indispensable to adapt and convert or sufficiently downplay their own cultural values in order to make them acceptable to sometimes widely different cultures. At the same time assimilating foreign customs and practices became an ever more pressing economic necessity.

This expansive movement was thus complemented by a corresponding assimilative tendency which focalized around a few cultural and translation centres – Antioch, Constantinople and, above all, Toledo – the sum total of all the learning accumulated by the Greeks, the Arabs, and the Jews. At the dawn of the Renaissance, western culture was paradoxically confronted by the necessity to assert its overruling difference and to transform itself in contact with those it had conquered. From that period, we date the beginning of polemic representations in the discourse about translation.[3] And this state of affairs has with few historical adaptations lasted until the present time.

One of the constants of the discourse on translation has been the polemic and ambivalent nature of its pronouncements as Savory (1957: 49–50) has clearly pointed out:

The truth is that there are no universally accepted principles of translation, because the only people who are qualified to formulate them have never agreed among themselves, but have so often and for so long contradicted each other that they have bequeathed to us a volume of confused thought which must be hard to parallel in other fields of literature.

To make plain the nature of the instructions which would-be translators have received, a convenient method is to state them shortly in contrasting pairs.

And there follows a list of contradictory statements about translation. It should be added that it is the systematic listing that reveals as contradictory what is nearly always expressed in the most persuasive manner in the literature about translation. The practice of translation, as opposed to the discourse about translation, is for most of its paradoxical defenders precisely the art of resolving contradictions, as Mounin seems to imply: 'Translation like architecture or medicine . . . is or can be or should be both a science and an art.'[4] This quotation points to another way of displacing the notion of translation characteristic of the polemic stage. It consists in assimilating it to some other form of activity such as, for example, architecture or medicine or in the case of Poggioli[5] in comparing it to musical interpretation, all of these comparisons highlighting the ineffable difference of the notion under consideration. It is obvious that the two tendencies are not exclusive of each other and combine in order to produce a discourse on translation which although fascinating is scarcely usable for the purpose of systematic definition.

Polemic representation of cultural conceptions made the contradiction of the realities involved in translation bearable or, to say the least, conceivable. What could no longer be made plausible in the ingenuity of mythical texts was now either perceived as ambivalent or alternatively represented in sharply contrasted discursive positions. Sides could safely be taken in the controversy about translation without jeopardizing the whole system; and the system itself could be vindicated by showing that the division of opinions could be reconciled by resorting to a less problematic concept. In the passage from the mythic to the polemic age, the illusion of homogeneity does not disappear, it merely coexists with the perception of contradiction. Although the polemic stage has never completely disappeared from the discourse about translation, it progressively gives way after the Second World War to a more technically oriented form of discursive construction.

3 The next stage in ideological representation corresponds to *systematic constructions*, in which the emphasis is clearly placed on internal

coherence and external relevance to practical data. Such is the orientation of Vinay and Darbelnet (1958) and a few others. In the case of Vinay and Darbelnet, it is obvious that the translations actually produced by the authors were generalized into translation techniques which in turn opened onto some generalization concerning the psycho-cultural characteristics of cultures. This inductive rationalization of practice which, in one form or another, prevails in most of the 'methods', 'theories', or even 'sciences of translation' is mainly concerned, as we are going to demonstrate, with the normalization of polemic representations.

It thus illustrates another function of the system of representation. In contrast (or in alternation or combination) with the uniformization process of the mythic stage or with the ostentation of contradictions in the polemic stage, the constructivist stage provides a pseudo-justification for these contradictions. The ideological bias consists in acknowledging superficial complexity, thus recognizing contradictions as surface manifestations ('exceptions'), while at the same time reaffirming the fundamental coherence of the system.

This coherence is based on what Pêcheux and Fuchs[6] call the 'omissions' constitutive of the meaning-producing subject. They concern:

the universality of meaning allowing for some minor, epiphenomenal cultural variations;
the production of meaning as originating solely from the subject and submitted entirely to his or her agency;
the conception of language and other semiotic codes as purely instrumental to the formulation of meaning and thus dissociable first in terms of 'content' and 'meaning', second as 'thinking' and 'expression' and third as 'designation' and 'reality'.

These ideologically induced illusions constitute the fiction on which the system rests and comes to be validated in the minds of its users. They determine in turn a variety of validating 'constructions' to account for referential phenomena which range in the case of translation from universal convertibility to untranslatability with partial translatability as a middle term. All these conceptions share the common postulate that meaning is universal and that translation consists in changing the culturally distinctive form of an otherwise commonly shared content.

Other constructions replicate the second 'illusion' and consider the translating subject as the sole justification for his translations; consequently, his theory should be the rationalization of his practice. Finally, other theories systematizing the last of the system-induced illusions defend the position that translation is a mere technological operation demanding strict analysis of the manipulations involved and a systematization of translating techniques, the ultimate development of this orientation being the complete algorithmization of the translation process.

All these systematic constructions share the same orientation: they derive coherence from the system itself rather than from relevance to the phenomena they claim to represent.

It seems, as we have discovered in Chapter 1, that the three types of historically relatable ideological conceptions, far from being progressively discarded, are either alternating, combining, or conflicting in the abundant current literature on the subject. Let us examine, for example, one of the most scrupulous studies on the subject, Nida's definition of 'Dynamic [as opposed to Formal] Equivalence' (1969: 166):

> One way of defining a D-E translation is to describe it as 'the closest natural equivalent to the source-language message.' This type of definition contains three essential terms: (1) *equivalent*, which points toward the source-language message, (2) *natural*, which points toward the receptor language, and (3) *closest*, which binds the two orientations together on the basis of the highest degree of approximation.

We find that, although the formulation is extremely meticulous, we are progressing from vaguely familiar notions to more unclear determinations as the definition is broken down into its constituents. The reason lies in the initial fuzziness of the concept of 'equivalence' which in turn spreads on to the notion of what 'natural' or 'proximity' can mean when it comes to comparing languages in cross-linguistic productions.

Does thinking about translation inevitably mean relaying or amalgamating ideological preconceptions? Is formalization impossible beyond the mere reshuffling of surface appearances? Are we necessarily manipulating representations in order to fit and justify our practice? Since, apparently, there is no way we can abstract ourselves from the world of representation, we can at least stabilize representations, prevent them from shading off one into the other, thus enclosing formalization in paralogical circles. The main objective of the historical perspective is to make us recognize the succession, combination, and rationale of representations. Our next step consists in discovering the socio-historical factors which determined them and which to a large extent continue to be prevalent.

Three sets of factors have combined to determine the representations in the forms and the development they have gone through. Economic, political, and religious determinations constitute the obvious prime factor. Although it is somewhat outside the purpose of the present study to go into details about them, it appears that a general socio-cultural objective seems to have presided at the definition of each of the stages in Translation representation. The mythical stage corresponds to the search for cohesion and justification in protohistoric communities; the polemic stage provides the ambivalence necessary to account for the successes and setbacks of a transforming society; and, finally, the constructivist stage tallies with the contemporary obsession with scientific rationalization and efficiency. The next predictable stage might involve, in the wake of cultural hegemony, a disappearance of the necessity of translation and a return to myths such as that of the 'global village'.

So far, translation does not differ in any way from all the other conceptions that can be formed about 'reality'. The cultural system at one and the same time *projects* reality for the purposes of the social subjects and *justifies* it in the social system. The contradiction of this double process defines cultural representations as both reflections and distortions. The 'images' of translation that we have reviewed so far share these two characteristics: they simulate and dissimulate translation.

To make things even more difficult to unravel, the system has also to supply an image of itself and of the instruments of signification as perceived by the social subject. This second-degree representation accounts for an increase in dissimulation. In the case of meaning-producing activities such as translation, the general skewing of reality may reach its ultimate stage – complete inversion or occultation.

Besides, a certain number of images specific to translation further contribute to confuse representations. Translation is evidently concerned with cross-cultural communication. Conceptions had to be constructed for individuals in society to be able to conceive of what lay outside the confines of their cultural world. To a large extent, this amounts to a contradictory proposition, since the system can only contribute to justifying itself and its referential basis. All the conceptions that have been historically devised to think of the foreign, alien, or strange in or outside societies are a direct reflection of the structures and conflicts prevailing within those communities. We saw for example that, in the tales of Oedipus and David, images of foreignness (the enigmatic, monstrous, and female common to both the Sphinx and the Queen of Sheba) corresponded to different stages in historical determination and to a shift in power relationships.

All these motivations contribute to making the discourse on translation one of the most complex and tangled formations in the history of culture. They account at the same time for the overabundance, the confusion, and the polemic nature of the literature on the subject. At this point, it would be pretentious and illusory to be simply moving from false to 'true' images of translation. Our aim is rather

to place the terms of our conceptual representation of translation in the cultural system (see pp. 23–8);
to explore the basic constituents of the act of translating (see pp. 28–33);
to propose a theory based on explicit concepts capable of accounting for and facilitating the process of translation (see Chapter 3).

THE CONCEPTUAL DEFINITION OF TRANSLATION

Since, in the case of translation, the process of epistemological clarification does not consist so much in discarding old concepts and proposing new ones but in redefining logical connections between existing notions, we intend to isolate:

the role of translation in the *production of meaning*;
its incidence in *communication*;
and finally, its specific function in *language*.

Our first objective will be to synthesize all the notions utilized but left unorganized in our preceding development. Our only excuse for such tardiness is that in order to understand the working of the System of Representation (SR), the notions and conceptions it generates have to be recognized and identified *before* being categorized as such. When one deals with our perception of the world, it is easier to admit the working of the cultural system in principle than to relativize its effects and the hold it exerts upon our thinking processes.

Following Eco's conception (1972), we posit a System of Representation (SR) through which men in any given society accede to the 'reality' of the world around them, of their relations with others, and of their own subjectivity. An adequate analogy would be the various visual projections that cartographers have given of the globe. Since, because of our particular relation to the world, we cannot command a global vision of the universe, a representation has to be constructed mediating our perception of reality and indeed constituting, as far as we are concerned, reality. That representation inevitably proceeds from a particular bias since it reflects the preoccupations of men in connection with world maps. If the main emphasis is, as is often the case, Europe or the New Continent, that particular segment of the map will be highlighted to the detriment of polar regions or the Third World, for example. Each of the geographical zones' individual shapes and sizes and their respective relationships are dictated by the particular angle adopted in the perspective.

In the same manner, all the values within the SR and their respective determination are fixed by the pragmatic objectives linked to socio-historical determinations. The coherence of the whole is meant to justify the social structure which underlies it. There are obvious differences: these objectives are evidently never tied to the decision of one man as in the case of maps; they result from the collective definition of social orientations. Most important of all, at any given time, a multiplicity of representations can be found to correspond to the projection of the same socio-political complex. There can be several and sometimes conflicting 'maps' of the same reality corresponding to the same socio-economic basis.

The production of meaning can be compared to all the possible routes that can be plotted taking the world map for a basis. In the same way, no meaning can be produced, in essence or substance, without resorting to the SR. This does not detract from the fact that routes like human enterprises are effectively conducted in reality, it means that no conception of them can be attained without the necessary mediation of the SR.

The SR is a projection of the social structures and more fundamentally of the needs and objectives of men in their relation with their environment. Conversely, the SR only exists and persists through the practice of men utilizing the system for the pursuit of their own interests – as an *axiological* system – or for the exploration of the world – as a *referential* system. These two distinct ways of resorting to the system are not exclusive of each other.

The SR is made up of a multiplicity of correlated conceptual fields which reflect the variety of men's individual, collective or institutional 'appropriations'[7] of the system. Each conceptual field is a construction of correlated referential and axiological values. Thus the highly charged lexical unit 'money' represents a variety of referents which are more or less tangible according to the perception of the man in the street or the economist; it can be associated to a wide set of axiological values ranging from the highly desirable to the most detestable. If we cut across the complexity of the conceptual networks, it is possible to imagine an identical referent being designated by several terms: thus, what is a crime or just an offence for some will appear as true action for others according to differences in axiological codes. Conversely, a same designation can correspond to different values or to a multiplicity of referents, as for example, in connection with the recent political evolution in the Eastern bloc countries, the use of the term 'conservative' to designate Communist Party members.

Multivalence in designation corresponds to the structural complexity of the system. It also accounts for the dynamic principle within the SR: people, individually or collectively, will attempt either to make uniform the system by excluding or integrating diverging subsets, to accentuate its divergences or further to complexify the existing systems of values.

Translation, in the extended sense of the word, has a fundamental role to play within the SR and between SRs. It insures the *conversion* between the several axiological or referential systems. Thus, for example, a patient will refer to a disease identified as nephritis by the medical profession as kidney disease, and a police officer will equally convert a 'moment's inattention at the wheel' into a punishable offence; similarly, a case of ecological thinning down of species will be considered by others as an aggravated example of cruelty to animals.

All these differences in values have to be converted. Translation regulates socio-cultural relationships and mediates ideological confrontations within a given community. It provides the necessary social interface between similar and dissimilar conceptions, failing which any cultural group would fall apart.

It logically follows from our description of socio-economically determined SRs that we place our reflection within the general framework of the Sapir–Whorf hypothesis. Language cultures[8] proceeding from different bases are thus fundamentally different and incommensurable with each other. Intercultural translation consists in taking into account and expressing in meaningful productions the fundamental difference between language cultures, as Nemer has shown:

> There would be some form of idealism in thinking that Translation could remain poised on the confines between linguistico-cultural systems, in a neutral space miraculously freed by the double backward surge of irreducible specificities. On the contrary, it is undoubtedly made up from the disjunction between these systems, evidencing, rather than identities, the deep ferment of difference.[9]

Translation is the exploration of an unbridgeable gap and of a tension between cultures, variable according to the historical time and the socio-economic motivations of the assessment. Its function is to develop cross-cultural constructions while at the same time bridging and underlining the differences. Intracultural translation has been presented as an operator of coherence; intercultural translation is the indispensable operator of *differentiation*.

Signification as a combined process of cultural reference and adaptation is never produced in the abstract. It is indissociably linked and conditioned by *communication* as the mediating structure between individuals and their environment.

This notion in turn needs to be briefly reassessed. We will exclude radical theories denying validity to the concept of communication, because they advocate either complete incommunicability or complete residue-free communicability. They equally invalidate the very principle of translation.

More acceptable for translation purposes is the theory of 'partial communication' which seems to stand explicitly or implicitly in the background of most contemporary studies about translation. In this perspective, communication can never pretend to transfer the totality of what has been originally imparted in the message. The division between communicable and incommunicable, though various in extent and nature, is generally conceived of in terms of the opposition between the idiosyncratic and the universal in signification. Intercultural translation, modelled on the same pattern, consequently, will principally give priority to content over form, matter over style, universals over cultural differences.

This conception is flawed because it is modelled on the economic pattern regulating the exchange of commodities. The information content and its transfer are solely considered without reference to the participants in the transaction. But it seems clear, in the wake of recent linguistic and philosophical studies, and particularly the work of F. Jacques (1985), that our conception of communication should be reoriented in this direction. There is no fundamental flaw in communication causing information loss or entropy. The message does not have to be oriented from a hypothetical origin to a still more problematic destination. It results from the interlocutory production of those involved in the act of communication and has to be interpreted as such. Communication should be conceived as 'co-significance' or the jointly-constructed, mutually negotiated production of signification: 'our relation to meaning is bound up with alterity . . . . Either we signify with the others or it is not meaning that we are producing.'[10]

This notion of communication as co-signification is invaluable to understanding intracultural conversion. It is evident in this perspective that translation *lato sensu* constitutes one of the most powerful means of negotiation between communication partners. The negotiated result of their encounter is a compromise between expression and exchange.

It is less clear in what way co-signification can be extended to intercultural translation. Since translation always applies to an already fully realized situation of communication in LC1, it is important to underline the meta-communicational status of the translator. He stands as the extraneous third party to the initial communication on the one side and his role is to establish a hypothetical situation of communication in the LC2 on the other. In both these positions, his role is both accessory and crucial to the communication process. Instead of co-defining signification with his interlocutor, he will *mediate* between two situations; that is to say, he will take it upon himself to define the norms and options that need to be established between two Language Cultures.

Finally, communication – be it intra- or interlingual – is overwhelmingly, though not exclusively, conducted through *language*. We intend to depart from the conventional conceptions of language as a 'projection of reality' or 'expression of man's thought', both of which contradict the notion of co-significance analysed above. The most evident proof of their invalidity is that they usually freely combine in order to reformulate the illusions that constitute the SR. In this conception, linguistic production is merely a question of formulation, adjusting linguistic 'means' to the expression of one's intention and to the designation of one's objectives in the world.

If we place ourselves in the perspective of meaningfulness as co-significance, linguistic operations can be described as a jointly defined selection and adjustment process which, within the slightly different conceptual frame of enunciative linguistics, has been finely described by Fuchs:

> The preconscious character of paraphrastic activity would be at work in all enunciative processes, that is processes involving production and recognition of linguistic sequences by enunciators. We think indeed that in order to produce a sequence, the enunciator doubly refers to the metalinguistic paradigmatic dimension first to select a semantic field (at the level of the utterance as a whole ... selection entails eliminating all that is 'different' ...) then in order to select, within this set, a subset, which presupposes eliminating all that is 'similar' .... Conversely, to recognize a sequence, the subject reconstructs the set of all possible similar alternatives and from then on to the set of possible different excluded alternatives.[11]

This process of comparison and selection associated with the production and recognition of linguistic utterances involves two types of linguistic operation:

1 *Designation* or resorting to preconstructed or linguistically constructed notions in the SR in accordance to a code or codes contractually accepted by both parties as corresponding to their objectives. Designation is inevitably bound up with the process of comparing and assessing possible alternatives. It negatively involves translation since communication is sustained through the inutility of resorting to code-switching.

2 *Conversion* is resorted to when this condition is no longer satisfied; when a hiatus, a discontinuity, and more generally a disagreement in communication intervenes, then there is a necessity for code-switching in order to re-establish the normal exchange of communication. Partners in communication resort then to conversion procedures whose main function is to stabilize communication.

Translation and all the intermediary stages that can be envisaged from the preceding analogy – partial, biased, imaginary translations – are obviously related to conversion procedures. But, in the case of intercultural communication, the objective is widely different. Because of the incommensurability of Language Cultures, the conversion strategy is no longer geared to the continuity of communication – this would presuppose that there is indeed a means of conversion between cultures – but to the multiplication of relationships between them. Instead of trying to define one unique medium of communication which would be detrimental to both cultures' specificities, the translator's objective is to diversify and motivate the possibilities of meaningful contacts between cultures. His or her ultimate aim is *cross-cultural multiformulation* rather than communicational adjustment. As opposed to intralinguistic meaning production, conversion procedures no longer simply contribute to the definition of meaning but to its diversification.

Since interlinguistic and intralinguistic translation belong to conversion or reformulative procedures, it is necessary (1) to study the general characteristics of this structure and (2) to isolate the specific properties which distinguish the interlinguistic factor.

CONVERSION AND TRANSLATION

We will unify for the purpose of our demonstration intralinguistic and interlinguistic translations under the general name of *conversion*. They share a common structure which can be described in two successive stages.

The initial motivation for conversion is a break-down, dysfunctioning or discontinuity (real, imaginary, or anticipated) in the process of communication. Apparently, this factor seems to be more applicable to interlinguistic than to intralinguistic situations; but the language difference should not obscure the fact that communication of some sort can always be established across languages. Similarly, within the limits of a single language, interruption in communication, far from being accidental, can in fact be thought of as constitutive of intralingual communication; in this perspective one does not think in terms of gaps in communication but of communicative strategies in order to fill in the gaps. In either case, the decision to convert (or not) reflects the communicants' perception of the necessity of continuity in communication. In all cases of conversion the extent of the gap in communication and the motivation for re-establishing contact have to be carefully assessed.

The second stage consists in providing an alternative sequence meant to bridge the gap discovered in communication before returning to the previous code or branching off into a new one. The substitution can be partial and incidental. In that case, we have to deal with paraphrase *stricto sensu* in the intralingual configuration and with what could be called 'spot translation' as practised, for example, by Ladmiral (1979, 219) as 'périparaphrases' in some of his translations. It can also involve the complete replacement of the original sequence and the adoption of a new code or again the juxtaposition of the conversion sequence, as in the case of explanatory paraphrase or interlinear or parallel translation. The finality of conversion strategies should not be, as Ladmiral seems to think, 'to allow us to dispense with reading the original text' (1979: 15), but on the contrary to establish a meaningful tension between original and translation, invalid and converted texts in, respectively, inter- and intralingual communication. Even in the most frequent case of complete replacement, conversion should always be considered as a *meta-text* or a text constructed upon another text.

Finally, the conversion can be established in various degrees of 'equivalence' with the original according to the objectives and intentions of the converting operators. It can range from a totally misleading and even erroneous or imaginary substitute to a wide variety of justifiable equivalents. It seems that assessing translations and paraphrases has always come up against the problem of equivalence in conversion procedures, i.e. what validates them in the last resort. Since the process of validation is bound to be saturated with ideological considerations, it is time to take into account not one or any criterion but all possible *forms* of equivalence. Then this problematic concept will be considered in a new perspective, no longer as a norm but as a continuum of possibilities that require to be justified and selected rather than unilaterally enforced.

Translation or interlinguistic conversion, sharing a great deal of structural characteristics with conversion strategies in general, will now have to be considered as the complex interplay between an insufficient (or rather unproductive in terms of communication) source text, a mediator, and alternative formulations in a different LC.

It is time to go beyond the simple process of analogy with conversion procedures and underline the distinctive features of interlinguistic translation.

We saw that in intralinguistic communication designation and conversion were complementary functions that insured continuity in interlocution. This is due to the fact that continuity is always potentially made possible because of the sequential (one notion leading to another) and synaptic (one notion belonging to two or more systems) nature of the semiotic chains in the SR. In translation, owing to the incommensurability of the SRs, the two functions are dissociated from each other. Conversion does not complement, it follows and replaces designation. The hiatus in communication is not bridged over but on the contrary materialized by the production of another but not a substitutive text. Translation is the persistence of communication in the disparity of codes.

The converting principle can no longer be *analogy*, or differences in likeness, but *homology*, or likenesses in fundamental difference, as underlined by Jakobson (1966: 233), and in keeping with Benjamin's intuition that 'kinship does not necessarily involve likeness' (1969: 74). Whereas analogy concerns the more or less exact approximations that can be established starting from a common basis of comparison: A' and A" being analogous with A; homology describes the various possible configurations of resemblances that can be established in two radically distinct systems of references: A'/B' and A"/B" would represent a homologous relationship between systems X and Y.

Besides, the initial text submitted to conversion is no longer clarified or rectified but completely displaced by the translated text. Conversion no longer contributes to immediate expressive or referential objectives, it duplicates an already fully realized situation of communication in order to fulfil different communicational purposes in a different LC. Translation is *second*, not in any way motivated by the initial situation, and it is *off-centred* in so far as the situation it institutes in LC2 is externally determined.

This particular configuration entails important consequences. First, the status of the initial text is radically changed. Instead of being a communicative text, it becomes a 'source text'. Being no longer a co-negotiated 'act' of reference, it is transformed into an 'object', as Ladmiral has rightly pointed out:

The nature of translation 31

Moreover Translation is a particular case of communication, it is a *meta-communication*, a second-degree communication which, from one language to another, is brought to bear on the first-degree communication which it takes as its object. Which means that translation proceeds to an *objectification* of the SL communication which it globalizes in order to make it the content of the message it has to translate into the TL.[12]

Its function is no longer to achieve designation but to serve as the basis for the construction of another situation of communication. In that case, the process of selective paraphrasing, which Fuchs postulates as being at work in the production and recognition of intralinguistic sequences, is no longer sufficient. It is the *complete* set of paraphrases – both dissimilar and similar – that must be reconstructed in order to account adequately for the initial SL sequence when considered as translation input.

Correlatively, the translated text is not the exact counterpart of the converting text in intralinguistic conversion. We saw that it was externally determined, which means that the motivation for signification does not arise from the TL situation but results from an outside cause. The translated text is always disconnected from its initial definition and so, transitionally for some translations and permanently for most, does not have any other justification but the explicit necessity to bridge a gap in communication.

In order to control the possibilities of parasitic distortions induced by this temporary *in vacuo* situation and to facilitate the possibilities of integration, it is again necessary to resort to the full range of paraphrases that the SL can give rise to in the TL.

Consequently, paraphrastic determination is not used in a complementary fashion, as in intralinguistic communication, but for oppositional purposes. Instead of contributing to the interplay of expression and comprehension, it defines the homological relationship as a comparison between interlinguistic options. At this stage, *translation can be said to consist in sets of homologically related paraphrases constructed on the initial ST*. Interlinguistic conversion is only one aspect of translation, the other being, as we have already indicated, the *insertion* of the converted text or rather, we should say at this point, 'text potentialities' into a different LC.

Our approach will be found to deal with the two aspects in conjunction, since the concept of variation (which could be compared to a parametered curve) at the same time implies an exploration of translation possibilities (the various points on the curve) and the conditions under which these possibilities can be said to be validated (the co-ordinates of these points on orthogonal axes).

If we take for example the concept of 'mainstreaming' in education, it will be found to be discursively related to that of segregated v. unsegregated tuition of handicapped/disabled/special/problem children as opposed to normal/non-handicapped children. This term will determine a set of possible French equivalents such as 'réinsertion', '(ré)intégration', 'remise dans le courant principal', or even 'mainstreaming', which are placed in various degrees of conceptual relatedness both with the SL and within the TL. The final choice of a translation can only be made by selecting the appropriate terms in keeping with an explicitly defined target context. The contextualization of homologies means bringing into play a certain number of determining factors.

Intralinguistic conversion was seen to be based on the harmonious correspondence between semiotic codes. Translation, on the contrary, underscores the radical disparity between LCs. Far from being a handicap or an obstacle to translation, this fundamental evidence has to be converted to meaningful purposes by the mediator. The act of translation will consequently inevitably include a 'Cultural Equation' or meaning-inducing tension between the SRs (see Chapter 6). Translation does not involve a process of transferring signification but a commitment to the disparity of two cultures under consideration. That 'tension' will be revisable according to historical and socio-cultural factors.

It is clear in any case that there can be no definitive translation (except those pronounced to be so for normative reasons), since the Cultural Equation relating texts across the boundaries of languages is constantly changing, thus contributing to the diversification of cultural values.

Besides, the insertion of homologies no longer regulated, as conversions were, by the co-participants' interaction is taken in charge by an exterior agency, the translator. The translator's place between one set of communicants and another totally unrelated set redefines the role of the converting agent. No longer exclusively committed to the continuity of communication, his or her function is invested with a particular status, that of mediator between intercultural situations of communication. That status, downplayed or overemphasized by former theories, will have to be accurately determined.

This function will be based on the translator's personal perception of the Cultural Equation and on intercultural competence. This competence can be said to be objective in so far as it is based on interlinguistic techniques accumulated through practice and instruction. It is also subjective in so far as the mediator can always be said to 'create' both the translation options and the conditions in which they are to be inscribed. Rather than resurrecting the contradiction of ideological images, we are proposing a concept associating contradictory elements.

The nature of translation

Translation can be neither an automatized process nor a complete creation. Though often unevenly balanced, the combination of functional and innovative aspects should always be considered as a choice characteristic of the translator's function.

Finally, conversion into a new SR does not simply mean branching off into a new code as intralinguistic conversion, but rather adapting to an entirely different set of *norms* – discursive, situational, and sociological. These norms have to be carefully elucidated both in the SL and in the TL in order for the mediator to assess the comparative values produced by the various translation options. This global critical perspective will enable the mediator to become properly speaking a translator, that is a producer of discourse in his or her own right.

The translated text finally produced should be seen (1) as a meaningful relation established with the SL original text and (2) as establishing a significant difference with the other excluded translation options.

Translation can thus be finally defined as the individually and interculturally motivated *choice* according to TL *socio-cultural norms* of a TT by a *mediator* among sets of *homologically* related *paraphrastic* options. A simple glance at the highlighted concepts in our definition shows the shift of emphasis that our approach introduces in translation studies. We pass from operation- (or product-) focused approaches to a systemic and comprehensive representation of translation.

The next stage consists in validating each of the concepts introduced in this chapter and building them up into a coherent and functional theoretical construction.

3 Building a theory of translation

REVIEW OF PREVIOUS THEORIES

In Chapter 1, we examined the conditions necessary in order to conduct a reflection on the problems of translating and translation. In this chapter, we will review some of the guiding principles which have been at work in the conceptions proposed to account for these phenomena. It is not our intention to analyse extensively all or even some of the translation approaches put forward by other theorists. The task would be both futile and self-defeating not to mention unrelated to our immediate purpose. We propose to group all the systems together and divide them into two antithetic positions in order to show at the same time the continuity and the comparative originality of our own proposition. As this is very much an overview we shall not be making specific references to individual studies.

We can divide the theories of translation in terms of the duality proposed by Steiner (1975: 235) between *universalist* and *relativist* theories. These two conceptions more generally seem to correspond to two fundamental processes used by human beings to come to terms with the problem of adapting to their environment.

The universalist approach is based on an extension of the economic concept of *contractual transaction*. We shall try in our exploration of this concept's potentialities to establish a constant parallel with translation.

This notion normally comprises two sides necessarily representing different positions (the two languages united by the translation process) and an act of conciliation of their respective claims, the contract (or translation), regulating their mutual relationships and supplying the basis for further transactions. In this perspective, each of the parties is considered to be endowed with both characteristic features and common universal properties. It is on the basis of the latter, but taking into consideration the radical disparity introduced by the former, that a common ground can be found. Translation, as a particular form of contract, is an agreement between the two LCs involved to transfer signification on a common convertibility basis in so far as it is not detrimental to the specific differences between cultures. The fundamental notion both on the economic and on the translational planes is compromise: that is, the agreement to remain separate in order to achieve a common goal.

The relative convertibility of meaning (as of goods through the conversion of currencies) entails a certain number of important consequences. If meaning can be generalized to the point of being transferred without major loss from one position to another, it follows that content is relatively independent of the form in which it has been expressed. It means also correlatively that socio-culturally determined differences do not constitute the essential of communication. Highly distinctive as they are, they must be sacrificed in order to achieve the transaction's objective.

The possibility of exchanging meaning similarly implies some degree of universality in the definition of thought and in the identification of reality. This does not necessarily imply that all men are supposed to think alike or that reality is exactly the same the world over. This would contradict one of the most glaring evidences of life in society and in international communities, and the obvious disparity between political systems and geographical realities. It seems, however, in that perspective, that universals which are more or less accessible to human enquiry can be traced in the process of cognitive definition and in the segmentation of reality. A further consequence of this position is the representation of language as an instrument for the formulation of thoughts and for the identification of referential reality.

Since the ideal contract can only be achieved within the confines of a single culture, the universalist conception envisages the relationship between cultures as possible but inevitably partial or flawed. The universals provide a sufficient basis of transaction which nevertheless excludes a total correspondence of interests. This regulated form of cross-relationship founded on a middle ground consequently precludes all kinds of deeper and wider interpenetration between cultures. The essential, i.e. what constitutes the specificity of cultures, is irretrievably lost, while only some expressly limited degree of correspondence can be achieved between cultural worlds. The main ideological emphasis is on coexistence and mutual benefit.

In keeping with the general idea of cultural relationships as contractual transactions, translation is conceived as a process of *transference* based on the criterion of *equivalence*. Not only can meaning be transferred as in the generality of communicational transactions but it has to be assessed in terms of equivalence or of a converting norm. The immediate pragmatic objective will hold precedence over the definition of semantic content and that in turn over the particularities of form, style, or idiosyncrasy.

Transference is necessarily partial since, fundamentally, translation is a losing or, in Levy's terms (1967: 1176), 'minimax' operation – a formulation which seems to encapsulate the gist of the contractual concept. Since both LCs are bound to lose some of their characteristics, the loss has to be kept to a minimum and if possible compensated by the maximalization of the common core of profit achieved in transferred meaning. It is clear, consequently, that translation consists in constantly perfecting this fundamentally unattainable compromise.

In order to further this goal, the ideal translator should be the impersonal operator who is able to suppress his own predilections and who ideally can be assimilated to a processing machine. Failing this ideal transparence, the translator can avail himself of a stock in trade of translation methods or techniques that can contribute to systematize his necessarily erring practice. It is the human factor that contributes to the entropic dysfunctioning of cultures.

An extreme radicalization of this position corresponds to the constantly resurrecting dream of residue-free transcoding between LCs as, for example, expressed by Weaver (1965: 18):

> One naturally wonders if the problem of translation could conceivably be treated as a problem in cryptography. When I look at an article in Russian, I say: 'This is really written in English, but it has been coded in some strange symbols. I will now proceed to decode.'

Paradoxically, but also significantly from the point of view of the student of ideologies, extremes seem to meet again on the plane of ideological delusion. This oversimplification asymptotically approximates an exaggerated version of the opposite conception, Benjamin's notion that

> For the great motif of integrating many tongues into one true language is at work [in translation]. This language is one in which the independent sentences, works of literature, critical judgements will never communicate – for they remain dependent on translation; but in it the languages themselves, supplemented and reconciled in their mode of signification, harmonize. (Benjamin, 1969: 77)

This analysis is interestingly close to Weaver's pronouncement, although the orientation of their thoughts is radically opposed. Weaver refers to the general convertibility of meaning, while Benjamin has in mind the possible elimination of linguistic differences in order to reconstitute through the regenerative agency of translation the ideal and long-lost *Ursprache*.

Thus, the opposite theoretical conception is perhaps not a fundamental contradiction of the former. In contrast with the economic paradigm based on pragmatic considerations, the relativist conception confronts us with the idealistic concept of *interaction* as an alternative to both separateness and confusion of differences. A contract aims at preserving specificities, interaction at capitalizing on them.

The main concept associated with communication in the relativist perspective is no longer transference on a contractual basis but *production* within an *interactive* structure. From that point of view, universals are not only perceived as non-existent, they contribute to the denaturing of communication. Everything that can be conceived as general or could in some way be generalized is necessarily unadapted to the purpose of meaning definition. The essential of signification lies in particulars and differences which can never be universalized away but only exist in proportion to their specificity. Consequently, signification can never be repeated, duplicated, or transferred, it can only be reformulated and adapted to the ever-changing conditions of meaning definition.

This conception of communication is based not only on the incommensurability of cultures but also on the radical differences between the individual participants and the specific conditions of the act of communication. In addition, each act of meaning production determines alterations in the factors involved in communication including the medium in which it is achieved, thus making the necessity of constant adaptation even more pressing.

As a logical extension of this particular position, language and reality are not conceived as distinct from the means of their expression. Fusion or rather correlation between form and content, expression and reality is inevitably associated to signification. Consequently, there is between man's intellectual processes and reality a constant interplay which at the same time commits him to and distances him from his linguistic productions. Correlatively, language and linguistic utterances do not exist independently of their actual inscription in the context of production. If meaning can be ascribed to linguistic productions they derive it from the parties involved in their definition rather than from intrinsic semantic properties. In the words of Humboldt, quoted by Steiner: 'Language is a "third universe" midway between the phenomenal reality of the "empirical world" and the internalized structures of consciousness' (1975: 81).

The relationship between cultures is a natural extension of this perception of the process of signification. Far from trying to discover an illusory middle term between opposite positions, cultures can only succeed in establishing contacts – be they of the harmonious or of the destructive sort – through and because of their differences. The discovery of otherness in foreign systems is not only crucial in order to establish the originality of cultures, it is also essential in order to enlarge and validate them. Cultural relationships are regulated by a complex interplay of attraction, repulsion, and cross-fertilization. When cultures do not communicate, they are bound to regress or at least lose some of their distinctive 'edges'. According to Steiner, the role of translation is determining in this process of cultural cross-determination, since 'In translation the dialectic of unison and of plurality is dramatically at work' (1975: 135).

Seen in this perspective, Translation can only be described as a *hermeneutic* process of interlinguistic production. The hermeneutic stance represents an attempt at conciliating the respective differences of the LCs concerned through the particular tension induced by the comparison between the ST and its envisaged translations in the LC2. For example, translation is perceived in Meschonnic's conception as a rapport and a tension. The 'tension' coincides with the unique sociocultural configuration that translation literally stages between two LCs. The 'rapport' concerns the individual operator's appropriation of that confrontation. It follows that translations are in no way perfectible, only renewable. This does not mean that they are justified by the mere fact of their existence. Large differences and consequently values can be revealed in the degree and extent in which they express that unique conjunction of rapport and tension (see Chapter 9).

Translations are thus perfectible, but this process cannot be effected through systematization or the correct application of translation techniques. The only way to improve hermeneutical production is through an increased perception of the respective cultural values involved in the conversion – through complexification of perception not rationalization of techniques. Similarly, the translator can only contribute to improving the conciliation of LCs by refining his or her own perception of cultural factors, not in any way by eschewing personal or idiosyncratic preoccupations.

It seems that in their contradictory ways, the universalist and relativist approaches – simplified as they may appear in our didactic presentation – neutralize each other and, in so doing, contribute to the present deadlock in Translation Studies or to its sterile reproduction in alternating cycles.

The *Variational* approach is an attempt at conciliating and synthesizing the merits of these contradictory options and regrouping them in a wider perspective. It was felt that precisely because they had produced so much, no new ground could be discovered if the same directions were preserved. A decisive conceptual redefinition was vital. We think that the concept of variation supplies the necessary reorientation.

Both universalist and relativist hypotheses unnecessarily and in their different ways distort the reality of the information which communication is supposed to convey. Indeed, the crux of the problem concerns the question of information transference between cultures. Posing the problem in terms of an alternative between universals as opposed to culture-bound specificities has locked the debate about translation into a stalemate. But the complexity of the phenomena seems to be pointing towards a different reality.

Although on the one side, objective statements do exist and every statement can be considered to contain at least some degree of indisputable objective evidence, it does not necessarily follow that this informational content is universal and so directly transferable from one language to another. Objective statements are necessarily set within patterns of culture-bound formulations, giving rise to differences which do not affect the phenomena in question but the conceptions that individuals form about them. The difference between 'L'eau bout à 100 degrés', and English translations such as 'Water boils at 212°F' or 'The boiling point for water is 212°F' or '212°F is the point at which water boils' are apparently slight. But, although they correspond to the same objective reality, they are expressed in different formulations, implying different emphases not to mention unit systems. These differences seem to be indissociable from our perception of these universally valid truths. They consequently have to be accounted for as such and not divided in terms of universals and particulars, truth content and formulation, because universals simply do not exist independently of the particulars in which they are inscribed. We might even add that for the purpose of linguistic communication, they are almost exclusively perceived in the particulars. Individuals appear to be more sensitive to variations in formulation and their consequences – that, for example, water should be the main emphasis in our first English translation as opposed to its boiling point in the second or the temperature in the third – than to its common application to a well-known reality.

On the relativist side, it will not do to consider with Steiner – in one of his exceptionally overextended arguments – that: 'The great mass of common speech-events, of words spoken or heard, does not fall under the rubric of "factuality" and truth .... Statistically, the incidence of "true statements" . . . in any given mass of discourse is probably small' (1975: 220). This is certainly applicable to 'truth statements' as such but not in any certain measure to the question of truth in statements, which is a totally different matter. All utterances must be conceived as containing some degree of truth designation together with explicit indications on the part of communication participants as to the degree of validity of their linguistic productions. This does not mean that there is always a definite amount of truth content which is transferable interlinguistically but that there are in every language various ways of signifying truth and untruth and the degrees in which they are supposed to be recognized as such in language. It is on these various formulational strategies that the translator works, not on the referential truths, nor on these particularities alone independently of the truth content they convey.

The concept of Variation appears to be particularly suited to account for this changed perspective. Variation could indeed be defined as the set of all possible formulations that can be associated with any given identifiable situation. Communication partners at any moment have at their disposal sets of more or less interchangeable, more or less applicable formulations in various degrees of paraphrastic nuances that they can freely adjust to their communicational objectives. Communication could then be conceived as the co-negotiated and contextually motivated *selection* of (more or less) *predictable communicational formulations*.

Consequently, meaning is not recognized in terms of informational content or reference, it is produced, controlled and identified in variations. This can be further developed as follows:

1 The participants in the act of communication have at all times some notion of the differences between the formulation options at their disposal and of their common core referential meaning. They collectively constitute the *variation range* made up of *variation options*.
2 They can relate these options to various contextual determinations or *parameters* that they can identify.
3 The variation range is supposed to correspond to the same segment of reality.

This new conception allows us to conceive of linguistic formulation as being, on the one hand, varied within certain limits while corresponding to a unique referent and, on the other, strictly determined in terms of context while allowing for a certain degree of formal predictability. It is not so much the exclusive choice of one type of expression among others that counts in our perspective as constant adjustments to situational requirements. What we will try to underline is not the *selection* of one formulation but the *interplay* of options within the variation range and thus the constant implicit relationship between selected and excluded options and of each of these with the variation range as a whole. The Variational concept provides a good compromise between cultural universals in the universalist approach and irreducible cultural differences in the relativist approach. The deadlocked contradiction between the two theoretical positions described above could then be satisfactorily resolved.

The Variational concept similarly provides a more finely regulated representation of cross-cultural relationships. Instead of being contingent on individual acts of creative adaptations, as in the relativist conception, or contractually negotiated through the neutralization of cultural differences in the universalist conception, they will be found to exist in a wide range of predictable cross-cultural configurations. These configurations correspond to the various ways variation ranges can adjust or fail to conform in different cultures. These predefined options do not exclude creativity in translation nor do they insure the translator against erroneous solutions; they actually enhance and motivate his or her practice as a cultural act.

As a consequence, the concept of translation is significantly restructured. We are no longer concerned with defining one or several translated 'equivalents' to any given ST, but with producing a variation range in LC2 corresponding to the reconstituted range framing the ST. This double process of relativizing translation and translated text is fundamental to our approach; it strictly defines the limits of systematic representation in Translation Studies. The production of translations, a more complexly and, above all, differently determined process, represents a further stage predefined by the Variational approach but in no way predetermined by it.

THE CONCEPTUAL BASIS OF THE VARIATIONAL APPROACH

Most of the theoretical concepts reviewed so far were associated in various degrees with the definition of a specific process 'translating', itself designed to account for the production of specific products, 'translations'. Translation theories or methodologies are, in the vast majority of cases, process- or production-oriented: that is to say, strictly determined on the empiric plane. Our reflection on ideological misrepresentations and on the current theoretical deadlock in translation research has led us to propose a new basis for theorization, no longer geared to observation and to the production of immediate results but constructed around the concept of Variation.

The Variational representation of the translation process corresponds to a complete change in model conception. Translation operations – whatever the conceptual framework within which they were situated – were conceived as a *linear, oriented* and *objective-determined* chain of operations. Our intention is to place systematic representation immediately before the ultimate determination of a translation product by the translator. This displacement of theoretical emphasis not only provides the necessary leeway for the translator's final free choice which largely escapes determination, but also generates a broader perspective on the rest of translation phenomena.

Emancipated from the largely unaccountable explanation of translation productions, theory can concentrate on the definition of a *systemic, bilateral, polyvalent* comparison between the ST and TT variation ranges. The translator's subsequent choice is to be conceived as being framed within a range of systematically parametered options. This construct represents the range of possible translation alternatives that can be associated in LC2 not only to the ST but to the full range of its reconstructible alternatives. These alternatives on both sides are associated with explicit contextual determinations defined on a comparative basis.

The relations established within the interlinguistic pattern of variations are not one to one but polyvalent – any item in the Source set can be meaningfully associated to any other in the Target set and vice versa. These separate and global relationships are not LC2–oriented but can be envisaged in both directions, from LC1 to LC2 and vice versa. It is the nature and extent of the translation comparison that are taken into consideration, not the justification of any separate item contained within the system.

At this stage, which we consider as the only formalizable portion of the translation process, neither the ST nor the intended TT are given any particular priority. They are resituated within the range of possible formulations that the act of translation has given rise to.

The construction of the Variational model of translation necessitates the development of a two-stage strategy based on co-ordinated sets of concepts. The first stage is a *generative* process describing the development of variations in LC1 and LC2 and the definition of correspondences between the two sets. The second stage is a *normative* process defining the socio-cultural parameters corresponding to each pair of correspondences between LC1 and LC2. Translation production proper is situated beyond these two operations.

The generative process in the Variational approach

Taking the ST as the initial basis, the Variational approach aims at establishing a double relationship spanning two or more LCs. The first one can be conveniently defined as *paradigmatic*. It describes the range of reconstructible alternatives from which the ST was originally selected (see Fuchs, 1982: 172) and, correspondingly in LC2, the range of possible options from which the subsequent TT will be chosen. This paradigmatic reconstruction in either case is based on *paraphrases*.

The second relationship develops along the *syntagmatic* dimension and concerns the crucial basis of comparison for ST and LC2 paraphrastic sets. It is founded on the concept of *homology* which, together with that of paraphrase, calls for reassessment.

Paraphrase does not refer to the rhetorical device sometimes considered as unnecessary reformulation or elegant variation; it is, rather, a generative process inevitably associated with expression. It is, besides, fundamental to the construction of the Variational model.

As we have seen, the ST submitted to translation is not directly accessible for translation purposes, or, rather, the translation project converts this ST text into the input stage of a transformational process. Its semantic content, organically related to the initial situation and context of production, has to be completely reconstructed. Similarly, once a correspondence of some sort – the object of our next development on homologies – has been established between SC and TC, as we have shown, this process does not correspond to the definition of one translation exclusive of all others but to a set as complete and as clearly defined as possible of translation alternatives. Paraphrase functions as a *clarifying* concept in ST and as a *relativizing* one in LC2.

This crucial notion, which has already been explored in the wake of Jakobson by Ballard (1980: 18), Choul (1980), or Bruce and Anderson (in Brislin, 1976: 209), needs to be re-examined in its logical foundation.

The naive conception of paraphrases complies with the stylistic judgements which we have quoted as being most commonly associated with paraphrasing. Everyone is generally prepared to concede that all statements can be more or less exactly paraphrased. Yet, there is a strong feeling that in keeping with a given situation there can be one and only one correct or apposite formulation and that all the other paraphrases are in some degree unadapted or deviant. Any native speaker should be able to select the correct and eliminate the parasitic paraphrases. Characteristically, the common ideological preconception emphasizes free meaning definition and individually, as opposed to culturally, motivated production of utterances.

The analytic conception discussed and to some extent relayed by Fuchs (1982: 53ff.) considers that paraphrasing establishes a process of conversion between utterances that dissociates meaning in terms of what remains unchanged under transformation (core meaning) and what is changed (peripheral determinations).

It is interesting to note at this juncture the close resemblance between this view and the theory of partial translation. In both cases reformulation does not affect the core meaning and only concerns the peripheral specifications which are either unreproduced or altered. The difficulty is that it is never quite possible to establish a clear division between core and peripheral meaning and that, even if it could be fixed, it is not sure that it would not be affected by reformulation. Besides, there are several degrees in paraphrasing that make the process shade off from quasi-identity into non-paraphrase. The problem in each case is further compounded by the fact that when one submits different paraphrases to native speakers for validation, there is no agreement as to identity or similarity, thus making any analytical distinction unrealistic.

Fuchs apparently found a solution to the difficulty of formalizing the concept of paraphrase by positing three different types of paraphrastic activities: paraphrase proper, that she defines as a preconscious activity 'which is necessarily reductive' (1982: 169); and the meta-linguistic 'constructed and conscious linguistic activity' (p. 127) that 'would take into account the totality of the semantic definitions' (p. 169); and between the two, she places the glossing process which describes 'the moment when the paraphrasing activity becomes conscious, i.e. when the subject becomes conscious that he or she is positing a relation of identification' (p. 170).

So it seems that the relevance of paraphrasing in the definition of meaning is clearly linked to the degree of consciousness which is being associated to the process. But, if it is probably indispensable to mark off limits between levels in human consciousness, it does not follow that they can be extended to the linguistic field. There is no proven possibility of conceiving any stage in linguistic activity that would *not* be consciously formulated in some way or another through the system.

In short, there is simply no ground for a belief that conscious metalinguistic paraphrasing could be more reliable than preconscious paraphrasing. In fact, we are merely insensibly shifting from one type of activity to another – from spontaneous process of paraphrasing in various degrees of explicitness onto reformulative practices explicitly related to well-defined conceptual fields such as linguistics. We change from the *practice* of paraphrasing – unaccountable and heterogeneous as it may seem, but deeply related to translating – to the development of a systematically constructed *system* of operations which Fuchs, following Culioli, considers as the proper object of linguistics.

We do not propose to minimize the linguistic definition of meaning nor do we intend to give it absolute priority. Linguistics will be considered as only producing one type of paraphrase – 'normed paraphrase' – to be associated and combined with other no less productive types.

Our conception is based on an application of Peircian semiosis and on an extension of the methodological guidelines defined by R. Martin which seem so harmoniously to complement each other. In this perspective, fundamentally, there are no *semantic* only *operational* universals: 'Universality is less in the noemes ... than in the operations which allow us to isolate them.'[1]

According to Peircian semiosis, signification cannot be isolated as such or defined independently of its formulation but is always contingent to a dynamic structure involving three terms: sign, interpretant, and object.[2] Meaningfulness does not pre-exist or outlast the act of signification; it is not associated with referents or defined by communicants, much less contained in words; it is connected to the SR and activated by the participants in the act of communication in order to serve their specific purposes. Thus reformulation constitutes the only way semiotic man can conceive of his existence and of that of the world around him. In this conception, paraphrase and paraphrasing are crucial to the definition of meaning or interpretant, which itself is linked to its infinite reproduction or semiosis.

Linguistic utterances are comparable not on the basis of nuclear meaning and circumstantial specifications (how could one define 'core' meaning without reintroducing the circularity of semiotic reformulation?), nor, for that matter, on the ground of the linguistic operations that they reflect (identifying operations amounts to corroborating or invalidating a system *exteriorly* posited, not assessing meaning) but through *variations*, both reformulation and difference and the judgement establishing that difference, which seems to correspond to Greimas's conception of meaning: 'Meaningfulness is nothing else but this transposition from one level to the other, from one language to a different one and meaning is nothing else but that possibility of transcoding' (Greimas, 1970: 13).[3]

Paraphrasing establishes at the same time continuity and differentiation in meaning. It is, in a more extended way that need not concern us here, the foundation of linguistic activity: we always produce meaning differentially on top of an already constructed meaning and in order to make some more or less differential contribution.

What is meaningful is necessarily produced and perceived as different. When there is no difference between two terms or utterances, there is no possibility of meaning construction or no possibility of conceiving of these terms as different. Meaninglessness can be conceived on the contrary as infinite difference – not absence of meaning – when there is no possibility of constructing a meaningful difference between two terms. It should be added that these two extreme situations are difficult to imagine or simulate, since there can always be found a pair of communicants who would produce meaningful differences between two perfect synonyms and create a significant relationship between otherwise completely unrelated terms.

This remark leads us to a fundamental consideration regarding paraphrasing. There is no pre-established, definable, or objectively identifiable relationship between paraphrases or, for that matter, between any linguistic utterances that is not mediated through the competence of a paraphrasing agent. All judgements concerning identity of paraphrases, whether spontaneous or based on systematic knowledge, come to us through the paraphrastic productions of a socio-culturally determined operator.

The advantages of this theoretical position are crucial for translation purposes:

we thereby dispose of the conception of meaning in terms of core and peripheral, semantic and contextualized paraphrases and replace it by the notion of *paraphrastic sets*;
there is no distinction between paraphrases, semi-paraphrases, and non-paraphrases but only *explicable degrees in reformulative differences*;
there is no difference in kind between paraphrastic and meta-linguistic reformulations, only differences in logical constraint and the paraphraser's degree and type of competence.

Considering its vital function in the definition of signification and its consequent relevance to the process of translation already underlined by Peirce himself – 'The meaning of a proposition is itself a proposition. Indeed, it is no other than the very proposition of which it is the meaning: it is a translation of it' (Peirce, 1966: V, 284) – the concept of paraphrase needs to be developed from a simple relationship between two elements – paraphrased and paraphrasing elements – into a more complex representation of paraphrastic possibilities.

We call the traditional type of paraphrase 'closed paraphrase' because it compares for specific purposes only two elements. We tend to consider it as a particular case or one particular combination within the *open paraphrase* which corresponds to the paradigm of all the elements that can be associated in varying degrees of similarity with any given statement. This paradigm is consequently an open-ended set since, potentially, it can be extended to the totality of producible utterances. The isolation of a set of open paraphrases will always be the expression of a locutor's individual choice.

We also distinguish the *syntagmatic paraphrase* which consists in developing – or synthesizing – any or all of the elements contained in an utterance. It is obvious also that for the same reason as for the open paraphrase, this is potentially a never-ending process, since any segment in a proposition can be recursively reformulated. The degree of explicitness or condensation is thus closely connected to the reformulator's choice and needs.

Finally, we resort to the *discriminating paraphrase*, or 'normed' as opposed to 'glossed' paraphrases in R. Martin's terms. These are reformulations according to the predefined concepts of a constructed system of reference such as linguistics, but semiotics or any other science might also be pertinently associated.

These three types of paraphrases will be amply utilized in order to define the meaning of the initial ST but also in order to produce a range of potential LC2 equivalents. They constitute, in their generative as well as their discriminative function, the indispensable basis for the definition of homologies, establishing cross-linguistic links between LC1 and LC2 paraphrastic sets.

Homologies

Following our analysis of the process of translation, no transfer or equivalence of meaning can be achieved across languages. There can only be homologies between paraphrastic sets, i.e. between the SL paraphrastic set 'framing' the ST and the LC2 paraphrastic set comprising the translation options. The nature of the homological link needs to be investigated beyond the simple provisional reference to Jakobson's notion of 'resemblance in difference'.

A good approximation of it can be reached through Steiner's reference to topology (1975: 425ff.):

> Topology is the branch of mathematics which deals with those relations between points and those fundamental properties of a figure which remain invariant when the figure is bent out of shape .... The relations of invariance within transformation are, to a more or less immediate degree, those of *translation*. (p. 426)

The only reservation that could be made in connection with this analogy is that although it gives a good image of the 'reshaping process' at work in translation, the reference to transformation seems a throwback to former misrepresentations. There is indeed no way in which the semantic content of the original language can be said to be submitted to variations in shape as are objects in the topological theory, nor are there any constants to speak of in the elaboration of a translation from a LC1 text. It is easy to diagnose again a resurgence of the persisting ideological notion that there are universals in communication and that consequently reformulation is a practice that affects the particulars without altering the fundamentals.

We rather think that, since cultures are radically different, it is more realistic to posit that there cannot be any common denominator or transference between them and that local coincidences can only be needlessly illusory. Consequently, it is impossible to conceive of a one-to-one correspondence between items contained in different LCs. Yet, if we take into consideration *sets* of paraphrastically related elements in separate LCs, thus explicitly excluding individual items on the one side and general classifications of the linguistic type on the other, it is possible to discover significant resemblances.

If we take, for example, the following list of syntagms

a brave
a hero
a man of courage
a brave/courageous man
a man who has courage
a man who knows no fear
a Hector

we can easily find, beyond the limits of lexis, syntax, and cultural associations, a common denominator relating these very disparate formulations. This common formula could be stated as the relation between 'a male human individual' and 'absence of sensitivity to danger'. This crude formulation can, of course, in no way be said to be the core meaning upon which all these expressions would be variations since this would reintroduce a conception of signification in terms of core and peripherals. Nevertheless, the mathematical notion of a common denominator is a rough and ready approximation of our conception of what a *homologon* can be in relation to a set of paraphrases. The common denominator provides a means to effect conversions, comparisons, and, more generally, manipulations between items in a set but has in itself no further justification beyond its very functionality. It is a converting factor and as such is not positioned hierarchically in relation to the elements within the set nor is it constitutive of any of them. They are, rather, to be considered as being differentially defined in relation to it; that is to say, enhanced and confirmed in their specificity. And it is, as we have seen, these specific differences that stand for 'meaning' in the practice of the paraphrasing subject.

Yet there are notable differences between a common denominator and our conception of a 'homologon'. Whereas a common denominator can be exactly computed and is strictly dependent in its definition on the items comprising a numerical set, homologon definition is affected in its adequacy by the extent of the paraphrastic set under consideration. The more elements in the set and the more finely discriminated they are, the more apposite the homologon will be. Since, in strict semiotic logics, sets can be said to be potentially limitless and so inevitably open-ended, and paraphrastic discrimination itself is a recursive process, homologon definition is bound to be incomplete and thus infinitely perfectible. Besides, whereas the common denominator is unaffected by whoever correctly applies mathematical rules, the homologon should be conceived as varying according to the competence and acquired cultural experience of the homologizing agent.

We believe, consequently, that the homologon, variable in extension and definition as it is, is capable of inducing a similar variation range in the TL. This does not amount to displacing the problem of translation onto the homologon, since homologous definition does not produce translations but variation ranges in LC2. *The 'homologon' or verbal equation of the ST serves as the basis for variations (not equivalents, much less translations) in a different LC.* For the same reasons that made the definition of the homologon strictly related to a variation range, homological generation can only consist in sets of paraphrastic related items. These variations are the 'TL paraphrastic sets'. The relation established between two variation ranges, we call a *homology*.

The production of homologous sets in LC2 is in turn strictly contingent on the translator's bilingual and bicultural competence. At the three different stages in the homologizing process – the definition of the homologon, the production of the TL paraphrastic set, and the discrimination of that set – the translator's intervention is crucial. We feel that it is important to emphasize the translator's contribution as this clarifies the difference between what is acquired and what is generated in the translation process, between competence and production. Homologizing procedures are useless without bicultural competence, but that same knowledge is insufficient in itself to produce homologies. Homologies correlate structures by establishing global correspondences of factors within different relational systems.

The function of the homologon is distinctly heuristic in so far as it is meant to induce in a different system a set or sets of correlated paraphrases. Any failure in producing acceptable TL homologies is supposed to determine the definition of a new, more analytic and productive homologon.

The various types of paraphrases – paradigmatic, syntagmatic, and discriminating – are equally suited, in various combinations, to formulate homologons. It seems, however, that, since the homologon's specific function is to supply an *explicating gloss*, some types of paraphrases are particularly adapted to treat certain aspects more than others. Concerning lexical problems, it will be found that the syntagmatic or 'definitional' paraphrase enables the translator to pass over the arbitrary boundaries between lexis and syntax; syntactic features will be best treated in terms of discriminating paraphrases, while the more diffuse effects of modulation will appear more clearly in sets of open contrastive paraphrases.

The specificity of paraphrastic types does not exclude the possibility of conversion or duplication of one item's characterization into more than one type of paraphrase. For example, if we have to characterize the difference between 'fuir' and 's'enfuir', it will be useful to rely on an aspectual designation such as inchoative or, alternatively, to propose a syntagmatic gloss for 's'enfuir' such as 'commencer à fuir' which will in different ways clarify the problem of its rendering in English. The homologon for a segment of ST can be presented in any meaningful combination and juxtaposition of the basic paraphrastic types.

The homologies established on the basis of the ST are, as we have already established, systemic, non-oriented relationships involving two sets of paraphrases. In this perspective, is there a point in isolating as more worthy of attention sets of statistically recurrent translations, translation patterns such as Guillemin-Flescher's 'tendances' (1981) or Culioli's 'gabarit' (template) (1987: 8)? It appears that for these authors such regularities can only be observed in relation to a *tertium quid*, the reference to linguistic concepts and operations. But even if we could eliminate the parasitic influence of the translation situation, it is clear that this procedure would only serve to corroborate the linguistic system as such and not in any way establish standard translations between languages. Though this type of information can be of interest in contrastive linguistics and for the perfecting of linguistic concepts, it is of no particular help to the translator or the specialist in Translation Studies. There is no possibility, directly or through some mediating system, of associating one item in one language to another in a different language. This would once again resurrect, albeit in a more logical form, the myth of complete, systematized conversion, thus excluding the human, situational, and socio-cultural factor unavoidably associated with that process.

The normative stage

The normative stage constitutes the next step in the definition of translation Variation. Once the Variation range has been generated, the several possibilities which it contains have to be parametered in socio-cultural terms. Each of the potential options must be appreciated in terms of its inscription in the TC.

Although the problem of translation referenciation has been to a certain extent outlined in Pergnier's study (1978: 290), it has for the most part been perfunctorily treated, never fully analysed, and frequently dismissed as an external criterion. We intend to give it a full development and ultimate priority over all other factors involved in translation.

In order to account more adequately for this referencing process, we have broken it down into three related concepts:

1 The **cultural equation** concerns the translator's conception of translation and its role in cross-cultural relationships. No translation is ever produced without reproducing, initiating, or reformulating a particular conception about translation. This general orientation has often been presented in a dichotomy opposing 'sourciers' and 'ciblistes' (SL- or TL-oriented translations). It seems that this conception is needlessly reductive because it obscures the continuum of extremely varied positions that can be imagined between these two extreme positions.

The cultural equation can never be eliminated. It should be taken into account whenever we have to appreciate the choices made in any situation of translation and explicitly considered when we propose our own choices. Its inevitable admixture to the translation process invalidates all translation procedures based on corpora and the direct generalization of regularities derived from the comparison of texts and their translations.

2 **Mediation**: No reformulation is conceivable without a reformulator or mediator. Beside his function as the vehicle of a certain cultural equation, his specific intervention can be defined according to two different lines of consideration.

He represents, whether he chooses to emphasize or downplay it, a distinctly psycho-socio-cultural stance which will be reflected in his productions. Translations are, because of this factor, inevitably historicized and, in the most extreme of cases, bear the imprint of the personality that has effected them. For that same reason, translations are bound to be renewed in keeping with cultural changes and they can coexist at one given moment in history, thus participating in cultural complexification.

The mediator also accounts for a specific capacity that we call translation competence, which all translators possess to a greater or lesser degree and which fundamentally influences to the nature of his productions. We distinguish between three types of competence:

(a) *Acquired interlinguistic competence*: no translation is possible without competence in at least two linguistic systems and a certain knowledge of the LCs associated with them. The totality of the Variational operations, both generative and normative, are dependent on the ability in the mediator to mobilize a certain amount of cross-cultural competence. The approach is mainly destined to organize that competence and to a lesser extent improve it. The same correct strategy will yield vastly different results according to the extent of basic linguistic knowledge which has been brought into play. If it is a well-established fact that bilingualism does not entail translation expertise, it would be absurd to pretend that this particular faculty incapacitates those who possess it for the purpose of translation. The sytematization of translation can only be validly undertaken if founded on some degree of bilingual proficiency. The reverse proposition is far from being true. Translation is not – or only minimally and indirectly so – as has long been thought, a means to acquire competence in a second language; it is, rather, as we will see later, a means to consolidate that knowledge in correlation with the native language.

(b) *Dissimilative competence*, which is the direct consequence of the systematic practice of the Variational approach, includes, consequently, (1) an aptitude to generate and dissimilate homologous statements and (2) an aptitude to define and recreate socio-cultural norms. This competence can be taught, and constitutes the object of the didactics of translation (see Chapter 10).

(c) *Transferred competence*, by which we mean all the dissimilative competence which has been accumulated and committed to translation auxiliaries such as translation methods, dictionaries, data banks, and expert systems. These invaluable aids constitute a rough and ready definition of homologies and norms, a sort of blueprint for the finer definition of translation processes. They should not be neglected, considering the complexity of the factors involved. But, they should be

Building a theory of translation 53

kept to the instrumental role and never considered as determining elements.

3 **Socio-cultural norms** constitute the key concept in the Variational approach. They subsume the preceding factors of translation referenciation.

Each item within the homology has to be assessed in terms of its insertion within the TL situational and discursive norms:

the discursive level or the insertion of any given text within an ideologically referenced family of discourses;
the functional level or the explicit function of the text within both ideology and the social situation;
the socio-cultural determination of the text or of its family of discourses, i.e. its insertion within the structures of society.

The main idea here is that no text and no translation can exist without explicit socio-cultural determinations. Thus, we denounce the illusion that there are more or less constraining norms as, for example, in the difference between normalized texts (regulations, patents, scientific texts) and apparently lesser determined or undetermined texts such as everyday conversations or literary texts. All these texts in various degrees and forms correspond to definite norms.

JUSTIFICATION OF THE SYSTEM

Internal coherence

The two successive stages in the Variational construction, complementary as they seem to be, are fundamentally based on opposite principles. Homologies, as an invitation to generate, compare, discriminate, are a direct antithesis to the normative, defining, and referencing attitude evinced in the second stage.

It seems difficult, on the one hand, to imagine that the discriminative stage could be accomplished in a total socio-cultural vacuum and, on the other hand, that clearly defined socio-cultural norms should not preclude the paraphrastic exploration by specifying one or several solutions. Or, to put it differently, it could be said that multiplying paraphrases contributes to diluting the applicability of norms, as we commonly do when, disregarding codes, we concentrate on the nature of the referent we want to highlight, as in 'C'était un gangster, un bandit, un malfaiteur, un malfrat, que sais-je?' On the other hand, it seems, if we consider, for example, scientific denomination as an extreme case, that alternative formulation is just a pretext for insufficient referential precision. We are vague or slack in our denomination because we do not mean or know how to be sufficiently discriminative.

But this representation of discourse phenomena seems to fall short of reality or, rather, again to relay the images of language as transparent expression of man's thoughts, on the one hand, or as reflection of reality, on the other. As a matter of fact, all forms of expression are mediated through largely predetermined discursive structures that specify what formulation alternatives to use and under what conditions they should be used. Scientific language is not by any means, as common belief would have it, a rigid system of designation, it allows for sets of meaningful alternatives for identical referents and, similarly, the expressions of daily life which we tend to consider as freely interchangeable are strictly regulated according preconscious social codes; who would think of adding to the long list of phatic greetings used in Anglo-Saxon communities, such as 'How do you do?', 'How are you doing?', 'How are things today?', a deviant, though acceptable, paraphrase like 'How do you feel?', which would imply a totally different social rapport?

Discursive productions are thus at the same time various and codified, linguistic expression creative and rule-bound. We feel, consequently, that the distinction of two stages in the construction of the Variational model is justified. It might even be considered in its systematicity as an efficient way of by-passing some of the omnipresent preconceptions that we entertain about discourse.

Besides, the generative and the selective stages are never as completely distinct as our systematic representation tends to make believe. They are always closely associated in the actual process of translation. Indeed, it is this constant back-and-forth movement between the two types of activities – however unsystematic – that characterizes the practice of translation in actual experimental circumstances.

So, despite the apparent contradiction and overlapping between the two stages, we must emphasize the *complementarity* that unites them. Paraphrastic reformulation corrects the potentially reductive tendency of the selective procedures, and selective norms qualify the impression of semantic indeterminacy produced by the study of variational ranges. Both aspects, kept apart for explanatory and heuristic purposes, jointly participate in the act of production/reproduction at work in translation. As opposed to preceding systems underlining one aspect of translation – the operation or the product of translation – this twin conception unified round the notion of 'homological variation' contributes to representing translation phenomena as one global configuration of factors including Source Culture (SC) and

TC, ST and TT, and the translation operator. The globality of approach is achieved by opposed and complementary means, by relativizing and systematizing perspectives. Each aspect, taken separately, would be artificial; combined, they provide a reasonably accurate simulation of reality.

Complementarity and globality are finally to be conceived in a dynamic perspective. This consists in the loopback effect that the system provides when placed in a heuristic perspective. Any failure (or anticipation of success) in the production of a translation is to be understood as starting (or reducing) the process of paraphrasing and normalizing until a satisfactory solution is ultimately found. Besides, paraphrastic reformulation is never a self-sufficient activity and should be conceived as an anticipation of norms and conditions of integration of a translation solution. The looser the anticipation of TL norm strictures – because they are unspecified or are open to adaptation – the more exhaustive the generation process will be.

Taken as a whole the variational model is at the same time a *representation* of translation phenomena, an *exploration* of translation potentialities, and a *heuristic system* to predefine translation solutions.

The Variational system criticized

Obviously, such a globality of representation is in apparent contradiction to one of the basic principles of epistemological receivability, the imperative of simplicity. Besides, the Variational system involves such a complexity of factors that it can be felt to be in striking disagreement with the simplicity and spontaneity of the act of translation.

An obvious argument in defence of the system is that theoretical complexity is a direct reflection of the intricacy of the phenomena under consideration. We can further justify our wealth of precautions by a shift in emphasis in systematic representation. Most of the former models were mainly oriented towards the production of a specific product and so toward pragmatic efficiency. Our construction, without excluding that obvious finality, is more particularly aimed at representing classes of phenomena, degrees of predictability, and conditions of convertibility. In a very evident manner, complexity is the price to pay for the perhaps excessive ambition of the project.

One of the problems that the Variational approach will have to deal with is to find ways to apply the system in the most economical way. But this objective does not concern or affect the theoretical plane; this is to be treated from the methodological angle that we reserve for the next chapter.

Among the evident drawbacks of the system one can mention a certain indecisiveness in the definition of certain concepts. Homologies and norms are in this respect particularly open to criticism. More prejudicially still, some of our concepts seem deliberately to associate in equal proportion definiteness and indeterminacy, such as, for example, the paraphrastic activity conceived as the product of both given and acquired competence and as being observable and open-ended.

Although we are quite prepared to acknowledge our imperfect theorization, we tentatively venture a justification in the form of a new epistemological definition. It is our belief that positivistic formalization in the field of the humanities is not only an illusion but a possible block to the further development of research. We prefer to conceive of human-related phenomena in terms of what could be called 'fuzzy' logics, providing at the same time for rigorous description and a certain form of unpredictability. Thus, it is hoped that man and his productions can be fitted in with rather than reduced to formal processes. To all intents and purposes, the general orientation of the Variational approach satisfies this double objective.

Finally, the most damaging objection concerns the possible indeterminacy of the system. Our representation is so general that its object tends to dissolve in the wider frame of semantic productions and their representations. In trying to counter the notion that Translation Studies do not exist except as the intersection of various scientific fields, we would have generalized its object in such a way that it would completely lose its specificity.

This risk, though serious, is perhaps inevitable since, as we have tried to show, translation lies at the core of man's faculty to produce signification. A global and wide-embracing outlook is consequently justified; it will be our particular objective in the next chapters to show that it opens new perspectives onto related fields of research and at the same time does not preclude, but rather encourages, practical applications.

Generally, we switch from a product-oriented approach to a systematic construction of translation phenomena. This change in perspective seems to justify some of the limitations discovered above and particularly to correct the blocks and simplifications discovered in the previous systems

The paraphrastic sets as a discriminative concept in Source Language (SL) and a predictive concept in Target Language (TL) offer a changed basis for the definition of meaning. They allow for an expansive description of semantic productions which surmount the deadlocked position of impossible or partial translatability and the inevitable obstacle of the incommensurability of cultures.

Homologies provide the necessary concept to position this expansive process of signification cross-culturally. This is achieved in correlated, bilateral, multifactorial constructions promoting creativity in each culture differentially envisaged. The challenge confronting the translator is no longer simply solving an isolated practical problem but mediating an intercultural proposition. The solution finally adopted – a translation – can no longer be individually determined, it is bound to be interactional.

The homologon is the key operator in this process of cross-cultural regulation. It is neither a neutral middle-term nor a converting element but a dynamic factor justified through its productivity in the confrontation of cultures.

The cultural equation puts an end to the different 'schools of translation' and the confusion that is normally associated with them. They can be seen as the inevitable cultural biases more or less consciously associated with the translation process. Since these preconceptions cannot be eliminated, they have to be integrated into the system.

Similarly, the translator's formerly under- or overemphasized role can be placed within the system. The mediation concept accounts at the same time for dissimilative competence, socio-cultural determination, and creativity, thus making translation a systematic and open-ended operation.

As for the socio-cultural norms, though they had never been questioned, they had generally been considered as secondary or determining in only limited cases. We give them full and final power in the definition of translation products.

The general emphasis of the whole system is less the production of a translation than the insertion or reinsertion of a complete productive process in a global context of cross-cultural references.

The validity of the concepts presented in this chapter needs to be tested in connection with translation procedures in contact with the actual process of translation. This what we intend to achieve in the next chapter.

4 Interlinguistic homologies

The study of interlinguistic homologies will, for practical considerations, be spread over two chapters. Chapter 4 will deal with intrapropositional relations and Chapter 5 with correlations lying beyond the scope of the proposition. In addition, introductory notes in Chapter 4 and concluding remarks in Chapter 5 will treat methodological problems related to the practical implementation of the system.

FROM SYSTEM INTO METHODOLOGY

Once the general conceptual background has been clearly defined, it is necessary to describe the conditions of application of the Variational approach to the field of Translation Studies. Methodology, or the conversion of a conceptual framework into a pragmatic set of rules destined to account for a certain field of enquiry, involves three separate orders of considerations:

First, the *field of operation* has to be recognized and limited – in our case the ST proposed for translating – and, if need be, modified or clarified for purposes of efficiency.

Second, methodological enquiry should make clear all the *instruments* that it proposes to use in the process of production.

Third, an operational strategy has to be determined in order to achieve the desired result, i.e. to produce a translation of the ST in LC2. This strategy will normally define the *object* (and possibly sub-objects) about to be produced and the *procedure* to be followed in order to generate these objects and relate them to the end-product.

The field of operation in Translation Studies

Any process of transformation has to start from an initial state which has to be transformed or processed into something else. When we say that, for the purpose of translation, the initial state is the ST, we seem to be stating the obvious. Yet if we read Larose's summary on the question of 'translation units' (1987: 208ff.), it is never quite clear at what level the ST is supposed to be treated, according to typographical (paragraphs, sentences?) or logical divisions. We do not intend to make an exclusive and definitive choice in the matter but, in keeping with our general approach, to reflect and, if possible, account for the complexity of the issues involved.

We should first make a clearcut distinction between four different orders of considerations in keeping with the ST. There is first the *observation* basis – the ST and its semantic determinations. To all intents and purposes, as we discovered in our study of the translation process, this text is inaccessible as such. It has to be disconnected from its initial situation and processed as an input product for the translation process.

The processing of the ST involves three types of manipulations: segmenting, structuring, and globalizing. Segmenting the ST will produce the *working* basis. Although, it should never be overlooked that, in our progressive approach, final decisions will ultimately be taken at macro-textual and contextual levels, we propose for obvious practical reasons to divide the text into a succession of 'working units' that will cumulatively make up the working basis. We consider the basic working unit as being constituted by the proposition or the combination of a subject and a predicate with related qualification and referencing elements that may also involve imbricated propositions. For example, the first sentence of the Sillitoe text[1] ('Many people in the country had twentieth-century brains and energy but were held under by the eternal sub-strata of hierarchical soil-souled England'), which will also be selected for a final recapitulation of different points at the end of this chapter, will be divided into two propositions: 'Many people ... had ... energy' and '[These people] were held under ... by ... England.'

This methodological decision, dictated by the necessity to define an expedient working basis, divides the observation basis into a succession of segments but at the same time predetermines the type of structuring which is going to be applied to the text. The choice of the proposition as the working basis creates an evident distinction between intra- and interpropositional relationships. These segments can be redesigned into more logically defined *planes of definition* corresponding to clearly marked discontinuities in linguistic description. Thus, in addition to the *propositional* plane that corresponds to the basic working unit and concerns traditional linguistic determinations, we will consider the *extra-propositional* plane that describes the proposition's contextualization, and the *strategic* plane that places the proposition within the macro-structures of textual strategies.

Each of the planes of definition will then be subdivided into *levels of description* or sets of homogeneous factors that can be treated separately in meaningful association. Thus the propositional plane will comprise the traditional linguistic divisions – i.e. the lexical, syntactical, and modulatory (or rhetorical) levels; the extrapropositional plane will be composed of the interpropositional, situational, and intertextual levels; and finally, the strategic plane will be described in terms of content, reference, and medium.

The segmentation of the ST observation basis into planes and levels, justified though it may seem for empiric and methodological purposes, could be felt to be excessively disruptive were it not compensated for by the *synthetic* function of the homologon. It is indeed the homologon's specific property to reconstitute the continuity and organicity of the text through a global explicating simulation.

The instruments of the homologizing process

Before defining the specific procedure that we intend to follow, it is necessary to redefine from the pragmatic angle some of the concepts which have been presented in our theoretical introduction.

Paraphrase and *paraphrasing* have a pivotal role to play in the definition of homologies. They are used, on the one hand, to elucidate and frame the semantic values of the ST and, on the other, to predetermine some of the translation options in LC2. Both LC1 and LC2 paraphrastic sets can be made up in various combinations of the three different types of paraphrases: reformulative (syntagmatic), comparative (paradigmatic), and discriminating (defining). Although, inevitably, the translation process begins and ends with a text, it is essential that at either end there should be sets of options. For it is only through options that the Variational aspect of translation can be fully explored both in its generative and its determinative aspects.

No less crucial to translation procedure is the *homologon* and the *homologizing* process. It consists, taking the ST as its basis, in logically formulating a gloss which is sufficiently explicit to produce a workable homologous paraphrastic set in LC2. Each level of definition corresponds to a specific type of homologon definition. The propositional level is mainly accretive in so far as it contributes the constitutive parts that are going to make up the homologon. The interpropositional level is relational and so builds up these parts into an integrated whole. Finally, the strategic plane orients this structure towards a function in the world of signification.

Thus, the main functions of the homologon are:

1 to homogenize in one reformulative gloss all the various constituents of signification in ST, thus cutting across the *dense* features of lexicon, the *discrete* markers of syntax, and the more *diffuse* constraints of contextual and textual configurations;
2 to serve as a basis or priming element for the reformulative process in TL. The homologon is to be considered as a *converting equation*.

Translation procedure

Procedure is meant to relate the *working basis* to the production of the desired objects, i.e. a LC2 translation, with the help of the necessary *instruments* described above.

We propose in accordance with our theoretical conceptions to replace the empiric duality of translated text and translating text by a constructed object – a homology – subdivided into two complementary sub-objects: the homologous sets of paraphrastic options in LC1 and LC2 and their parametered values in their respective socio-cultural contexts. Chapters 4 and 5 will deal exclusively with the definition of homologous sets. A homology between a LC1 text and any of its imaginable LC2 translations is then to be considered as an *intermediary* object on which, in the second stage (see Chapters 6, 7, 8), socio-cultural norms will be made to apply in order to account for the various contextually definable translated texts. Eventually, out of the homology and in accordance with translator-specified TC norms, a translation will finally be selected.

A homology is composed of three components sequentially related by translation procedure. We first reconstitute the *ST definitional set* by dividing the ST into propositions, isolating planes, and levels of reference, as previously indicated. Each level and each plane will generate a paraphrastic reformulation of the values they contain and combine in order to define a *homologon*. The homologon in turn is used to generate in the LC2 a *set of paraphrastic options* in which the values elucidated in the homologon will be reflected in various degrees and combinations of paraphrastic reformulations. The complete sequence can be represented as follows:

ST definitional set → homologon → LC2 paraphrastic options

This linear procedure, strictly observed in the subsequent study, is in reality bilateral and recursive in so far as the process of homologon definition can be renewed almost indefinitely until the necessary pragmatic objective is reached, i.e. a LC2 paraphrastic set usable for translation purposes. The completion of the homologizing process is thus to be understood as heuristically activated. Failure to achieve a satisfactory result will automatically start the reformulative process on the ST at a deeper or different level.

Conversely, in the actual practice of translation based on the Variational approach, all the levels and planes that are now going to be systematically investigated are virtually never resorted to all at the same time. It will be seen that, not infrequently, several stages in this quite complex procedure can easily be by-passed or telescoped because they either do not apply, are duplicated at another level in the process, or are rendered unnecessary by immediate dictionary or other accessible levels of equivalence. The reciprocal of recursivity in homological generation is the possibility to shortcut through some of the levels and planes in order to pinpoint only those translation factors relevant to homological purposes.

This can be illustrated with an example from the Zola text in Appendix 2. When the translator comes to 'dès qu'on les tenait par la tête', he may feel that he has at his disposal most of the equivalents he needs to translate this proposition except the information concerning the subject. He will thus initially concentrate on the reformulative values of 'on'. But as he explores the unspecified agentive values of (Fr.) 'on', this may in turn start a kind of loopback effect into the reformulation of the aspectual values that can apply according to the predicative relation selected: 'when they were (being) held by the(ir) head(s)' with an unspecified agent will thus be found to be more naturally compatible with a variety of aspects than the construction with a collective plural agent: 'as soon as they held them by the(ir) head(s)'.

Homologon definition is then a flexible, bilateral, and adaptative system designed to produce a translation result graduated according to the translator's competence. It facilitates the expert translator's concentration on well-defined translation obstacles by corroborating intuitive choices and helps the translation instructor in reconstructing the necessary translation steps for the benefit of the neophyte translator.

It should again be emphasized that the crucial process of homology generation is based on the translator's competence and thus varies in productivity according to the extent of his linguistic and dissimilative expertise. The objective of the Variational procedure is not and cannot be to devise a translation-producing system. It would inevitably lay itself open to the strictures of Quine's radical objection[2] that at any time two coherent but different translation systems can be devised to justify the same translation and, correlatively, two different translations can be related to the same translation system. As we have shown, this conception relies on a one-to-one form of equivalence between text and translation. We have shown that, in order for the full range of parameters involved in translation, including the human factor, to be properly accounted for, the relation between text and translation has to be homologous, i.e. systemic and parametrable. Our methodology merely consists, starting from a translator's competence, in rationalizing, ordering, and explicating the chain of choices that are at work in the Translation operation.

THE VARIOUS PLANES AND LEVELS OF TRANSLATION HOMOLOGIES

We now consider each separate paraphrastic level within each of the cumulative planes clearly classified in terms of propositional, extra propositional, and strategic relationships. Our examples will be taken from a set of six texts, not a 'corpus' but a 'field of observation' providing adequate contextualization and a good variety of text functions.

The objective does not consist in presenting a complete and in-depth study of all the contrastive problems pertaining to each level. It is clear that a whole volume of obervations would probably not be sufficient to complete the task. More restrictedly, we will try:

to justify and illustrate each level available for paraphrastic reformulation;
to demonstrate the variety and combination of options that can be generated at each level;
to trace their progressive and cumulative aggregation into a homologon;
to show the organicity of all these homologically related options within the ST and their projection in the LC2.

The paraphrastic sets proposed at each level as homologously related in LC2 are to be considered as sets of translation *options*, later (see Chapter 9) to be reconsidered and assessed from the point of view of one or several socio-culturally referenced translation *versions*. Thus, Chapter 9 will indicate for four of the seven above-mentioned texts how one can proceed from finely nuanced options on to translation choices consistent with identifiable textual strategies and contextual determinations. The other three texts, used in Chapters 4 and 5 as illustrative material and not selected for final determination in Chapter 9, will be given translations in the Appendix consistent with the analyses proposed hereafter.

It is important to note that the emphasis in this analytical part will be on paraphrastic elucidation of ST, whereas Chapter 9 will understandably concentrate on TT-relevant paraphrastic sets. But conversions into LC2 in one case and back-reference to LC1 in the other could easily have – and will in some isolated cases – be supplied.

Besides, and again for obvious space-saving considerations, each level has had to be considered on a separate basis independently of the homologon in which it has to be finally integrated. Yet, it should be clear that the translation options envisaged at each level are to be seen as progressively building up a homologon and determining homological projections. We will attempt to compensate for this limitation by cross-referencing whenever possible, and most particularly in the step-by-step translation that we intend to give for the Lufthansa publicity text which concludes Chapter 5, together with a recapitulation of the main aspects of the propositional level in connection with the translation of the first sentence of the Sillitoe text at the end of this chapter.

Placing a special emphasis on lexicon also calls for some introductory justification. It appears that lexical definition has been largely ignored by previous linguistic enquiry because it was considered unformalizable or situated outside the realm of linguistics. Most serious contrastive analyses so far have concentrated on syntactic problems with infrequent observations on lexical problems mainly restricted to morphological elements. We intend to reverse this tendency by dealing more cursorily with already well-documented syntactic problems and concentrating on the less widely explored lexical determinations. Besides, although the distinction between lexicon and syntax is artificial from a technical point of view, it is our belief that for paraphrastic reformulation, lexical units contribute the greater part of the proposition's semantic content and that syntactic relationships only add on peripheral modifications. Finally, our methodological angle, based on homologies, is explicitly conceived in order to bridge the difference between the two orders.

Lastly, our explicit or implicit reference to various linguistic systems will be deliberately empiric and eclectic. The aim is not to confirm or invalidate any system but rather to apply the available linguistic knowledge to the definition of translation-relevant levels of definition. Although, from a strictly linguistic point of view, some of the categories will be felt at times to be overlapping or needlessly duplicating each other, our justification in choosing them was their contribution to the definition of an explicit and productive homologon.

Lexicon

Reformulating the lexis

Although there is some degree of overlap between the following categories an initial distinction should be made between (1) *lexes* as culturally preconstructed pre-enunciative packages corresponding to the intuitive conception that 'words have meanings' for which we spontaneously supply paraphrastic equivalents; (2) *functions* or the conversion of lexes into the linguistic system as 'substantives' and 'predicates' or other categories; and (3) the actualization of these functions as *lexical items* to be found in dictionaries. If we take the word 'fouiller' (Zola, (Appendix 2) which is going to be our object of study during this first development), any native speaker of French can give a rough and ready paraphrastic reading of the term that we call the lexis; this lexis is independent of the function it can play in the system, either verbal 'fouiller' or substantival 'fouillis' or agentive 'fouilleur'. These functions in turn can be variously represented on the lexical plane as 'fouillis', 'fouille', 'fouillement', etc. for the substantival function.

The lexis, or potential meaning, is a more or less structured and exhaustive paraphrastic complex taking, in the case of translation, a ST lexical item as its starting point. It corresponds to R. Martin's (1983: 55–6) conception of paraphrases or to what Grunig and Grunig (1985: 152, note 2) have described as 'énoncés légiférants' (legislating utterances). It is founded on (and thus limited to) the translator's paraphrastic competence supplemented by what lexicographic data he or she may call on.

Lexis expansion is the necessary consequence of the semiotic principle which we have established as being the basis of semantic reformulation. It follows that the absence of meaningful variation between two linguistic units is either impossible or incompletely defined. Thus, when R. Martin (1976: 78) equates: 'Pierre a ôté sa veste' and 'Pierre a enlevé sa veste' (curiously leaving out other verbal equivalents such as 'quitter' or 'retirer'), this must be considered as a case of confusing contextually irrelevant distinctions for semantic equivalence. More specific contexts would exclude 'ôter' and specify 'enlever', as in 'enlever un graffiti du mur', because a 'graffiti' cannot simply be taken off as other three-dimensional objects such as jackets or hats. So, potentially, a lexical unit can always be given a *lexis expansion* either paradigmatically in the form of a differentiated synonym or definitionally as an expanded periphrasis.

Lexis expansions should not be confused with the 'lexical definitions' that can be found in dictionaries. Whereas lexicographers try by specific means to establish and differentiate the words' various meanings, the lexis is used as an enabling element in order to generate the full range of paraphrases comprising the homologon. These widely different functions dictate diverging objectives, reductive on the one hand, expansive on the other. The lexicographer aims at establishing a core or average signification whereas lexis definition explores the various facets of meaning definition.

Neither should lexis expansion be assimilated to componential analysis, since the linguistic elements that contribute to its making are not given any special status as distinctive features or classifying elements, for example. The lexis is a paraphrase like all the other paraphrases constituting the TL dissimilative set. The only difference is that it forms a complex of correlated paraphrases submitted to the exigencies of exhaustivity and explicitness.

Finally, the lexis expansion is an ordered set of paraphrases which should not be understood as duplicating in a different form the essentialists' distinction between core and peripherals in semantic definition. When we use the term 'nucleus' in syntagmatic paraphrase, this term is to be conceived as a 'locus', in the geometrical sense of the word, that is as a set of points entertaining specific relations in several geometrical figures; in this case, the nucleus is what stands in common between all the paraphrases associated to a given lexis.

There are different ways of formulating the lexis expansion.

1 It can be expressed *definitionally* by rewriting the lexis as a complete sentence.

In order to achieve this objective, it is necessary to divide the lexis into structuring categories. These categories are:

the 'left collocate' (or words most commonly expected to the left of the word under consideration);
the 'nucleus' or the invariant preserved in paraphrastic reformulation;
the 'modifiers' applying to the nucleus;
the 'peripherals' or additional elements that are felt to be associated with the ostensible meaning such as connotative, affective, intensity or historical markers;
the 'right collocate' or indications as to right-contextual compatibility.

All these factors should be envisaged when formulating a lexis but need not be always represented in their totality.

If we take, for example, the word 'fouiller' in the Zola text (Appendix 2, line 2) the lexis can be reformulated as follows:

left collocate (**agentive subject**);
nucleus (**parcourir**);

modalities (**avec soin**), (**en tous sens**), (**pour trouver**);
specification as to left collocate: (**un objet enfoui**) thus implying a *milieu* in which that object could be said to be 'enfoui';
no specific peripherals.

We should note that contextual information will have excluded the interpretation of 'fouiller' as referring to the earth as most natural implied milieu. Our reading will then be oriented towards metaphorically assimilating what is being submitted to the 'fouiller' process ('les trous') to earth-like substances (or metonymically to containers susceptible to hold such substances), thus excluding specifically tangled or untidy media such as are implied in 'rummage', for example. Paradoxically, it will appear later (p. 90) that this lexeme could be adopted for the translation of the second appearance of this word (Appendix 2, line 9) where the relevant milieu is 'seaweed', thus creating for the textually conscious translator a problem in consistency. The decision will have to be taken at the textual level but can obviously not be validly taken if some of the options have been excluded or, in case repetition is adopted, without envisaging the irregularities in collocation that Zola has built up.

2 The lexis can be defined *parasynonymically* (more rarely antonymically), the ST item being situated and discriminated within a parasynonymic set comprising, for example, in the case of 'fouiller': 'explorer', 'inspecter', 'sonder', 'rechercher' – all these items more or less sharing the same nucleus and thus being equivalent to 'fouiller' minus or plus one or several modifiers.

If we proceed to the generation of a homologous set in English, it so happens that the three lexemes that could finally be selected as constituting a good SL approximation show in their paraphrastic differences different emphases in modifiers: 'explore' gives priority to *wide-ranging* examination (as opposed to merely 'avec soin' in the more spatially restricted 'fouiller'); 'search' lays the stress on the *objective* of the examination, the hidden object explicitly designated as 'to be found' instead of simply 'caché' as in 'fouiller'; and finally 'probe' predefines the hidden object as potentially harmful and highlights the *instrument* of investigation left unspecified in 'fouiller'. This discrepancy between a ST synonymic set and closely homologous LC2 options corresponds to our theoretical postulates. In most cases, as in R. Martin's example of almost perfect synonymy, these different emphases should not preclude the adoption of any of these items as valid translations. This suspended translation choice does not imply that they are all exactly synonymous but that in the generality of cases the context might not be sufficiently specific and thus exclusive so as to block the use of one or the other of these terms on the basis of the specific pattern of modifiers they contain. Should more specific contextual constraints apply, a more specific lexeme would be needed or, failing this, any of the lesser specific ones supplemented by appropriate circumstantial modification. Thus, if 'explore' was felt to be lacking in (or insufficiently explicit as to) the modifier 'avec soin', 'thoroughly', 'exhaustively', 'carefully', etc., could be added in order to reduce homological discrepancy. Thus we pass insensibly into the third type of lexis definition.

3 The lexis can finally be formulated *hyperonymically* (more rarely hyponymically), one generic lexeme covering the nucleus with one or several modalities in various degrees of specificity attached to it, as for example: 'explorer en tous sens avec soin pour découvrir un objet caché'. Note that some of the modifiers already contained in the hyperonym ('en tous sens' normally included in 'explorer') can be freely added, thus creating redundancy. If, for example, the verb plus particle 'go through' can be considered as an undertranslation because it only refers to a specific movement, 'scour', 'ransack' or 'rummage' will appear, on the contrary, as overspecific as to respectively the mode and the objective of the quest. It is important to observe that, whereas the more specific items can scarcely be despecified because this would create conflicting influences in modifiers such as in '(?)rummaging carefully', the less specific items can be supplemented with the relevant modifiers, thus strictly reproducing in various combinations the definitional homologon. In this way, 'thoroughly go through every nook and cranny' might be considered as an acceptable, though unnecessarily expanded, solution.

We can propose a tentative diagram of the 'Fouiller' homology – the first box is the definitional paraphrase, the second paradigmatic, and the third syntagmatic (see Table 4.1). The three types of lexis formulations will have to be used in various combinations in the definition of the homologon. The more developed and versatile it will be, the more

Table 4.1 Fouiller

parcourir en tous sens avec soin pour trouver un objet enfoui	carefully go through in all directions in order to find some hidden object
explorer inspecter sonder	explore search probe
explorer en tous sens	explore carefully

productive the definition of the TL paraphrastic set. It is clear, furthermore, that the reformulating activity is potentially a neverending process theoretically ranging through the complete chain of semiosis since each hypo/hyperonymic, definitional, or parasynonymic operation can be indefinitely repeated. The only limit fixed to paraphrastic expansion will be heuristic, i.e. geared to the definition of a productive homologon.

Lexicalizing the lexis

Besides the fact that the lexis can be diversely expanded, a certain number of specific manipulations can be resorted to when it comes to lexicalizing the lexis in LC2, i.e. concretizing the lexes into lexical items. In our generation of English equivalents to 'fouiller', we have implicitly taken for granted that there is a word-for-word and even function-for-function correspondence between the ST item and its LC2 equivalents. This is one of the most persistent and least challenged assumptions in the field of Translation Studies. But, it is bound to be limiting in the generating phases that we are investigating.

As Jakobson has shown in his seminal but undeveloped article 'On Translation' (1963: 82), translation is based on generalized conversion between linguistic categories, from syntax into lexicon and vice versa. Thus in the Sillitoe text (Appendix 1), the verb 'had' ('had twentieth-century brains'), which can be given a very simple lexis reformulation, will of course have to be compared with 'avaient' and 'possédaient' but also with the prepositions 'chez'/'pour' and the possessive 'leur' or the relative 'dont' ('Chez/Pour beaucoup de gens, l'intelligence . . .', 'Beaucoup de gens dont l'intelligence . . .', 'Beaucoup de gens appartenaient par leur intelligence . . .'). Failing a linguistic explanation discriminating these variations on the notion of possession, it is important that the translator should be aware of them as translation choices.

In the same way in the Delisle text (Appendix 3), 'resemble' in 'make it more nearly resemble' is aptly translated by 'le rendre à peu près semblable', a variant of the also homologous possible 'ressembler', no doubt chosen because of the presence of an approximator. Conversely, in Sillitoe (Appendix 1), the translation of 'hierarchical' as 'hiérarchique' or 'hiérarchisée' in 'hierarchical soil-souled England' should also be compared with 'la hiérarchie d'une Angleterre . . . '. Rather than thinking in terms of obligatory transfer procedures or, on the contrary, excluding certain possibilities as deviant, it is vital that the translator be informed of all these reformulative possibilities and of the differences they entail.

Besides, in the process of lexicalizing the lexis, various lexical possibilities – either *dense* or *discrete* – will be found to be available such as in 'dream' and 'have a dream' or 'expertly' and 'in an expert manner (way)', 'like an expert', or 'with expertise'. These lexical variants, which are rarely studied in the linguistic or lexicographic literature, could be considered as relatively interchangeable since they correspond to the same lexis expansion. Yet, when it comes to translating: 'elle regardait dans son panier' (Zola, Appendix 2), the translator might want to consider a choice between 'have a look into' or 'look into'; in the same way in Sillitoe (Appendix 1) for 'Many people in the country', 'Beaucoup de mes concitoyens' (associating 'people in the country' to a situational feature 'this ["my"] country') cannot be outrightly excluded for the more obvious 'Beaucoup de gens dans ce pays'.

Finally, as we have already hinted at (see p. 68), it is always possible to duplicate some of the categories of the lexis, thus creating a degree of *redundancy* that might be justified by the TT socio-cultural definition – legal documents, for example, demand more specification. We should simply add that the reverse procedure – *contraction* – can be an equally justified procedure and thus well worth consideration. In Delisle (Appendix 3), for example, in the space of one sentence our translation will be less explicit for 'the skin where the breast had been removed' ('à l'endroit de l'opération antérieure') and more explicit for 'the new one' ('au sein artificiel') due to an overall shift in the system of referenciation.

Multiple lexis expansions

The situation is altogether different when one SL lexeme may be related to several lexes, thus potentially creating a situation of ambiguity or multiple reading. Several cases have to be envisaged.

1 When these lexes are found to be closely related and thus can be integrated in one extended lexis regrouping these various reformulative possibilities. The variants are sometimes significantly contrasted by the original text itself as in the Albee text (Appendix 4) the closely juxtaposed presence of 'lovely' and 'handsome' for the same referent in the differently accented languages of Honey and Nick.

2 When the lexes are found to be different yet congruent as, for example, in the interpretation of the passage from Zola (Appendix 2), '[Elle] les glissa très bien elle-même', in which the modality of appreciation can be found to apply either or both to 'glissa' and to 'elle-même'. Failing a solution preserving this ambiguous reference, a choice would obviously have to be made by the translator according to explicit criteria.

3 The most difficult case is when lexis definition produces widely divergent readings of the SL unit, as in the case of 'triumphant reassumption' (Lawrence, Appendix 5) or in 'soil-souled England' (Sillitoe, Appendix 1). Two solutions will have, in these cases, to be considered: either finding a homologous TL item compatible with the two lexes or constructing a expanded periphrasis combining the two lexes. The choice between the two procedures will largely depend on textual strategies (see Chapter 5, pp. 96–100).

Lexis specification

Lexes can finally be culturally or conventionally *specified*, i.e. instead of being largely adaptable to a variety of contexts the use of the lexical item is strictly limited to certain specific conditions. The difference between cultural and conventional specifications should be perceived less as opposite poles than as extremes situated at either end of a continuum.

An adequate lexis formulation and its homologue in LC2 can sometimes fail to produce an acceptable translation solution in LC2. For example, in Albee (Appendix 4), George's aggressive offer of a drink to Martha, 'Rubbing alcohol for you?', will have to be appreciated not only on its lexis definition but on the LC2 culture's notion of what a distasteful drink can be. An adequate French rendering could be: 'Et pour toi, Martha, un doigt d'alcool à brûler?' More insidiously still, the lexis elucidation of certain cultural attitudes such as 'I can finally look at myself in the mirror without wincing' (Delisle, Appendix 3) will fail to produce any significant homologies in French. So, different equivalents will have to be found based on the situational relevance of the lexis rather than on its actual paraphrastic content such as:

'Je peux enfin me regarder dans la glace sans avoir à baisser les yeux.
                               sans appréhension (crainte).
                               sans éprouver un choc.
                               sans avoir froid dans le dos.'

More generally, the cultural dimension should be considered not as an exception to homologon definition but as an ever-present factor which should be taken into account and assessed in relation with socio-cultural parameters.

Specification can also be the result of an individual group's collective decision to mark out its productions from mainstream designations. *Conventions* are instituted whenever a restricted group wishes to create certain lexical items or redefine others extracted from the common stock in order to achieve certain specific goals.[3]

When these goals are *pragmatic* they correspond to various approaches to reality which in turn involve varying degrees in technicality. If we take the Delisle text (Appendix 3) for example, it is clear that the translation proposed has systematically rewritten the technically 'multilayered' text on 'Breast Reconstruction' into a uniformly high level of technicality. Thus the contrast in specification is ignored between the introductory paragraphs destined for the layman and the more technically oriented rest of the article that is so typical of a *Time* or *Newsweek* article. The clear distinction in both technical reference and intended target audience which is implied in the juxtaposition of 'Rebuilding the Breast', 'Breast reconstruction', and 'Mammoplasty' or in 'the removal of her left breast', 'breast surgery', 'amputation' and 'mastectomy' has been not only altered but sometimes curiously jumbled. The averagely specific 'removal of her left breast' is transformed into the highly technical 'ablation' and the more specific 'implanted' into the less technical 'inséra'. An overall definition of the various planes of specificity is obviously needed in order to define the several technical levels in that text and their interfaces.

Conventions can also be adopted by certain *social* subgroups in order to highlight their own specificity in opposition to the rest of the community (i.e. sociolects). Social specifications can also be used in a micro-situation such as that used in Albee to describe a complexity of subrelationships linking various pairs of characters within an apparently homogeneous social event (see Chapter 5, pp. 99–100).

Generally, then, lexis definition, duly complemented with the necessary specifications, should satisfactorily account for the *notions* involved in the translation unit under consideration. Syntactic features need now to be introduced in order to further determine the *relationships* pertaining between these notions. Thus the homologon progressively builds up from a succession of lexes to an articulated chain of correlated notions.

Syntax

1 *Preconstruction.* Syntax normally entails applying the rules of the linguistic system to the notions singled out for communicative purposes in relation to referential objectives. But we must take into account a double set of culturally predefined syntactic constraints that somewhat limit the strict application of the rules of the system: on the one hand, most lexical items are predetermined in terms of syntactical construction – Eco speaks of 'magnetisation of cultural items' (1972: 107); and on the other hand, some items are already preconstructed in the practice of a linguistic community and so impervious to further syntactic modification.

These two configurations have to be envisaged before coming to the study of syntax properly speaking.

Presupposition and collocational factors explicated in the lexis as left or right collocates regulate the compatibility between the different notions over and above the formal relations that can be established through syntactic means. This collocational predefinition is of paramount importance for the purpose of translation, since LC1 terms such as 'violemment' in Zola (Appendix 2), 'crevettes rouges, qui sautaient violemment', could be translated by different terms such as 'violently' or 'frenziedly' if the subject or left collocate was not identified as a non-agentive animate substantive, thus excluding 'frenziedly'. Similarly, in Delisle (Appendix 3), failure to recognize collocational correlation between '*rebuild* her missing breast' and '*restored*' leads Delisle into an unjustifiable periphrasis – '[Je voulais] simplement qu'il élimine les traces de l'amputation' – while a simple translation like 'reconstruite', 'restaurée', or the more colloquial 'remise à neuf' or even 'retapée' would have preserved the desired metaphorical vein.

In accordance with the dynamism of the homologon, the collocational ties can in turn contribute to increased productivity in LC2. In Sillitoe (Appendix 1) 'songs of yesteryear', the simple word-to-word translation 'chansons d'autrefois' has to be supplemented by translations such as 'succès d'antan' or even 'rengaines (chansonnettes) du temps jadis' whose justification does not simply rest on lexis expansion but also on a process of synergy induced by congruent collocational features.

In the examples that have been analysed so far, syntactic rules can normally apply once the collocational constraints have been observed. The next step in preconstruction is when syntactical relationships can no longer apply since both notions and relations have been preconstructed by usage. This is the case of clichés, stereotypes such as in the Kiwi text (Appendix 6) 'non-drivers come into their own', or in Sillitoe 'They didn't even know how to pull themselves up by their own bootlaces', which have to be analysed as one lexis associated to deactivated metaphoric power (see Chapter 4, pp. 77–85). These preconstructed entities can also be reactivated in order to fulfil various textual objectives such as the wordplay on 'say cheese' in Lufthansa (Appendix 7) or the humorous development of one cliché into another in the Kiwi text, for example 'In a country that relies so heavily on the auto for its bread and butter and most of its honey', which will have to be appreciated at a higher level in textual determination.

2 *Construction*. The next level describes the linguistic construction of notions and relations through linguistic means. These procedures

regulate the complexification of lexemes in the process of being adapted to the requirements of specific referential situations. The difficulty for translation purposes does not lie so much in the concatenation of the constituents involved in lexical construction – that is normally dealt with in the homologon – but in the *nature* of the semantic link introduced in the process.

If we take the example of Sillitoe (Appendix 1) 'twentieth-century brains and energy', it appears that before making a translation choice, the translator should consider the three ways these three notions can be combined: through the idea of *filiation* ('leur intelligence était issue du . . .'/'ils tiraient leur intelligence du 20ème siècle'); that of *congruence* ('leur intelligence était en accord avec/accordée au/s'accordait au 20ème siècle'); and finally the idea of *belonging* ('leur intelligence appartenait au 20ème siècle'). The same holds true for the choice of relations that can be produced in equivalence to 'une passion de femme' (Zola, Appendix 2) as for example: 'a woman's passion', 'a womanly passion', or 'the passion of a woman'. The problem confronting the translator is not categorically to opt for one or the other of these solutions but to be *able to choose between these options*, a decision ultimately based on the information he or she can gather from text, cotext, and context.

In addition, or as a substitute, to formal description of the informational content induced by lexical construction, we should be able to formulate the list of *reformulative variations* corresponding to one given combination of lexes: for example in the case of 'man' and 'courage', we should be able to produce 'man of courage', 'courageous man', 'man with courage', 'man who has courage/who is courageous, who acts (is acting) with courage/courageously'. These paraphrastic options can not only be productive of LC2 options, they also contribute to solving the particular problem of lexical specification. If, for example, in Delisle (Appendix 3), the text clearly develops three levels of specificity (vulgarized, technical and specialized) and we have to situate the translation of 'removal of the left breast' on the first level, then among the possible nominalized reformulations for the 'removal' lexis 'après s'être fait enlever (opérer du) le sein gauche' or 'après avoir été opérée du sein gauche' will prove more appropriate than the more technical 'ablation du sein gauche' selected by Delisle.

3 *Predication*. These few examples prove that the distinction between lexical construction and linguistic predication (the combination of notions and relations) is very fine, if not non-existent, and in most cases bridged over by various transformation procedures. Our intention again is not to be rigorously consistent from the linguistic point of view but to

multiply the reformulative possibilities in order to enrich our own specific objects – the homologous variation ranges. A good example of the continuity between lexicon and syntax lies in the possible paraphrastic reformulations for 'Car ces bêtes si vives l'inquiétaient' (Zola, Appendix 2). The nature of the predicative link uniting 'vives' and 'bêtes' – whether essential, 'these so intensely lively creatures', or circumstantial, 'these creatures [which were] so intensely lively', or implicitly explicative 'these creatures lively as they were' – will completely change the relation that obtains between that composite subject and the following predicate.

The next degree in linguistic structuring consists in relating the predicative structure to certain aspects of the communication situation through the use of *referentiation* markers (or 'shifters') that will in turn contribute to the homologon definition. It is in that particular field that paraphrastic reformulation should be particularly meticulous, since this set of situationally sensitive linguistic features are particularly prone to alteration in the translation process. Indeed, whereas first-degree linguistic structuring (predication and topicalization) can be said to be relatively limited in combinations and fairly stable cross-linguistically, the referencing factors constitute properly speaking the 'idiomatic' character of languages. These factors are particularly volatile in translation, since in the reformulative process an inevitable referential 'gap' intervenes in the transfer between ST and TL allowing for parasitic translator deformations.

Modalities, or the enunciator's judgement on predicative content with regard to a set of linguistically determined criteria – assertivity, probability, latitude, or gradability – are relatively well documented both in the linguistic and in the 'translation-studies' literature. The combination of these types of modal modifications, though less studied, more directly concerns the translator, who is always confronted with the globality of linguistic data. Thus in the Lufthansa advertisement (Appendix 7), the restrictive particle 'just', limiting the reference to the semantic content of the verb it modifies in 'We just can't say cheese', will discursively take an intensive function when applied to another modality calling for such LC2 homologies as: 'Nous ne pouvons tout de même pas . . .' which would not so aptly reproduce the surmodalizing factor [accumulated modals] as anteposed modals such as 'Pas moyen (Impossible) de . . .'

As to the distinctive functions of the types of modalities, it is particularly clear in Albee (Appendix 4). In this text, the characters' various social preconceptions are neatly distinguished in terms of the surassertive modalities (modalities reinforcing either a positive or negative value) in the case of Honey and Nick to express social embarrassment and appreciative modalities 'simulating' positive or negative assertive values such as 'She really is', 'What it is, actually, is it's a pictorial representation...', 'I don't think I mind', or 'I don't know if that's exactly the right word for it', suggesting the deviousness of George's style of expression. Evidently, such a distinctive use of modalities has to be documented in the homologon definition.

Tense and *aspectual* markers can also be difficult to account for in translation. If we take the example of the numerous 'imparfaits' used in Zola (Appendix 2), in contrast to the more evidently predictable aoristic 'passés simples', we should take great care to distinguish between values indicating steadiness of intent and secondarity (i.e. at second remove) in narrative emphasis as, for example, in 'De leurs filets étroits, ils fouill*aient* les trous. Estelle y apport*ait* une passion de femme. Ce *fut* elle...' rendered by 'With their narrow nets, they *were* explor*ing* [steadiness of intent] the holes. *Meanwhile* [secondarity], Estelle put the passion of a woman into it. It *was* she who...'. Similarly, in Lawrence (Appendix 5), the presence of a pluperfect in 'the moon had exploded' amidst preterites or aspectualized preterites poses the problem of the possible homologous equivalents for antecedence in French which can range from 'imparfait' (in its backgrounding value simulating antecedence), 'plus-que-parfait' (or indefinite antecedence), and 'venait de' (or immediate antecedence), which will be eventually adopted in our translation.

When it comes to *determiners* and *quantifiers*, there is no lack of fine comparative analyses on the subject though some specific cases can be difficult to resolve. In Sillitoe (Appendix 1), in two instances – 'the eternal sub-strata of hierarchical soil-soiled England' and 'The soul of indoctrinated England' – 'England', though highly determined contextually, is treated as a conceptual notion; the same holds true in the same text for the appositive 'spew created by intellectual semi-demi-masterminds'. It seems that this last instance could be easily dealt with by the French appositive 'vomissure'; but since it would also translate the more commonly expected 'a spew', this, together with the preceding examples, raises the more general problem of notional designation in French. Should the right determination be 'l'–la/une/cette [Angleterre/vomissure]'? Again, a different type of determination should be taken into account in order to solve these local problems.

No difficulties are generally associated to *allocutors*, or the determination of the persons linguistically designated as being involved in the predication, although the 'We' in the Lufthansa advertisement (Appendix 7) can cause a certain amount of perhaps not unintended confusion. Indeed, it is never quite clear whether the company or the company's passengers are addressing the enigmatically smiling hostess or whether the company and the hostess in conjunction are to be associated with that statement. On the other hand, it is important to take into account the inclusive (all of us decent caring business people) and the exclusive (as opposed to our competitors) reference of the personal pronoun. The introduction in French of 'chez nous' could come very close to reconstituting most of these values.

Both predicative and referential markers ordering or modifying the notions and predicates should be added to the lexical determinations in the form either of linguistically determined concepts (defining paraphrases) or explicitating paraphrases. It is indeed the specific justification of the homologon to enable the translator to aggregate in one cumulative reformulation all the pertinent features identifiable at preconstructed and constructed levels.

The final intrapropositional level could be defined for the sake of sustained comparison as postdetermined construction, which we are going to analyse under the general concept of modulation.

Modulation

Once the lexical values have been selected and given the necessary syntactic determinations, the enunciator still has to determine the type of modulation according to which these values are to be considered. Modulation does not so much concern meaning definition (lexicon) or meaning specification (syntax) as the comparative values to be imparted to the several constituents of the utterance. Choices are between a wide variety of modulating options ranging from the total absence of modulation or unmodulated expression to a wealth of superimposed additional effects. These complementary manipulations do not modify either the lexical content or the syntactic inflections studied in the preceding paragraphs; they merely introduce a semantic overlay, creating variations in intensity, contrasts in emphasis, and, generally, increased complexity in meaning definition.

These effects, sometimes dismissed from the field of linguistics as 'stylistic', are not to be considered as 'deviations' since that position would confront us with the intractable problem of defining a recognized and especially definable 'norm of reference'. So, in accordance with the general orientation of our approach, we will envisage modulations as variations within a paraphrastic set. The emphasis will not so much be on deviation from a standard as on meaningful variations between separate items in a paraphrastic set. These variations concern the way each element in a linguistic proposition is affected not in its lexical content or in its syntactic value but differentially in relation to all the other elements included in that proposition.

Consequently, modulatory modifications will be studied as *dual structures* regulating comparative degrees or types of emphases. Modulations will typically divide a proposition into two blocks contrasting a highlighted segment to a relatively de-emphasized segment. Because of the imbalance thus created – or not – some specific semantic increment will have been generated. These dual structures can be observed syntagmatically as significant *ordering* of the elements contained in a proposition or, paradigmatically, in the *superimposition* of elements upon certain segments of the proposition. These two types of modulation procedures can be freely and variously combined as we will try to show with concrete examples.

To take in Zola (Appendix 2) a fairly obvious but widespread example – 'Ce fut elle qui prit les premières crevettes' – it is clear that 'elle', through the focalizing anteposition, is placed in high relief above the rest of the proposition, which is consequently de-emphasized. It should be equally evident that the special status given to the subject implicitly designates that it was '*She* [of all people] who caught the first shrimps', that is explicitly in opposition to the rest of the party who could not catch any, at least before she did. A double pattern of contrastive values has been established. The subject is meaningfully opposed to all the other possible subjects in the referential situation and its importance in the propositional content is redefined as pre-eminent over the ensuing predicate in opposition to the normal end-of-sentence focus. One could produce the following homologous set in English which corresponds in varying degrees to the values observed in the ST:

'It was she who caught the first shrimps';
'She was the one to catch (who caught) the first shrimps';
'She it was who caught the first shrimps'.

The translator's final decision will have to rest on contextual clues in order to account for his or her choice of a translation notably concerning the individualizing of the subject present in all these options.

Less noticeable and most frequently overlooked is the anteposition of the prepositional phrase, which is often considered as characteristic of the French narrative style and one of the most affirmed 'tendencies' in the comparativists' observations (Guillemin-Flescher, 1981: 117). It is thus almost systematically returned to its canonical position at the end of the sentence in translation into English. Yet, if we examine this so-called 'stylistic device' in terms of ordering modulation, we realize that anteposition contributes to de-emphasizing the circumstantial phrase (instrumental in that particular case) and thus giving full end-focus informational force to 'fouillaient les trous'. It so happens that on a textual level this referential action becomes one of the main motifs progressively building up through that scene towards symbolic status prefiguring the perturbing but delightful discovery that the two young people are going to make (that they are falling in love). There is consequently no reason whatsoever why the English TT should not preserve this altered emphasis through specific means which inevitably include anteposing the prepositional phrase.

The same contrastive emphatic structure can be used for opposite effects. Thus the writer can choose for reasons of his or her own to downplay instead of highlighting a few segments in a given proposition. In Albee (Appendix 4), the use of ellipsis in George's language, as in 'Anywhere... furniture, floor... doesn't make any difference around this place' in the middle of more voluble and chatty small talk, immediately implies that some part of his expression has been withdrawn from public attention, conveying a kind of subdued resentment which the translator would be wise not to normalize in the French translation.

'This right-little-tight-little offshore island' in Sillitoe (Appendix 1) provides us with an interesting complex of modulations. This string of qualifiers acquires some increased cohesiveness and thus some form of plausibility in its application to 'island' through the use of the maliciously slanted parallelism between 'right' and 'tight' and the stronger emphasis produced by repetition, a more primitive but also most effective type of modulation. The two consonant modulations are placed on the syntagmatic plane. At the same time, the assonant juxtaposition of 'right' and 'tight' alternating with the full consonance of the repetition imprints on the whole expression some kind of ironic twist, thus undermining the plausibility acquired by other means. It looks as if the implicit alternating rhythmic pattern paradigmatically projected on this statement at the same time enforces and undermines its semantic content. This is the kind of modulatory complex that we have tried to preserve in 'cette petite, droite, petite et étroite île côtière', but other solutions could have been equally possible, such as 'cette petite, juste, juste petite île', based on a different rhythmic pattern. The main objective is to reproduce these highly emphatic overlaid modulations which take precedence in Sillitoe's strategic objectives over the ostensible lexico-syntactic content of the ST.

This particular complex is also an interesting illustration of the complementarity between modulations of the first type based on syntagmatic relationships and those of the second type that create meaningful differences in the paradigmatic dimension.

In the most typical of cases, such as in Lawrence (Appendix 5) 'Rapidly, like white birds, the fires all broken rose across the pond', a discontinuity is more or less forcefully induced in the reader's contextual expectations. This in turn creates a semantic gap at the same time equating and distancing the two notions 'fires' and 'birds'. As we have already noticed with the ordering modulation some significant meaning increment is in the process added to the proposition: the 'fires' partake of all the attributes of 'birds' while continuing, maybe more distinctly, to be conceived of as 'fires'. The only difference being in the present case that modulatory accretion is not contained in the utterance itself but more diffusedly based on the receiver's ability to validate the required contextual expectations. The modulation is then confronted with a double risk: the risk of the underlying discontinuity's being not perceived and its being accepted as normal by the receiver.

This phenomenon (i.e. 'metaphoring') can be more widely envisaged as covering all types of contextual discontinuities ranging from on–off interruptions marked out by linguistic markers such as 'like' or 'as' or, as in the previous example, embracing commas, to more diffuse and unstable discontinuities such as 'held under by' (Sillitoe, Appendix 1), 'Many people in the country had twentieth-century brains and energy but were held under by...', which largely depend on the reader's capacity to activate them.

In this latter example, the hiatus created by the use of 'held under' over the normally expected 'dominated' could correspond to a French paraphrastic set comprising items such as 'écrasés', 'enfouis', 'dominés', 'refoulés', which all reproduce the 'repression' homologon plus the modulatory difference by resorting to the corresponding commonly expected clichés. Yet, a closer analysis of the text's strategy might reactivate the full force of the reference to 'keeping somebody's head under water in order to drown him' and thus call for a wider discontinuity. This would then specify the more explicit translation that we finally adopted: 'coulés' or 'noyés' or 'enfouis' if one wants to extend the 'earth' simile contained in 'soil-souled'.

A lesser degree in contextual discrepancy would bring us back to pre-constructed structures or clichéd phrases which are nothing else but normalized discontinuites that we have already studied in relation to lexical definition. The only thing that needs to be added to our previous remarks is that in that case the semantic increment is no longer perceivable, although these expressions are felt to be endowed with an extra charge of expressivity due to residual metaphoricity, as, for example, 'non-drivers come into their own' in the subtitle of Kiwi (Appendix 6) which could be translated as 'Le non-conducteur retrouve ses droits' or with a compensatory ordering modulation, 'c'est l'avènement du non-conducteur'.

Substitutive modulations create similar semantic overlays when contextual discontinuities which are deliberately introduced by the writer and recognized as such by the reader are then, as it were, ignored by the writer, who thus proceeds as if what he or she has written is perfectly logical and consistent. This could be considered as a case of inverted metaphoring. The added semantic charge does not result as before from a process of accretion but through the enlarged perception induced by the discrepancy: the two superimposed segments are not perceived in their resemblances but in their disparities. It is clear that the difference between these types of effects (as in the case of over- and underemphasizing ordering modulations) is a fine one and easily reversible. It is for the reader to decide whether, for example, the Kiwi in the *Time* article subtitle is placed in an exalted or ridiculous position as a result of his being 'in the catbird seat', or possibly both at the same time.

The sheer provocativeness of this subtitle is obviously meant to tease the reader into reading the article, which is part of its most fundamental strategy. The rest of the article in its baroque orientation builds on that initial effect by accumulating pretendedly unrecognized discontinuities: 'When the bloom/ was on the roads', 'doomed to a life of dependence on alien wheels', 'camshafting egregious OPEC', etc., in order to emphasize the particular turn of economic events that caused the formerly ridiculous non-drivers to be recognized by the community at large as meritorious citizens. A translation restricting itself to the simple restitution of this banal observation and neglecting to simulate the ambiguous strategy which uses it as a pretext would undoubtedly fail to reproduce the distinctive tenor of this article.

Before passing from intrapropositional to extrapropositional determinations, we will demonstrate the progressive construction of a homologon and envisage some of the corresponding French options. This will enable us to synthesize the progressive findings that we have built up at each successive step in our previous development.

If we take the first sentence in Sillitoe (Appendix 1),

Many people in the country had twentieth-century brains and energy but were held under by the eternal sub-strata of hierarchical soil-souled England.[4]

we can capitalize on some of the observations already proposed:

82 *Redefining Translation*

1 '**Many**' as a quantifier indicating 'great quantity' will be found to correspond to a wealth of expressions in French such as 'beaucoup', '(un) (grand) nombre' (one of the parenthesized words optional), 'bien des', 'plusieurs'. A closer study of the LC2 paraphrastic set will make it clear that 'many' merely indicates 'great quantity' as an objectively high degree situated on the quantitative scale with no further special emphasis on the exceptional character of that quantity such as could be found in 'bien des', or on its designation as in 'un grand nombre' or on simple plurality (opposed to unity), as in 'plusieurs'. Thus, clearly at this stage of the homologous definition 'beaucoup' seems to be the only word to duplicate the values indicated in the homologon.

2 We already mentioned that '**people in the country**' – once 'country' has been contextually identified as not referring to rural as opposed to urban areas but to the fictional character's own nation, and once '**people**' has been reformulated as 'unspecified individuals', thus excluding 'individus' and 'personnes', but qualifying 'gens' and 'hommes' (with neutral gender designation) – could be either reformulated in discrete elements as 'beaucoup de gens dans [(ce) (le) (mon) – the choice of determiner would have to be defined at the macro-textual level taking into account cross-cultural designations] pays' or in a more condensed form as 'beaucoup de mes concitoyens'.

3 The reformulative possibilities of the predicative link '**had**' attaching the ensuing attributes to the 'people in the country' have already been mentioned and need only be re-examined at this stage as introducing varying semantic values in the ordering of 'brains and energy' and 'twentieth-century'. Thus 'avaient [possédaient] une intelligence et une énergie du vingtième siècle' subcategorizes 'intelligence et energie' in terms of the modifier 'vingtième siècle'; 'tiraient leur intelligence et leur énergie du vingtième siècle' gives precedence to 'vingtième siècle'; 'chez beaucoup de gens dans ce pays, l'intelligence et l'énergie appartenaient au vingtième siècle' has shifted the emphasis a little further up, to 'gens'. The solution adopted will have to take into account the relative confusion introduced by a translation such as 'intelligence du vingtième siècle', which implies that there might be several types of intelligences characterized according to centuries, and so contribute to excluding that obvious solution. The translator will thus have to rely on one of the 'by-pass strategies' studied subsequently (Chapter 5).

4 We have also shown how the semantic connection introduced by the nominal compound '**twentieth-century brains and energy**' might generate

several congruent but different LC2 options that would have to be discriminated at a higher macro-textual level.

5 Sufficient indications have also been given as to the nature of the contextual discontinuity introduced by the predicative link '**held under**', though one further remark would have to be added concerning its passive status and the aspectual determination that would normally have to be associated with it. On these two points, homologous projections in French are bound to produce different options – the aoristic or frequentative aspects '<u>furent</u>' ou '<u>étaient</u>' and the agentive or non-agentive (even with a specific cause introduced by 'par') passive can freely combine: '<u>étaient/furent noyés</u>' or '<u>se trouvaient/se trouvèrent noyés</u>'.

6 The explicitation of the causal agent '**the eternal sub-strata**' should lead us into exploring the geological paradigm: '<u>stratification sous-jacente</u>' (incidentally, an expanding paraphrastic formulation), '<u>sous-couches</u>', '<u>strates inférieures/sous-jacentes</u>'. Considering the general ironical strategy of the whole text, our preference would go to the more pejoratively connotative terms such as '<u>strates inférieures</u>', for example, a justification which would also qualify '<u>sempiternelles</u>' over '<u>éternelles</u>' thus combining to produce: '<u>les sempiternelles couches inférieures</u>'.

7 As opposed to the synthetic nominal compound that we analysed previously, the analytical compound introduced by '**of**' leaves no ambiguity as to comparative emphasis between the two nominals involved. 'England' clearly bears the sentence's end-focus, a structure that will be preserved in LC2 reformulations.

8 We also mentioned the difficulty that would be encountered in giving full notional power to '∅ **England**', the choice in French LC2 being between various degrees of determination – '<u>une /l'/ cette Angleterre</u>' – whose diverse potentialities will have to be assessed in relation to the general orientation that the translator will choose to impart to the text.

9 The first qualifier, '**hierarchical**' will give rise to two related lexes – 'relating to hierarchy' and 'arranged as a hierarchy' – which would separately correspond to TL 'hiérarchique' and 'hiérarchisée', a duality obviously calling for a choice that needs to be textually or contextually justified. Another option based on a shift in grammatical categories – 'la hiérarchie de . . . ', – beside being clearly patterned on the second lexis, would also entail an undesirable modulation in emphasis.

84 *Redefining Translation*

10 The second qualifier, '**soil-souled**', is more complex in its structure and in its lexis definition. The syntactic pattern on which it is constructed is probably a cross between the 'adjective + souled' paradigm (on the 'great/high/mean-souled' model) reformulable as 'who/which has a [adjective] soul' and the 'noun + noun + ed' paradigm (as in 'giant-sized') reformulable as 'who/which has [physical attribute] the size of a giant'. This structural overlap (and possible modulation) creates the basis for the ambiguity which is more evidently conveyed in the plurality of lexes that can be associated to the lexical unit '**soil**'. They can be classified into two sets: those referring to 'earth/soil' and those referring to 'dirt/dung'. Besides, the ambiguity is 'slurred over', so to say, and made plausible by the overlaid modulation alliteratively associating the two substantives. Homologon specifications, no doubt largely induced by LC1-specific features, make it very difficult for the translator to reconstruct a similarly signifying complex in LC2. But at least the constitutive elements of the homologon are clear and so are the priorities to be given in their restitution. The various paraphrases that will have to be generated can consequently be justly assessed in terms of their reformulative adequacy. Thus, in the solution finally adopted – 'à l'âme

Table 4.2 Homologies

Beaucoup de mes concitoyens	Beaucoup de gens dans ce [le, mon] pays	Chez beaucoup de gens dans ce pays
tiraient leur intelligence et leur énergie du vingtième siècle	avaient une intelligence et une énergie du vingtième siècle	l'intelligence et l'énergie appartenaient au vingtième siècle

mais

se trouvaient	étaient	
enfouis	noyés	coulés

sous les

sempiternelles couches inférieures	éternelles sous-couches/strates inférieures	stratifications sous-jacentes
d'une	de l'	de cette
Angleterre hiérarchisée	de la hiérachie d'une Angleterre	

à l'âme tout aussi terrienne que terreuse

Interlinguistic homologies 85

aussi terrienne que terreuse' – the alliteration and the basic lexis values have been simulated but the paradigmatic ambiguity has been projected on the syntagmatic plane.

The homological set of options shown in Table 4.2 could be proposed in French. This particular homologon expansion will no doubt appear inordinately ponderous and needlessly meticulous in its determination. Indeed, in many cases, some of the developments or explication will not have to be conducted in full. As we have already indicated, the homologon's 'telescopic' properties provide at the same time for the shortcuts and retroactive loops that may be necessitated by variations in difficulty occurring in the definition of LC2 paraphrastic sets. The translator's competence is again the foundation and the complement of homologous definition. It is, moreover, fundamental to the Variational approach that the translation options should be kept open as long as possible in order for motivated decisions to be taken at the highest possible level in the translation procedure.

5 Extrapropositional relationships in homologon definition

Translation Studies are the problematic offspring of the sciences which have contributed to their definition and of the practitioners who have treated translating and translation from the pragmatic angle. There seems to be little and often no common ground between the two traditions. As a consequence, translation procedure has been either compartmentalized in linguistically inspired studies or generalized in syncretic overviews. In order to compensate for these limitations, the Variational approach has contributed (1) an analytical and progressive analysis of all the translation-relevant levels in meaning definition independently of boundaries between research areas and (2) a synthetic construction of these levels in the homologon definition.

Among the indirect consequences of this former state of the reflection on translation was that what lay outside the necessarily limited preoccupations of the linguists or beyond the empiric considerations of the practitioners was excluded from consideration. Among the problems commonly ignored were beyond-the-sentence determinations and textual strategies that we propose to integrate within the general model of homological construction under the general name of *extrapropositional determinations*.

Concerning these problems, what characterizes the Variational approach is that it completely reverses the *order* and the *nature* of operations in the decision-making process regulating translation choices. In most of the previous methodologies, determinations were fixed from the lowest level, i.e. lexical and syntactic choices, upwards. Once the basic constituents of meaning had been selected, then a certain number of other considerations were envisaged peripherally in order to modulate this basic definition according to rhetorical, stylistical, or textual and even contextual criteria. If these determinations could not be fitted in or could only be partially integrated, it was generally felt that the essential, i.e. the basic, meaning definition had been safeguarded.

Although we stress the crucial importance of the lexical level and we proceed cumulatively from that level onto larger structures, it will be clear by now that the Variational approach is based on a totally different strategy. Instead of working on Levy's 'minimax' principle (1967: 1176) of progressively reducing the choices in order to find the most productive one, our methodology is aimed at opening up the options, defining ranges of variations, and fixing the conditions of their application. Consequently, the higher levels of definition – contextual and textual – are bound to be built into the homologon not as complementary, optional, or secondary features but as fundamental, although more diluted or far-ranging constituents. They can easily be integrated as explicit sets of constraints regulating the *chaining* and overall *patterning* of the choices generated at lower levels. Thus, instead of cumulatively built translation texts, we produce meaningfully constructed and referenced sets of alternative translation sequences.

This overall construction of options is finally submitted to sociocultural norms in the LC2 receiving context. One should note again that the usual perspective is reversed, since in previous methodologies, the translator started from an overall notion of the receiving context and then proceeded to formulations that would be in accordance with his or her analysis of the relevant factors. The Variational procedure aims at opening up the options sufficiently in order to determine the greatest number of possible conditions of integration in the LC2. This does not imply that previous solutions were necessarily wrong or incomplete but that the emphasis has been changed in order to reduce parasitic distortions. Instead of starting from a predefined conception of what the receiving context is going to be, the Variational approach tends to predict a variety of LC2 language insertions. The orientation is no longer *prescriptive* but *prospective*.

The homologon as we have described it seems to be particularly well suited to account for the extrapropositional dimension. Not only does it contribute to homogenizing the various parts within a proposition but at the same time it can formulate interpropositional relations. Its systemic nature offers the possibility of accounting for exterior correlations as extensions, reformulations, or further variations on the homologon. Between each homologon developed at the propositional level, we will try to establish chains of sequences themselves integrating textual strategies. This progressive concatenation of signification seems to correspond to the empiric apprehension of meaning through comprehension or reading. It is our belief that this process, erratic and unpredictable as it may seem, nevertheless conforms to some basic objective patterns that we will now proceed to develop both at the interpropositional and at the textual levels.

THE INTERPROPOSITIONAL LEVEL

At the *interpropositional* level, we no longer take into account the *construction* of meaning from lexical selection, syntactic ordering, and modulatory shifts of emphasis, but we try to account for the indispensable complement of meaning construction which is meaning *referencing*. If we refer back to the System of Representation (SR), we can conceive meaning production as a double process of abstracting and resituating cultural values through the mediation of the linguistic system and semiotic codes.

Meaning has to be extracted from the SR in order to become adapted to the communicators' *specific* objectives in a given situation of communication. Meaning definition in its first stage can only produce significantly distinctive results by isolating notions and relations from the whole *and* by cutting off all existing ties with the original common structure. Fuchs and Pêcheux (1975: 19–20) have clearly demonstrated that it is an illusion constitutive of the 'subject' that he should consider himself as not only the originator but also the creator of his meaningful productions. The subject 'naturally' conceives of himself independently of the receiver of his discourse, of the general context of his enunciation and of the cultural background of reference in which it is situated. He perceives his enunciations as meaning-producing, i.e. expressing his thoughts, accounting for reality and serving a purpose, according to the 'ready-made' preconceptions that the system provides.

Accounting for that aspect of meaning definition in isolation would then be vastly misleading. Meaning definition is at the same time *productive* and *differentially produced* within the system, an expression (according to the readily available stereotype) and an imprint on something else. There can be no assessment of meaning without measuring the difference introduced by the linguistic expression upon the semiotic frame of reference: the situational, textual, and intertextual contexts.

Meaning is thus determined on a first level of definition by *selection* and on a second level by *referencing*.[1] This process should be clearly distinguished from the socio-cultural parametering that considers the totality of the outside situation in order to determine its incidence on the production of meaning.

This extension of the homologon can be described in three different manners: *contextually, situationally* and *discursively*.

1 *Contextual* extension entails the redefinition of ST-internal paraphrastic sets in keeping with interpropositional networks of meaning such as can be reconstructed by the reading process.

If we reconsider, for example, our study of the first sentence of Sillitoe (Appendix 1), in order to introduce beyond-the-sentence relations, we are led into redefining some of the paraphrastic sets described in the preceding chapter. It is easy to identify, for example, meta-textual entities known as 'characters' that can be considered as contextually binding. If we contrast from that point of view John's excessive judgements to Frank's more sedate perception of the British soul, we can confirm some of the choices that have been proposed. 'Bon nombre' and 'beaucoup' can still qualify as being homologous to 'many' with a slight preference to 'bon nombre' corresponding to Frank's counterfactual impression that such an objective quantity could be found despite John's sweeping judgement to the contrary. Besides, both John's and Frank's expatriate status and the LC2 necessary 'foreignness' to the British context make us favour the distancing deictic 'ce' as a determiner for 'pays'. So contextual determination contributes to specify some of the unattached options previously generated at the propositional level; but it should be made clear that this form of specification does not exclude other options, it only creates more or less probable bonds between propositions.

Other more pervasive but less obvious contextual determinations can be found. Since they are not so easily recognizable as the literary entities known as 'characters', they tend to be overlooked, though they contribute powerfully to our construction of signification in the reading process. In Sillitoe, the structure repeatedly enforced in the context preceding the sentence selected for homologous exemplification, based on a pattern of the type: 'they (the British) were + nominal identification' (such as 'they were insular plain-speakers') is abruptly interrupted by the introduction of the 'had' structure in 'had twentieth-century brains and energy' (Sillitoe, *A Tree on Fire*, p. 414), which turns the previous objective description into an attributive statement. This textual feature should lead us into reconsidering the LC2 paraphrastic formulations for 'had'. Clearly, a new, more restricted set of LC2 options including 'avaient', 'possédaient', and even 'étaient *nantis* de' for increased contrast with 'étaient' patterns would have to be formulated. This raises again the problem of the unwanted ambiguity introduced in the second part of the proposition by 'intelligence et énergie du vingtième siècle', which indicates a case for adopting one of the shift strategies described later in this chapter (pp. 100–4).

Conceptual, as opposed to structural, constraints also contribute to homologous redefinition. Thus still in Sillitoe, the obvious parallelism between 'except the chosen few who are buried under the common mass' in the preceding context and 'were held under by the eternal sub-strata' is sufficient invitation to reconsider our preferred choice of 'enfouis sous' and requalify all the predicates describing metaphorically a similar position though referring to different elements such as 'noyés' or 'coulés'. For the same reason, the presence in the previous context of 'who muddled through by clan and hierarchy' may justify us choosing for the sake of parallelism 'la hiérarchie d'une Angleterre' over the adjective solution, thus clarifying the ambiguity contained in that phrase.

These chains of structuring elements are based on contrastive patterns acting as guiding-lines delineating the text's construction. In Zola (Appendix 2) a steadily more compelling conceptual pattern is established through the opposition between two parallel and contrasted sets of features: those associated with the young woman opposing awkward, fumbling activities such as 'fouiller' (twice repeated) and nimbler manipulations such as 'on les tenait par la tête', '(Elle) les glissa ... dans le petit panier', 'Elle triait les herbes délicatement, les rejetant par minces pincées', on the one hand; and those describing the object of her quest, the shrimp perceived at the same time as brisk and crisp in 'si vives', 'un bruit sec', 'un petit bruit d'ailes', and in association with viscous, slightly offensive things: 'un paquet d'herbes', 'là-dedans', 'enchevêtrement d'étranges feuilles, gluantes et molles comme des poissons morts'. Both sets of features converge on the two young people's vague perception (through the shrimping activity) of their progressive amorous involvement, seen as the same time as exciting and perturbing. This wide-ranging textual construction is of crucial importance for the overall redefinition of the choices produced at the propositional level. 'Fouiller', which we used as an example for lexis definition will have to be reconsidered for its contrastive value to 'triait ... délicatement', 'rejetant par minces pincées', thus possibly reactivating 'rummage' for the kind of confused, disorderly activity it describes. Similarly, if we take the translation of 'les rejetant par petites pincées' as a case for dense or discrete lexicalization (see Chapter 4), 'flicking it off bit by bit' will be more convincing as indicative of brisk fastidiousness over the more objective though adequate 'throwing it away in small pinches'. For the same reason, the assonantly related translation of 'paquet' and 'enchevêtrement' by 'bundle' and 'tangle' would certainly bring in a not unwelcome overtranslation (see below, p. 103).

The case of the last two qualifiers in the sequence mentioned above ('feuilles *gluantes et molles* comme des poissons morts') is even more interesting since it is submitted to the double determination of close right-contextual determination through 'comme des poissons morts' and through more far-ranging contrastive relations to the shrimp's movements. The difficulty is compounded by the fact that paraphrastic reformulation and homologon explicitation fail to produce satisfactory LC2 homologous options. The possibilities for 'gluantes' are 'sticky', 'slimy', 'gluey' and for 'molles', 'soft', 'limp', or 'flabby', thus constituting a fairly heterogeneous assortment. Clues will have to be sought in the contextual determinations, privileging strongly connotative terms in LC2: viscidity and repulsiveness in the case of 'gluantes', thus favouring 'slimy', and absence of firmness and energy for 'molles', thus indicating, rather, 'flabby'. Still, the options should be felt to be very much open to translator's individual predilections.

Finally, Lawrence (Appendix 5), as we will more fully develop (see Chapter 5, pp. 98–9), combines the full range of *continuous* and *contrastive* possibilities studied so far in Zola and Sillitoe together with an extraordinary array of progressive paraphrastic variations contributing to the text's distinctive *metamorphic* development, such as the chains of cognate predicates 'Flying – rose – fleeing – fleeing out' in opposition to 'forcing their way in – came in heavily – running under towards the centre'. In this particular case, the exact degree of progressiveness has to be fixed in close conjunction with the lexis definition of each item included in the set.

Thus, the two main aspects of the homologon structure – syntagmatic and paradigmatic – are clearly represented at the contextual level. A text is a macro-proposition based on constituent units (propositions or sentences). This much has been made clear by contemporary studies in Text Grammar or Discourse Analysis.[2] Our contribution from the Variational perspective is that macro-structural correlations are systems involving patterns of *similarities/contrasts* and *variations* that we consider as the extended formulation of the ST homologon.

2 In all the texts that we have selected for analysis, the *situational* factor cannot be envisaged directly but only through various forms of textual simulations and, in only three of these texts, it is of any significant relevance. In its characteristic novelistic strategy, Zola (Appendix 2) divides the evocation of the material conditions of the shrimping party into described and implicit details. The same holds for the Albee text (Appendix 4), which is an invitation for the reader to reconstruct the full situational determinants of the scene. Only, in the case of drama, the producer of the play has to take into account the conventions of the theatrical world for which he or she is staging the play and the fundamental fact that he or she, in colloboration with others, is

mediating that scene for an audience. Our last example (the 'Lufthansa' advertisement, Appendix 7) is apparently closer to the conditions of the basic situation of communication with its photographic reproduction of reality. But we will see in our analysis of the document that this is also an illusion which has to be decoded by the 'reader' of the photograph. All our other texts are based in various degrees and for different purposes on generalization of situational references.

Situational determinations will act in close association with contextual ones, as will appear clearly in one particular example taken from Zola. The last sentence of the excerpt relating M. Chabre's casual remark, 'C'est particulier . . . je n'en pêche pas une', cannot be assessed through the lexis explication alone of its ambiguous present tense which is bound to produce acceptable LC2 homologous equivalents, such as 'I can't (even) fish (get, catch) (a single) one'. It has, of course, to be related to contextual references to his wife's repeated catches. The situation so created connects in the reader's mind M. Chabre's bad luck with his total unconsciousness of the young people's growing mutual attraction. This aspect of the situation would be humorously set into relief in 'I'm not getting a single one' self-consciously referring to the 'activity' introduced by the aspectual rather than to the inability designated in 'can't', which could be felt to be too explicit, although that aspect of the situation might be thought to be glancingly evoked in the choice of the verb 'get'.

Situational specifications can be more or less determining according to types of discursive situations. When for example, it comes to translating dramatic texts such as Albee (Appendix 4) a double dimension has to be taken into consideration. On the one hand, more or less explicit situational information is commonly supplied by the dramatist in the form of stage directions indicating the particular way in which the characters' texts are to be related to the scene. On the other hand, the dividing-line between these two types of meaning definition – linguistic and behavioural – is not easy to draw in so far as the human body is the most immediate 'setting' for the character's utterances. Some linguistic expressions such as George's 'Brandy? Just brandy?' would be needlessly inexplicit in French LC2 and so could be made more specific: 'Du cognac, sans rien d'autre (avec des glaçons?)'; other texts such as 'Martha: "Ha, ha, ha, HA!"' would have to be reconverted as stage directions: 'Martha (partant d'un gros rire [s'esclaffant])'. It is clear, in any case that the overall distribution between text, stage direction, and supporting action will have to be redefined in terms of the theatrical norms of the receiving context.

For example, if we examine at the beginning of the Albee text, George's feigned attempt at saving face after Martha's gross explosion, because of cultural differences in order to translate George's 'Ahhhhhhh!', the French LC2 will call for a steady flow of mellifluous banalities in order to drown and highlight Martha's obscenity, thus justifying our rendering: 'Tiens, vous voilà tous les deux, quel bon vent!' Also, most of the self-conscious small talk that the young couple are exchanging and the accompanying stage directions will be rendered as effusive and lavish urbanities in French. A case in point of this transfer of meaning between expression and situation can be George's retort: 'George [innocent and hurt]: "Martha!" ' which would be clearly felt as insufficiently explicit if strictly patterned on the LC1 original. Some transfer from the meaning contained in the stage direction would have to be effected: 'George [feignant l'innocence et l'indignation]: "Martha, voyons, tout de même." '

Contextual definition will be seen to be even more determining in our concluding and cumulative study of the Lufthansa publicity (Appendix 7). A comparison between the quality of smiling displayed by the air hostess on the photograph and the business smiles lavishly served by the other airlines is crucial to the understanding and homologous definition of the accompanying text. It will be seen that this type of situation leads to the extreme case in which the formulation of the linguistic part of the advertisement is to be reconsidered in keeping with the explicit and implicit situational factors conveyed in the semiotic codes of the photograph.

3 *Intertextual referencing*, finally, consists in situating linguistically contructed meaning in relation with the preconstructed texts of all sorts that any particular text can marshal. Again, as in the other two types of referencing, the connection between text and intertext is the product of the reader's/translator's reading activity and should be perceived as strictly circumscribed to his or her reading capacities. Intertextual determination can be added to the homologon in the form of an explicitating paraphrase with additional notations defining the specific relationship which is established between text and intertext.

Contextual, situational, and intertextual referencing should be seen as complementary, sometimes overlapping, sometimes interlocking determinations as we are going to show using an example taken from Albee (Appendix 4). When Martha says toward the end of the passage: 'Sure. "Never mix – Never worry" ', she is quoting Honey's silly transparent excuse to have more drinks and so deriding her shallow hypocritical cant; but she is also, at a second remove, quoting intertextually from the common stock of social phrases condoning excessive drinking supposed to be mitigated by a certain uniformity of choice. Finally, at a further remove, Martha is humorously alluding to her own situationally obtrusive drinking problem and to the advanced degree of alcoholic intoxication she finds herself in at the moment. Considering this multilayered accumulation of references, it is all the more important that the corresponding LC2 text should be adequately selected. 'Jamais de mélanges!' could be an acceptable solution.

Certain texts are essentially based for meaning production on the ability of the reader to reactivate the built-in intertextual references dispersed through the sequence of propositions. This is the case of the Kiwi text (Appendix 6) which, on the basis of its propositional value, develops a very simple paradox of contemporary life – the non-driver – who used to be a scandalous rarity, but has, because of the oil crisis, become a kind of social hero. Apart from that very obvious point, the text acquires its particular brand of humorous signification in the wealth, complexity, and heterogeneity of its cultural and intertextual references. As a matter of fact, this is the type of culture-bound text which is often considered by traditional translation analysts as being barely translatable. Yet once it is made clear that the process of intertextual referencing makes up the essential of the text's semantic contribution, it is less difficult to propose homologous paraphrastic sets in the LC2.

First, it is essential to elucidate the types of references that the text conjures up in the reader's consciousness. We will isolate three levels of intertextual perception. There is first the type of vague cultural knowledge that stands halfway between paraphrastic reformulation and the basic encyclopedic knowledge that everybody is able to associate with certain cultural notions. Thus the 'kiwi' is associated with the ludicrous property of being a bird deprived of the ability to fly. On this basis, a certain number of clichés such as 'to be in the catbird seat' are reactivated and made to signify both at their face value: the kiwi is some sort of catbird (so a bird nevertheless) and, according to their stereotyped value; the ridiculous kiwi occupies a prominent position. The cultural reference to the common stock of knowledge contributes to infusing additional meaning references and consequently increased enjoyment into this fairly trivial social paradox. Such overlaid referencing is of course a challenge to homological reconstruction but should not inhibit production once the referencing procedures have been made explicit. While 'le kiwi est aux premières loges' would only reproduce the clichéd value, 'le kiwi est (traité) comme un coq en pâte' or 'tel le phénix, le kiwi renait de ses cendres' reconstitute most of the referencing determinants of this sentence's signification.

The reference can also be to what we will call 'social texts' in various forms of explicitness and stability. They can be circumstantial, i.e. linked to some specific event in a given society such as in Kiwi 'he can be said to have heeded official pleas to share the ride', referring to the energy-conserving measures that were more or less strictly enforced on the public during the successive oil crises. The double style of address contained in the intertextual reference – administrative 'heeded official pleas' and persuasive 'share the ride' – will have to be simulated. The allusion can also be to social phraseologies whose exact reproduction can provide the required semantic contribution, as in Honey's exclamatory comment (in Albee, Appendix 4) on Martha's alleged infidelity: 'Honey [to save the situation]: "Oh, ho, ho, ho, HO." ' They call for an appropriate LC2 social text such as: 'Tiens, tiens, voyez-vous ça!' Finally, the reference can be to clichés which constitute the inevitable social intertext on which the humorous writer can reinscribe his or her own particular contribution, as we saw in the 'kiwi in the catbird seat' allusion or in the humorous fusing of two clichés in 'a country that relies so heavily on the auto for its bread and butter and most of its honey'.

Other types of intertextual referencing are based on the ludicrous association between a trifling subject and a miscellaneous assortment of extraneous literary references. Thus 'When the bloom was on the roads' will be apty reformulated in French LC2 as referring either to some well-known stereotype – 'Quand les routes étaient à la fleur de l'âge' – or to some sixteenth-century poetic purple piece, such as 'Quand les routes n'avaient point encore perdu cette vesprée' according to the humorous charge necessary to produce the desired reaction in the text's final receiving context. Similarly, the cultural references to *The Merry Wives of Windsor* in 'excessive gasoline consumption has become offensive to nostril' or to Wordsworth's '*Ode on Intimations of Immortality*' in 'trails clouds of self-esteem as palpable as the carbon dioxide he has forsworn' call for a homologous rendering in LC2 either in the form of a stereotype – 'la consommation excessive de carburant porte atteinte à nos narines' and 'traine derrière lui des nuées de bonne conscience/ porte sur sa tête une aura de bonne conscience' – or any similarly slanted quotation.

What is especially flagrant about this particular text is in various degrees true of all types of signifying structures. They are characterized as much by the nature of the semantic construction that they evince as by the type of referencing that they suggest to the reader. They define signification by abstracting cultural units from the system of reference and by more or less extensive references to the system as a whole, to the situation in which they are situated and to themselves as ordered sets of propositions. *The text itself becomes a system designating the common system and displacing it.*

The systematic construction of texts which translation has to account for has finally to be envisaged as being oriented towards a finality expressed in textual strategies.

TEXTUAL STRATEGIES

Both formulation and referencing as constitutive of meaning definition are finally organized in the perspective of overall textual strategies which gear texts to their often complete referential functions and objectives.[3]

Meaning construction consists in abstracting notions and relations from the System of Representation in order to serve the enunciator's and co-enunciator's negotiated semantic purposes. This operation was seen as projecting individual signification on the background of a common cultural conceptual network of references. Referencing recreates links between constructed meaning and the various constituents of signification – the cohesiveness of its verbal structure, its contextual reference and the degree of intertextuality that it encapsulates. In this way, the constructed text is at the same time made up of reappropriated cultural material and resituated in its own specific and individual way within the System of Representation, *collectively determined and individually modulated.*

This process of adaptation which so intrinsically characterizes semantic productions corresponds to four 'textual strategies' reflecting the semiotic configuration of the SR. If the SR is hypothetically conceived as a multiplicity of systematically related values grouped together in a 'semantic universe', then in Eco's terms:

> (a) in a given culture there can exist contradictory semantic fields ... ; (b) the same cultural unit can itself become part of complementary semantic fields within a given culture ... ; (c) within a given culture a semantic field can disintegrate with extreme rapidity and restructure itself into a new field. (Eco, 1976: 80)

If we try to follow up on Eco's conceptions, there are only two possibilities of connecting these units for the purpose of communication. Either the semantic texture will explore the continuity of semantic chains, thus disregarding (or rather 'backgrounding') their oppositional value to the other semiotic chains, or it will develop on the contrastive dimension that singly or multivalently connects each value and cultural chain of values, thus ignoring (or again temporarily 'downplaying') their sequential potential.

The first procedure corresponds to the 'consecutive strategies' whose function is to produce new values and relations both on the cultural and referential plane. In this case they will be called *logical* (the name 'logical' should be understood in the widest possible acceptation as describing all types of sequential concatenation of propositions, including those which are traditionally considered as logical). These sequences can also be made to confirm and reinforce pre-existing values and relations, and will be designated as *analogical*. Consecutive structures can thus be either productive or reproductive.

The second procedure corresponds to 'ambivalent strategies' that are based explicitly on the contradiction of cultural values. Their function is either to produce new or more complexified contrasts between semiotic chains – in that case, they will be called *aesthetic* or to reveal and highlight existing contradictions already present in the SR thus corresponding to *ambiguous* strategies. It is clear that ambivalent structures can, like the consecutive, be either productive or reproductive.

Each of these strategies predefines a characteristic type of meaning organization which regulates (1) the interpropositional dimension in our previous section; (2) semiotic inscription, the intertextual and contextual dimension; and (3) the type of commmunication established by the text. We will henceforward refer to these three aspects of textual strategy as *Content, Reference, and Relationships*.

If we take the Kiwi text (Appendix 6) for example, we have to recognize that on a very thin informational basis, the journalist has constructed through various linguistic manipulations and intercultural references a dense sequence of ambiguous structures destined to make us explore, assess, and finally distance the contradictions of our privileged but precarious position in contemporary industrial societies as car-owners using up a precious raw material.

The content of this distinctly 'ambiguous' text is obviously poor in conventional informative terms; we can even say that it is intentionally counterproductive in this respect. This is because the essential of meaning definition is based on recognition of submerged contradictions as opposed to the definition, confirmation, or production of cultural values as in the 'logical' strategies. The characteristic type of reference is pluri-associative tending to call on the greatest number of cultural values in order to vindicate its particular objective. Finally, in terms of relationships, the ambiguous strategy calls for a certain form of conniving participation as opposed to the process of intellectual conviction which characterizes the logical strategy. Ambiguous strategies explore the extent to which the isolated contradiction is reverberated and dispersed throughout the SR. Logical strategies, such as the Delisle text (Appendix 3), on the contrary, isolate the text from the complexity of cultural references in order to verify the continuity and the referential productivity of specific chains of values as in that particular case the correlation between cancer/mastectomy/trauma and plastic surgery.

D.H. Lawrence (Appendix 5) follows a different type of productive procedure in the exploration of the SR. This production is based on the validation of some specific form of contradiction. But, instead of leading us to recognize and measure some existing ambivalence within the system, its objective is to construct new systems of ambivalences or refine and extend the existing ones. Thus Lawrence is founded on the exploration of a double and complementary contradiction between centrality and dispersion on the one side and between conflict and reunification on the other. This typical 'aesthetic' structure is superimposed on a very distended logical narrative sequence – one character has thrown a stone into a pool in the presence of another – which links up that passage with the continuity of the eminently 'logical' plot developed in the rest of the novel.

It should be clear that these specific strategies contribute further to determine the homologies which the translator is able to produce in his or her treatment of any given ST. Extrapropositional relationships tend to create textual networks or chains of related homologous options. But these chains, although connected, are not oriented. Textual strategies, which we postulate as being part of the co-enunciators' competence to produce and recognize, impose on these unattached chains of elements and options a single or multilayered complex of textual forms that have to be considered in order to appreciate the finality of the text. These general forms, however complex their combinations, correspond to the common intuitive feeling shared by every producer of discourse that his or her productions carry a 'purport' or 'convey a meaning'. These intuitively recognized forms should in no way be confused with the socio-cultural determinations which act upon both production and reception of discourse. If it is normal that a certain amount of congruence should exist between textual strategies and socio-cultural norms, there is still ample room for discrepancies, as we will see in our concluding study on the Lufthansa advertisement and more extensively in Chapter 9.

If we take the case of Lawrence in particular, and this would be equally true of all textual configurations, the translator will have to determine the text's homologon successively in terms of propositional, interpropositional, and strategic determinations. Thus, if we choose the following passage, 'It seemed to be drawing itself together', towards the end of the text, this particular segment will have to be assessed in its lexis and linguistic content but also in its left-contextual proximity with 'not quite destroyed', 'not even now broken open', 'not yet violated' as a negative definition and also with 'a white body of fire writhing and striving' as a positive forward orientation. Possible LC2 homologies will then be formulated: 'Elle semblait se reformer/se reconstituer/se resouder/se rétablir/se reprendre/se ressaisir' which will have to be discriminated in the perspective of the final coalescing ambivalence produced by the text: 'triumphant reassumption'. As we will try to illustrate in Chapter 9, the ultimate choice of both initial and concluding notions in the chain linking 'drawing itself together' and 'triumphant reassumption' is no doubt largely a question of individual sensibility and perception. What is not open to interpretation is the overall orientation and the necessary coherence between each stage in the development of that transformation.

We have seen that in most of the texts under consideration the strategies were expressed in dual, alternated, successive, or multilayered structures hierarchically positioned in terms of ostensible and underlying patterns. The strategies can also be used contrastively in situations of communication such as in Albee (Appendix 4). Thus Martha alternates opposite types of strategies in keeping with her various communicational orientations. She tries to make the young couple feel at home and so verbally goes out of her way to be charming and hospitable through a characteristic mixture of bossy logical structures (Do this or that!) and of analogical structures in which the guests themselves are the privileged value ('C'mon in, kids'). On the other hand, she strongly rebukes her husband in a similar blend of authoritarian logical statements complemented by analogical segments in which George stands for the negative value of her discourse. The logical structure of persuasion and orders which is clearly her favourite medium of expression can be easily overlooked in the translator's otherwise justified desire to offset contrasts in her attitudes. A case in point could be the juxtaposition of the two contrasted values in 'Just ignore old sourpuss over there. C' mon in, kids ... give your coats and stuff to sourpuss.' We mention an attenuated version of the contrast in parentheses: 'N'écoutez pas ce casse-pied' ('Ne faites surtout pas attention à ce vieux bougon'). Entrez, les enfants (Donnez-vous la peine d'entrer, les enfants!) et refilez vos affaires au casse-pied ('Donnez donc vos affaires à ce vieux bougon').'

George's expressive strategies are as contrary to Martha's as their characters. Instead of ostensibly changing modes of expression, he seems to adopt various dissimulative strategies and even at times to impersonate other people's speeches. The ostensible orientation of George's expression is thus quasi-tautological in, for example, 'You must be our little guests', or imitative when repeating Martha's words,

'Anywhere . . . furniture, floor . . . doesn't make any difference around this place', or when parodying Honey's laughter. But, this appropriation of the other characters' language is submitted to an ambiguous strategy. Their expressions are made to stand in isolation or embedded in his own deceitful discourse. Thus they are unfairly judged at their face value instead of their social values. In a play like *Who's Afraid of Virginia Woolf?* communicational strategies are at least as important for the reception of the play as the content of the words exchanged by the characters. Considering the differences in expressive emphases and theatrical conventions between LC1 and LC2, the problem confronting the translator is to decide to what extent and in what forms he or she is going to simulate these structures. Will he just rely on the actor's talent for meaningfully highlightling these passages or on the audience's recognition of George's tongue-in-cheek repetition of 'You must be our little guests', or will the translation be inflected towards a more textually explicit version, such as 'On dirait que ce sont nos petits invités'?

These are some of the options raised by identification of strategic objectives. Like the rest of the linguistic or referencing determinations we have studied so far, they constitute ranges of paraphrastic choices but, in the circumstances, they do not concern the content or the coherence of ST homologon but its overall orientation.

TRANSLATION SHIFTS

The analytical process that we have tried to track so far leads to the formulation of a fully referenced ST homologon definition and in turn to the production of similarly referenced homologies in LC2. At this point the generative stage in the Variational approach could be said to come to an end and give over to the final normative stage.

A last dimension needs to be taken in consideration though. Homological reformulation is at the same time productive and manipulative and consequently the methodology defined above is open to various modes or *techniques*. Particular precautions should be taken when referring to this term. Up until recently, Translation Studies were nearly exclusively devoted to the definitions of practical devices that could systematize the translating operation; the natural extension of these instrumental approaches was that if these devices were sufficiently refined and logically ordered they could be fed into automatic translation machines. Similarly, the translator her- or himself compensated for a certain lack of systematicity by various time-saving shortcuts in the decision process.

Our approach is markedly different in so far as translation techniques are never envisaged as an end in themselves nor for that matter as susceptible to being mechanized. They are not supposed to be applicable in all circumstances in connection with any type of texts. This would run against our initial theoretical foundations. On the contrary, they proceed immediately from our conception of homologies as referenced sets of interlinguistic paraphrases. Homologies constitute a fund of potential options to be submitted to socio-cultural determinations and ultimately to the definition of a translation choice. This decision can be guided and inflected by a certain number of translation shifts which we propose to study below.

These translation 'shifts' are to be considered as predefined by-pass techniques which should inform the translator's decision in certain specific circumstances. They can be characterized as cases in which the translator feels the necessity of departure from the strict homologizing production. These situations can be described under three headings:

1 The ST in its complexity or specificity compels the translator to choose among the conflicting values which he or she has analysed and thus some kind of escape strategy has to be marked out for him or her. This is a case already mentioned in connection with the translation of Sillitoe: 'hierarchical soil-souled England'.

2 LC2 limitations prevent the production of homological paraphrases or even evince 'voids' (see Dagut, 1981). In that case, a by-pass strategy has to be arranged, as when translating 'le [parisian] périphérique', for which a choice of translation would be still possible in British LC2 either in the form of a borrowing like ' "périphérique" ' or some indigenous reference such as 'ring road' with the necessary contextual adjustment, but would be more difficult to evoke in the American urban context of easily penetrable cities.

3 Finally, for reasons that are specific to his or her own communicative intention – as for example Delisle's 'analyse exegétique' (1984: 69) in relation to pragmatic texts – the translator may choose to deviate from strict homological definition (see Chapter 8).

All translation by-passing strategies have to be predefined and proposed to the translator as a choice of possible translation alternatives and not, of course, as surefire universally applicable or ready-made techniques. These alternative strategies are easy to define within the homological concept itself. If we bear in mind the fact that homologies are systematic cross-cultural ranges of choices, then the strategies will be simply conceived in terms of *shifts* between the various levels and planes that we analysed before, mere variations within the variation range.

Thus, a certain number of specific strategic orientations of translation methodology are easily predictable. We can first envisage the simple but extremely common *shift within the TL homologous set* – be it at the lexical, syntactic, or extrapropositional level. We should never forget that the LC2 paraphrastic set must always be considered as a *simulation* of LC1-observed values, never (as the difficult-to-eradicate naive conception would have it) as a reproduction or equivalent of the ST. Consequently, the LC1 homologous set, as we have seen for the translation of 'gluantes et molles' in Zola, constitutes a range of acceptable options that the translator can freely interchange in accordance with his preconceptions, the objectives of the text or the specific constraints of the LC2 context.

For example, in Albee (Appendix 4), the translation of the last word in the stage direction attached to George's first intervention, '... but really satisfaction at having MARTHA's explosion *overheard*', will avoid the more evident 'entendue' for its paraphrastic cognate 'ne passe pas inaperçue' which underlines the underhand character of George's remark. It is easy to imagine why such a conversion to the antonymic paraphrase would of course be impossible in a text like Lawrence in which we saw (see p. 98) that concepts were metamorphically evolving from antonyms or negated lexical items into various shades of the same lexis as in the end: 'not yet violated – getting stronger – reasserting itself – inviolable – strengthened – triumphant reassumption'.

In the same way, in Zola (Appendix 2) there will clearly be some justification for the translator's reading into the specific strategy of the text associating shrimping and some fascinating danger dawning on Estelle's mind when he or she has to choose between the neutral 'informed' or the more explicit 'warned' to translate 'un bruit sec... l'avertissait... qu'il y avait des crevettes au fond'. These shifts are not only easy to predict but also, as we will see later (Chapter 10), easy to instil into a learner's developing practice.

The second possibility in translation manipulation, already hinted at in our study of the lexis (see p. 65), should now be generalized to the whole homologon definition. It involves *expansion* or *contraction* of homologon material. Potentially, any item in the homologon reformulation can be expanded along the syntagmatic dimension or, on the contrary, contracted into more specific lexical item or phrases. This translation strategy is evidently the complement on the syntagmatic dimension of the preceding which consisted in shifts within the paradigmatic set. It is clear, consequently, that the two strategies can be freely combined and in fact there is always some continuity between them.

If we consider Delisle's translation (Appendix 3) of 'Mrs. Joan Dawson, 54, of New York City' by 'Une Newyorkaise de 54 ans, Mme

Joan Dawson', we notice that the syntagmatic explication of the person's identity has been condensed into a more specific item, 'Newyorkaise', thus adequately adapting the American magazine phraseology to the French style. On the other hand and taking into account the observations that we made earlier in relation to 'Elle triait les herbes délicatement, les rejetant par petites pincées' in Zola (Appendix 2), when it comes to translating 'Avec de grands cris, elle appela Hector pour qu'il l'aidât', it would be inadvisable to propose a lexically condensed version of the predicate and prepositional phrase idiomatically apposite as it may seem, as in 'She called out to Hector for him to come and help her.' Preference should be given to the more cumbrous 'With screams/loud cries (or "Shrieking, screaming"), she called (out) to Hector for him to come and help her', putting greater emphasis on the characterization of the young woman.

In the Kiwi text (Appendix 6), the translator will have to assess a choice between the rhetorically expanded 'Que ce soit parce qu'il refuse d'acheter une automobile' and the more laconically nominalized 'Refus d'acheter une automobile' according to the effects or the variation of effects that he or she will think fit to introduce into this very motley text.

Once again the shift strategies are inscribed in the very nature of homologon reformulation. They should be regarded as readily available devices that may prove necessary because of unexpected difficulties or specific expressive requirements.

The third possible strategy is a choice between what is commonly known in translation literature as *undertranslation* and *overtranslation*. In this case, translation options will either redouble emphasis on one or several aspects of the homologon definition, as in Zola (Appendix 2) 'un petit bruit d'ailes' might be homologously reformulated in growing order of emphatic explicitness as 'a light fluttering of wings', 'a sound of fluttering/flapping wings', 'a sharp sound sound like fluttering/flapping wings', in which the resources of the preceding expanding and contracting techniques are combined with redoubled emphasis on certain features such as the quasi-obligatory but redundant association between 'wings' and 'flutter/flap'. On the other hand, when reconsidering Delisle's translation (Appendix 3), 'I didn't want to be made into a sensational beauty', it is perhaps advisable to underspecify the final reference in order to give it more power and greater clichéd recognition: 'Je ne voulais pas devenir une beauté.'

As opposed to the terse and objective formulation of this informative text, a more luxuriant text such as Kiwi (Appendix 6) would justify all overlaid additions that would contribute to the humorous objectives of the text and to different conditions of receptiveness to humorous effects. Thus, in order to produce an effective French homologon of 'self-decreed cripple' beside 'invalide volontaire', an expanded reformulation would be well worth considering, such as 'condamné volontaire à l'invalidité' or even 'en quelque sorte comme quelqu'un qui se serait volontairement condamné à l'invalidité.' Let us note once again that the various techniques analysed separately are nearly always combined when it comes to particular translation cases.

The over-/undertranslation technique is neither an idiosyncratic choice nor a specific technique: it is an option that the translator should be prepared to justify in terms of the necessities of adaptation to the LC2 receiving context.

Finally, the translator can also rely on the *'implicating'/'explicating'* technique that consists in shifting certain elements from the linguistic to the situational level and vice versa. Explication will occur, as we saw in our translation of Albee (Appendix 4), when meaningful elements are transferred from the situation into the staging text (stage directions) or integrated into the characters' words; or, in Delisle (Appendix 3), as is often the case with pragmatic texts, explication will be introduced in order to clarify referential data such as the objects involved in 'make it more nearly resemble the new one' translated by 'pour le rendre à peu près semblable au sein artificiel'; or indications of chronology, as in the reference to the two reconstructive surgical operations that might call for a more explicit ordering of events in the French translation: 'En deux opérations successives, *tout d'abord*, il implanta sous la peau à l'endroit de l'opération *anterieure* un sac rempli de silicone, *puis dans un deuxième temps* . . .'. The redundant information will, on the contrary, be subtracted whenever the reference will be felt to be perfectly clear in the TT, as in 'rebuild her missing breast', which will become in our suggested version 'lui refaire un sein'.

The examples of slanted translations could easily be mutiplied and deserve more detailed investigation as to the cases when they apply, the conditions of their combination, and their practical implementation. But, as in most of the subjects we have raised, this particular line of enquiry would in itself justify a complete study. Our main objective has not in any way been to cover fully all the subjects but to give a clear account of the theoretical and methodological issues at stake. Concerning translation strategies, these extremely versatile manipulations should be studied within the frame of translation homologies, observed in actual translation, and recognized as part and parcel of the translator's options. They cannot be considered as systematized techniques or reproducible translation blueprints, much less as indicative of differential features characterizing languages and worse still psycho-cultural preconceptions. This would amount to confusing the freedom in the translator's choices for linguistically or culturally enforced restrictions. It is in this alternative between a qualified decision process and restricted patterns of choices that the characteristic difference of the Variational approach lies.

In order to synthesize the observations that we have built up in Chapters 4 and 5, both at the propositional and extrapropositional levels, we propose to follow the different stages in the generating process in the following short but revealing publicity text.

Let us briefly recapitulate what translation methodology aims at producing:

1 In its *generative* stage, it constructs a homological representation of the ST combining (a) all the *explicating* texts that define the ST's meaning and (b) the TT *variational range* of all the texts that can be found to simulate the values defined in ST. The explication of the ST is achieved through the use of three complementary types of *paraphrases*: the reformulative, the synonymic, and the defining paraphrases. The TT variational range can also be seen as a combination of the three above-mentioned paraphrastic types.

2 In its *normative* stage, it defines the applicability of the translation options generated above in relation to the available norms of the LC2 socio-cultural context.

This is what we intend to demonstrate in relation to the Lufthansa text (Appendix 7). For the purpose of this application, we will consider that in this semiotic complex all that needs to be translated is the linguistic text at the top of the page; although this provisional working proposition will have to be questioned when we reach the higher levels of homological definition, i.e. textual and strategic.

In order to produce an explicating reading of the original ST, or a homologon in our terminology, we proceed through levels of definition in the ST – linguistic, contextual, and textual – not in fact to be perceived as independent levels but rather as progressively more embracing integrative structures.

1 The *linguistic* level can be broken down into three distinct segments:

(a) the predicative relationship: [say + {something}];
(b) the content of the act of saying: ['cheese!'];
(c) the various 'shifters' relating the predicative structure to the enunciative situation: [We], [just], [can't].

(a) *Say* relates to enunciative verbs comprising an illocutionary and a locutionary value, the latter being explicated by 'cheese' between inverted commas indicating a change in discursive status. *Say* should be compared to *tell* and *speak* in order to show that it gives comparative precedence to content over implied addressee or the act of enunciation itself. The French language offers a choice not so much of verbs as of addressee statuses in the option between enclitic or implied addressee:

> Nous ne pouvons tout de même pas dire/lui dire

(b) *Cheese* is one of the words quoted by Jakobson as defying reformulation. It so happens that a ready equivalent can be found in French. The *exclamation mark* could be left like the 'cheese' to 'fend' for itself in a literal translation yet it is well worth analysing as a form of complicity established between addresser and addressee that might be developed into incitative formulas like: 'Alors/Eh bien! Souriez!' or 'Souriez donc!'

(c) The allocutive marker *we* refers to a collective extension of the first person singular, which can be exclusive or inclusive of the addressee. Although this ambiguous designation will have to be examined further down in its complex set of contextual references, we have a choice in French between: 'nous' (exclusive) and 'on' (inclusive).

Just and *can't* can be treated in conjunction since they stand as modalizer and surmodalizer. The deontic value of *cannot* implies that the subject is in no position, physical or moral, to achieve what is expressed in the predicative content. Because of the restrictive *just*, that confessed inability is the only modal designation that was found to pertain to the situation, which contributes, in fact, discursively, to reinforce the applicability of the deontic value. A few LC2 alternatives could be proposed in French in growing order of surmodalizing emphasis:

> Nous ne pouvons vraiment pas
> Impossible/Pas possible de
> On ne peut se résoudre à
> Que nous le voulions ou non

At this stage a variation range could be produced if a preconstruction factor uniting *say* and *cheese* did not have to be taken into consideration. It is worth mentioning that this preconstructed value might very well be overlooked by the translator, which once again underlines the crucial importance of the translator's competence.

We do not have a predication uniting *say + cheese* but *say cheese*, a preconstructed cliché referring to the photographic situation in which the operator tries to elicit a smile from his subject. The evident French equivalent is 'Souriez!', which does not resort to phonetic simulation but to requesting the act itself. As a matter of fact, a French adaptation has been facetiously introduced in accordance with the French phonetic system: 'Dites ouistiti!' which, were it not so unusual, would qualify as a possible translation for the ST clichéd expression.

But we happen to be placed in a situation of *modulation* (replacing the contextually predictable expression by another belonging to a different context), creating a discrepancy between the original context designated by the cliché and the present situation simulated by the photograph. This produces a double set of consequences:

(a) The smile is required in a situation as artificial as the photographic pose, although it naturally calls for spontaneity. The artificial semantic factor is produced by contextual displacement and could suggest in French such options as:

> Forcer quelqu'un à sourire
> Faire semblant de sourire

(b) But, once the displacement of meaning has been recognized, it is necessary to appreciate the 'remanence' of the original situation designated by the cliché which contributes to what is sometimes called the 'picturesqueness' or 'expressivity' of this formulation. In this perspective, the reference to the photographic situation might not be the only one, or the only one applicable, for the purpose of the publicity text. Other culturally charged and conventionally recognized stock situations might be alluded to:

> Sourires de façade/sourires de convenance
> Le sourire n'est pas seulement de façade
> Le sourire n'est pas une simple façade

2 If we consider the *contextual* level, we soon discover that we are not confronted with a real situation but with a simulation associating a text and a strongly oriented photographic representation of a situation. In order to interpret its signification we are divided between two contradictory logics of decoding, which we will designate as:

(a) the 'cartoon' logic, the most obviously culturally enforced, which proceeds from addresser – to photograph – to text,
(b) the 'visual' logic which proceeds from text – to photograph – to addresser,

whose competing pertinence will have to be appreciated at the next strategic level.

In the visual logic reinforced by the diagonal set-up of the semiotic materials pointing to the bottom left-hand corner on which our page-turning fingers are supposed to be placed, the *we* is highly saturated with multiple references to the airway as addresser with optional association with the air hostess and the addressee himself or herself, and an adversative designation of the competing airways.

The possibilites in French are those already mentioned in the linguistic section to which could be added another option, the absence of person definition ('Même les sourires ne sont pas forcés!') whose all-purpose, open-ended designation might very well prove a possibility.

The complex association of *just* and *can't* to the hostess's half-smile can be understood to refer to the competition who may have found a smile enforcement policy a cheap substitute for more tangible but also more costly air-transport services. The restrictive *just* makes it clear that in spite of competitive pressure, for ethical reasons that we are supposed to share, the company cannot resort to such gross strategies. A translation such as

> Le sourire de convenance (forcé) n'est pas notre affaire

would adequately stress the two preceding points by associating 'trade' and 'forced smiles'.

Finally, the reference to the hostess's Mona Lisa smile as being not of the kind that can be forced into a broad smile is, like Leonardo's model, difficult to elucidate (not to mention perhaps completely bungled by the advertising agent!). Indeed, on further consideration, it is not clear:

whether this (the half-smile) is an alternative to or substitute for the commercial smile that other airlines are known to encourage;
or whether the company desires to be recognized for other more tangible services than the superficial and impersonal cordiality of its hostesses;
or whether the flight attendant has grown so tired of supplying the multiple services offered by the airline that we should be grateful for the wan smile that still lingers on her face, etc.

The options so far in French could be:

> (Chez nous,) pas de sourires de commande (de façade)
> (Chez nous,) le sourire, c'est naturel
> Nous ne savons pas faire semblant

or explicitly underlining the third option defined above:

Et, en plus, on ne peut (tout de même) pas lui demander de sourire

3 As to *textual* strategy, it is clear that this text belongs to the Analogical as opposed to the Logical type. This identification is based on three types of considerations:

(a) As far as content is concerned, no production of 'new' information is involved, as publicists would like us to believe when they refer to their texts as 'messages', 'tips', 'advice', or 'counselling'. On the contrary, this text proposes a reinforcement of a 'value' already present in the socio-cultural context but insufficiently recognized. This recognition can at the same time be seen as:

positively enforced, although we saw how unclear the reference of the advertisement could be. Yet, it can be further elucidated through two orders of consideration:

(i) through the 'family of texts' to which this particular text is associated in a global publicity campaign. This text more than any other should not be considered, as we are spontaneously made to believe, as a self-contained entity but as a fragment or, rather, 'offshoot' of a global but scattered publicity text comprising all the advertisements in the same vein. From that point of view, the emphasis is clearly on 'smile' and should therefore be preserved;

(ii) through the levels of perceptibility (or readability) of the publicity text that contribute to reinforce the logotype or the firm's name recognition.

negatively, through the already implicitly designated references to competitors.

In this perspective, new more affirmative solutions could be proposed:

> Nos sourires sont de vrais sourires
> Nous ne savons pas faire semblant

(b) The second strategic consequence lies in the role structure imposed by the text. Instead of being explanatory as a logical text, the role structure proposed by the analogical text is implicative, tending to force or solicit our approval through the use of the already analysed *we/just can't/!* and other related means, such as the much abused but inevitable appeal to feminine charm.

(c) Finally, the specific strategy of the Analogical text as regards medium tends not so much to order or to hierarchize semiotic masses from text to context as the logical text but to amalgamate these entities. Instead of being illustrated complementarily in the diversity of media, the same value is repeated at all levels. A case in point is the various references to the firm's logo on the plane's fuselage, the air hostess's button and uniform colours and in the logo + firm's name in the bottom right-hand corner of the page.

Once the homologous potentialities have been generated, it is necessary to fix the socio-cultural determinations that might qualify one option rather than another in keeping with a given LC2 configuration. Here are some of the factors that would have to be envisaged:

The legal and current state of competition and of publicity strategies in the transport business – whether, for example, adversative or comparative publicity is legal, tolerated, or practised at all.

The nature of the strategic objectives to be achieved by a publicity text in that particular field and in relation to a specific segment of the market. One would have to investigate, for example, the cultural preconceptions associated with 'smiling' and to 'women's smiles' in a given culture; and assess the difference between the ubiquitous smile in American communities and its more ambiguous and rarefied counterpart in French commercial circles. In case the associations should not be found suitable, it would become necessary to change the semiotic and/or linguistic content of the advertisement.

The style of address of the advertising discourse family; whether it can, for example, accommodate punning or deceitful statements, would have to be documented in the publicity literature in order to determine the best possible means to influence audiences of potential customers.

Obviously, the iconography of airline publicity in international magazines would have to be consulted in order to choose the most effective semiotic compositions and their relationship to textual material.

Once these parameters have been made clear then a selection could be meaningfully made among the homologous options defined above. And this could be considered as a justified translation of the Lufthansa text.

6 The Cultural Equation

INTRODUCTION

The focus of our study now shifts from the generating capacities of language to the selection and elimination procedures which must be undertaken in order to produce a final text in the second language. We shall attempt to examine all the different criteria that the translator must consider when coming to choose his or her definitive text. But before coming to consider these criteria, it is important to reassess our whole way of thinking about the relationship between two Language Cultures, and to enlarge our view of what translation necessarily includes in the selection process that interests us here. In this chapter, therefore, we shall be seeking to explore what we call the 'Cultural Equation'. This new concept – which must, in our view, be built up and defined in every translation situation – is essential both in translation theory and practice. After some general remarks about LC relationships, and in particular the more traditional notion of the LC 'gap', we shall (1) look in some detail at the various 'actors' always present in the Translation situation; (2) examine the importance of the discourse family; and (3) then discuss the relative importance of LC1 and LC2 influences on the translator – these are all elements to be included in the Cultural Equation. In Chapter 7, we shall consider the translator – or Translation Operator (TO), as he or she will come to be called – as a Cultural Operator, and in Chapter 8 we shall examine the various socio-cultural parameters that must always be borne in mind when choosing a definitive Target Text.

LANGUAGE–CULTURE RELATIONSHIPS

We spoke in some detail in the opening chapters of our book of the different approaches to Translation theory, and in particular how these

112 *Redefining Translation*

have come to be reflected in a series of key terms and oppositions such as 'equivalence', translatable/untranslatable, faithful/unfaithful, etc. Our aim here is not to cover the same ground again, but to underline how Translation theory is often based on an unscientific notion of an LC 'gap' which the translator must 'bridge'. Now our own theory, as we pointed out in Chapter 2, is derived from the Sapir–Whorf hypothesis, and thus rests on the basic incommensurability of LCs, but is geared towards the reality of practical translation production. Therefore we redefine what might have been thought of as a 'gap' first of all as a 'relationship' – i.e. the bringing together of two or more LCs through the work of the translator – and then at the end of the chapter as an 'equation', or complex of variable factors which must all be defined and redefined for each new translation undertaken.

If saying that translating means creating a relationship between LCs is stating the obvious, what is not so clear is that a cultural relationship is never a limited and stable reality, but a complex of factors dependent first and foremost on the communication circuit being instigated by the translator. This goes beyond what is called traditionally 'contextualization', or in broader terms 'co-textualization',[1] and will be seen to include every element going from the genesis of a text to the foreseen or actual receivers in LC2. At this point in our development, it is enough to stress that our whole focus constantly includes as wide a range of elements as possible, and thus transcends both the limitations of *general* theories advocating transfers between different LCs, and, of course, the restrictive vision of the LC 'gap'. Thus if, in the first case, translation is possible as a principle, nothing is said about the variables that have to be taken into account, and in the second, the translator is faced with both an insurmountable and *unreferenced* chasm which he or she will try to 'cross' as best they may.

We begin our exploration of the translation situation by identifying the different 'actors' who are necessarily involved in each act of translation, and by exploring the different roles which they may be called upon to play.

THE 'ACTORS' IN A TRANSLATION SITUATION

Previous studies have tended to take the 'actors' in any Translation situation for granted, and in fact to reduce them to one – the translator. The translator himself is often taken to be some kind of idealized operator (divorced from his own socio-cultural and linguistic background, always operating in the best possible conditions), and as such his role is taken for granted – producing an 'optimum' translation (whatever that might be) at all times. We shall have more to say about his importance and role in the next chapter. Sometimes one finds references to the receiver of the translated text, but if so, he is usually only briefly considered. As for the sender of the ST – not to mention the original receiver in LC1 – they tend to be completely passed over, as if a text, and the whole communication circuit to which it belongs, could somehow be taken for granted. Moreover, there is one 'actor' who is totally absent from Translation theory, which we call the Translation Initiator (TI) – as the term indicates, this is the driving force behind the act of Translation, and whose identity and express wishes have a fundamental influence on the Translation operation.

The Translation Initiator

We can illustrate the fundamental role of the TI by starting from the premise that translation does not just 'happen', but results from (1) a need, and (2) an order. The need quite simply corresponds to a foreseen or actual breakdown in communication; the order corresponds to the instructions given by the TI to ensure that communication takes place. Once one has identified the TI as the driving force behind the Translation operation, it becomes clear that his identity (his 'position' in socio-cultural and LC terms) is of prime importance, as the actual translation will (theoretically, at least!) be fashioned to suit his order, and that very order can be determining in itself if it is of a restricted or specific nature.

Let us then look at some of the positions which the TI can occupy. On many occasions, the translator is his own TI. He does not translate because of an initial breakdown in communication (he understands the ST and does not himself need a TT) but because he *foresees* a communication problem, or because he wishes to make a work accessible to speakers of another language who otherwise would have no way of discovering that work. Such a translator has sometimes been referred to as a craftsman or an artist – one who is not primarily working for a mercenary motivation, but who is preoccupied by the transmission of an aesthetic message. Whatever his motivation in fact may be, it is important to see that the translation is carried out within the framework set by the translator himself,[2] rather than within a predefined set of conditions.[3] This can have an important effect not just on the way a translator works, but also on the choices he will make in his translation.

Conversely, when the translator is not the TI, he is dependent – to a greater or lesser extent – on the formulation of the Translation order. In other words, he acts on someone else's instructions and within a *pre*defined (and therefore analysable) framework. The choices which the translator will make will no longer depend on internal (or in fact personal) criteria, but on a whole series of parameters which will be more or less clearly expressed in the Translation order.

It immediately becomes apparent that the socio-cultural identity of the TI is of prime importance, and, of course, the LC to which he belongs. If he belongs to LC1, he will (presumably) fully comprehend the ST, and be seeking to inform (defined or undefined) receivers in the LC2. As he fully comprehends the ST, he will be able to emphasize certain cultural features of the text he wishes the translator to preserve (or bring out, or modify, etc.[4]). If, on the other hand, the TI belongs to LC2, it is quite probable that the Translation order will reflect his partial or total non-comprehension of the ST and will thus simply be a request for information ('I do not understand this text, please translate').

We will now show, using an example, how we conceive of the LC relationship which is dependent *in the first instance on the TI*. We have chosen this particular example because *when decontextualized*, it could be cited as one of the many cases where near total transfer is possible, where there is apparently a one-to-one relationship between different (European) languages.

Our SL here is French and the example very simple:

> Cette semaine on tue le cochon!

The only apparent problems when translating into English are the value to attribute to (Fr.) 'on' (which of course is well documented both in linguistic and translation theories[5]), and the choice of tense/aspect ('are going to'/'will', etc.). No problem, however, for 'tuer' → 'kill' and 'cochon' → 'pig', and one can produce some good textbook answers:

> This week we kill the pig!
> This week we're going to kill the pig!
> This week we will kill the pig!

One can, of course, add variants according to the value given to 'on':

> This week the pig is going to be killed!, etc.

However, the moment one looks at the context of this utterance, the LC relationship takes on its full force, and must initially be defined in relation to the TI.

Once a year one can find such an utterance (and certain variants) displayed in food shops in France to attract customers into buying pig products. The reference here is to a cultural event: killing the pig in villages, which used to occur annually at the beginning of winter, and which was and still is synonymous with celebration, plentiful, fresh pork meat, group identity, feasting. Clearly a literal translation would be quite impossible in England, given that the required effect ('buy!') is the same: the impact on the potential consumer might range from incomprehension to downright hostility. It is only by identifying the TI and by analysing the sort of Translation order he or she might make that one can weigh up the different Translation variants available.

If the TI belongs to LC1, the request to translate will reflect a certain communication goal, such as to create a similar publicity message in the second language. In this instance, the LC relationship consists of weighing up a 'full' situation ('tuer le cochon' in French culture) with an 'empty' situation (no comparable cultural event in LC2). The translator will have to consider suitable advertising strategies to bring across the perceived message – at the various levels at which it functions – of the original. To the incitation to buy, he or she would have to add all the positive connotations received by the native French speaker on reading the utterance: cheap, the auspicious time to buy fresh pork, festivity, etc.[6] The translation, then, would be subject to two conflicting forces: the brevity of the publicity message, the richness of the original text (requiring several utterances of 'explanation').

If the TI is English, a different LC relationship is instigated. The English native speaker who sees the original in France may well understand the words used to make up the message, yet be incapable of decoding the meaning – an 'empty' situation must be replaced by a 'full' (i.e. meaningful) one. The request for a Translation is not so much for the production of an equivalent message (with a 'buy' incitation) but for an explanation which would include both the cultural event in question, and the specific place held by the different varieties of pork-meat and 'pork-meat butchers' ('charcutiers') in France.

In this perspective, the LC relationship is not a constant, but a definable, dissectable, and dynamic face-to-face of two cultures. This has the immensely practical consequence of narrowing down the focus of the extremely daunting 'gap' seen in a general and decontextualized way, and of controlling the otherwise infinite developments that can ensue when comparing two realities which, quite simply, are not directly comparable. Translation comes to be seen not just as a culture-bound activity, but as dependent on a *specific culture pairing*. If, in the present example, the LC2 is Serbo-Croat, a literal translation initially seems possible[7] as a comparable cultural event still takes place in Yugoslavia. But once again, the *whole* socio-cultural framework has to be compared, and in particular advertising strategies – or the comparative lack of them in this country. The point here of course is that the

116 *Redefining Translation*

translator has to take into account predictable discourse forms in LC2, as we develop below.

Enough has been said at this point to show the importance of the TI in a theory of Translation. We shall be looking more closely at the socio-cultural definition of the TI and at the different aspects of the role he or she plays in translation in Chapter 8. We now consider and briefly discuss the importance of the other actors who must be taken into account.

The Translation Operator

When one considers the place of the translator himself in Translation theory, one is struck not so much by the fact that he is absent, as is the case of the TI, but by the simplicity of the assumption commonly made, which one might sum up by saying: the translator 'translates'. In fact, this tends to become polarized into two possibilities: in Translation Criticism, he tends to translate 'badly' (i.e. he is a deficient operator), and in theories he quite simply disappears, i.e. his role – and indeed his aim – is taken for granted. To distinguish our own approach from previous ones and to bring out his fundamental and active role, we call the translator the Translation Operator. Our aim here is to define his position in relation to the LCs in question.

The TO can, in fact, never be some idealized and theoretical individual working in optimum conditions and fully aware of all the problems raised by different texts. He is naturally bound first and foremost by the *position he occupies in relation to the languages he operates between*. It is often said that the TO should be 'bilingual', or at least highly competent in what is for him the foreign language. But we must examine this truism to see what it hides. Indeed, we work on the assumption that a 'bilingual' individual as such cannot exist, simply because any language-learning situation will preclude this possibility.[8] More importantly, there cannot be equal competence in every field, simply because no one speaker has intimate knowledge of and access to all types of discourse. In other words, the TO is more firmly rooted in one LC than in the other(s), which is, of course, highly significant when one comes to analyse the operations he undertakes. The ST will normally[9] be seen from the perspective of LC2. The whole process of decoding the ST will be done from a biased angle. Suffice it to say for the moment that the TO is just one of the variables that one must take into account when trying to have an overall vision of Translation.

LC1 Sender, LC1 Receiver

Having considered the TI and TO, we must now briefly turn our attention to the Source Text. Now the ST is not an aleatory collection of arbitrary signs, but a means of communication between a sender in LC1 and an original receiver in LC1, using discourse – or, to be more precise, a certain family or type of discourse – as a communication medium. Part of the TO's task is to analyse the position and purpose of the original sender, and the characteristics of the original receiver of the ST. This is, of course, what we have done when considering 'Cette semaine on tue le cochon!', in that we identify the sender as a producer of advertising discourse, and the receiver as belonging to the mass of potential consumers of pig products. In many cases, the LC1 sender may be identified as a socio-culturally positioned individual who is writing to fulfil a definite function, or as an institution, government body, etc. A precise identification of the sender together with an analysis of his or her aims can only further the task of the TO. The same holds for the LC1 receiver, who sometimes belongs to a restricted class of receivers, with particular demands or needs. This last point is developed from the LC2 perspective in the following section, and more general considerations about the importance of situating the ST in its production context will be examined in Chapter 8, pages 173–6, when we come to look at the different factors to be weighed up in the final choice of a TT.

LC2 Receiver

It may seem a little obvious to state that the aim of Translation is the TT, produced therefore for the receiver in LC2. But one cannot fail to be struck by the assumption that tends to be made that the receiver is everyone, or anyone, or that all receivers have the same needs and capacities. But it should be clear that the range of possibilities is very wide here, going from the broadest possible public, via identifiable segments of the population (i.e. an age group, or social class, or men or women, etc.), to the individual, with his or her specific needs and limitations. If the TO knows he is translating a document to be read by a certain institution, and that that institution has certain norms, he will respect these, despite what he might consider to be more important general criteria.[10]

THE SOURCE TEXT AND THE DISCOURSE FAMILY

Having considered the different 'actors' necessarily involved in each Translation situation, we come to look at another element to be built into the Cultural Equation – this is the ST itself, with its relationship to a discourse family in LC1, which will be put opposite a discourse family in the second LC. What interests us here again is not an abstract and general relationship between two cultures, but the tension induced by considering a ST – and its potential intralinguistic paraphrases – in relation to a series of potential TTs.

Our departure point for considering the ST, as we have pointed out, is Eco's description of the SR.[11] In this view, each text is both a reflection of the SR, and a (partial) restructuring of this latter. There is obviously a dynamic perspective necessary here, with the historical gap (however small it is) between the first production of a text and its consideration in the context of Translation. This two-stage model (a SR, a text) is, however, not sufficient to constitute this part of the Cultural Equation, as one has, on the one hand, the very general notion of SR and on the other hand the highly restricted example of a particular text. On the other side of the Cultural Equation we find an equally general notion (the SR of the second LC, or SR') and a series of paraphrastic possibilities, with no culture-specific guidelines to help us eliminate unsuitable versions of the future TT. We therefore introduce a third level of analysis, which is that of the discourse family.

The *discourse family*, as we perceive it, is a convenient label for describing an extremely complex reality. It corresponds in the first instance to the 'naive' perception of the translator who 'knows' that journalistic discourse does not function in the same way as literary or scientific discourse, and will (consciously or unconsciously) choose an appropriate 'style of writing' in his translation work. More importantly, it provides a framework both for judging the *potential* and *predictable* forms which will occur in a language in a given situation and for assessing the departures from these forms. Each family is composed of a number of subfamilies – journalistic discourse, for example, can be divided initially into the different media (television, radio, newspapers, magazines, etc.), each subfamily being divided yet again into smaller groups (newspapers into tabloids and non-tabloids, for example).

Several points need to made: the families and subfamilies are not definitive groupings, but need to be able to be redefined at will; the families cannot, of course, be in watertight compartments, as literary discourse permeates advertising and journalistic discourse (and vice versa) etc.; in the final analysis, it is (1) the *linguistic characteristics* and (2) the *textual strategies*[12] of the discourse which will retain the translator's attention.

As a final introductory point, we can consider the case of literary discourse. When one compares literary productions in different countries one is tempted to come to the conclusion that any author has full creative licence to do just what he or she likes – and the history of literature is undoubtedly the breaking out of established frameworks (or subverting in humour or parody). But, as Foucault pointed out (see, for example, Foucault 1971), there is a limit to what can be said at any one time, to which one can add the fundamental role of translation in broadening the 'possible' in any one culture.[13] The ideal TO would be able to judge the originality of a work in relation to the LC1 out of which it springs, and to produce such an originality in LC2 – something which manifestly did not happen when Kafka was first translated into French, as the translator, – reflecting his own preoccupations as a young writer,[14] produced a melodramatic text reading more like a version of Zola, as we will show below.

The discourse family can be approached through a double classificatory perspective. We look at the general type of discourse to which a text belongs (literary, scientific, journalistic, etc.). Then we consider the textual strategies operating within the text. This double classification has the advantage of keeping categories general while allowing for more explicit determinations, and also enables direct cross-cultural comparisons to be made without falling into the trap of putting 'equivalent' types of discourse on the same footing. A brief look back to 'Cette semaine on tue le cochon!' will serve to illustrate the point.

We have seen (1) how this utterance activates the SR on the level of 'an activity which happens (has happened, used to happen)', and (2) how the message is 'translated' within LC1 as 'Buy cheap fresh pork products!' We identified the family of discourse as being that of advertising, and we can complete this by adding that the text belongs to a subclass of this family – posters or notices appearing inside or outside shops. The textual strategy is an analogical one functioning initially by inference (because there is cheap fresh pork available, I am invited to take the opportunity to buy), but has now become a virtually dead cliché which is predictable at this time of the year, and now virtually only used by shopkeepers to attract customers.

The discourse family has a vital role to play as a focusing element within the Cultural Equation. In this particular instance we are comparing advertising discourse in the two languages, and, of course, the textual strategies available to a producer of discourse.[15] On a very general level, one can notice how advertisements in the UK often exploit ambivalent textual strategies, whereas in France, the discourse tends to use consecutive strategies, or to associate the promoted value (or product) to such obvious culturally recognized values as [women], [power], etc. In the UK, the identification of the product being advertised is often delayed, whereas in France it is usually immediately obvious.[16] So when in France one might expect to find an equation of the type X (product) = Y (quality, or culturally recognized value), the focus in English is first on a quality/value which is posed, in order to deduce what the product must be. Rewriting this as an equation, we are either first presented with the unknown element, corresponding in fact to the product – X = ? – which is then immediately equated with the value/quality – X = Y (quality) – or we are presented first of all with the value or quality itself – Y is subsequently identified or developed (Y = A, B, C), leading the receiver to draw the inference, X = product having Y.[17] Now 'Cette semaine on tue le cochon!' is interesting because it goes against what has just been said, given that at one degree, an inference must be made. One might therefore expect a literal translation here. Now we know by comparing SRs that this is impossible – and this can be confirmed by comparing the subclass of advertisements placed in shops. One is immediately struck by the *restricted choice* of discourses available in the UK and by the *immediate identification* of the product in question, either by naming it, or by the position of the notice in relation to the product. Such notices typically resort to direct strategies where something is being presented as an *offer*, where the *price* is low, or based on a *comparison*. Some examples:[18]

trial/sale/free/tax-free, sensational *offer*;
two for the *price* of one, unbeatable/give-away/rock-bottom/warehouse/lowest *prices*, *prices* the family can afford, save £'s, *cut-price* bargains, Mr *Price-fighter*;
X costs Y pounds less than Z, etc.[19]

A direct translation into a shop notice would therefore almost certainly involve a dramatic simplification into a 'special offer/reduced prices' notice displayed over the products in question, with, in this case, perhaps an indication of 'freshness' and 'abundance'.

It can be seen, then, that the use of discourse families and subclasses is a limiting, controlling and focusing device enabling the translator to choose between paraphrastic possibilities. We must briefly turn our attention again to the ST to understand the *double focus* that the Cultural Equation brings to the translator. We discussed in some detail in the first chapters of the book the concept of the homology, and the 'opening' effect that this has on a ST. By paraphrasing the ST, one is both opening up a multitude of possibilities, which, as we showed, are virtually unlimited in their scope. By establishing the Cultural Equation, one can not only control the ST in relation to its potential paraphrases (i.e. produce a series of measures to 'situate' the ST as accurately as possible) but also limit the likely LC2 paraphrases which can then be subjected to all the other socio-cultural parameters (see Chapter 8). This does not, of course, preclude the TO from 'inventing', or from producing 'creative' work, but introduces a measure of the creativity by the gap induced between the *predictable* forms in LC2 and the form finally chosen by the TO. 'This week we kill the pig!' would indeed be a creative advertising form in English, especially if displayed in a shop window.

We are now in a position to reconsider the culture 'gap' in the light of the Cultural Equation. What must necessarily be perceived as a virtually uncrossable chasm becomes, at the very least, a controllable phenomenon which is directly related to the various actors of the Translation situation and brought down to manageable proportions by the introduction of discourse-family to discourse-family comparisons. This does not, of course, imply some utopian vision of Translation whereby 'perfect' transference is obtained, and this, if for no other reasons, because each reader will bring a particular set of criteria. It is tempting to take literary discourse as the most obvious 'problem' case by evoking the richness of the literary text, the multitude of possible interpretations, etc. But there is nothing to enable us to say why a literary text is *per se* richer than other texts, and the very discourse family of 'literature' is the hardest to define, or limit, in any case (each family being a collection of subclasses which can also belong to other families). But it is precisely the richness of literary discourse which allows a TO not only to generate a wide variety of potential TTs, but also to choose in relation to existing discourse. But before illustrating this rather complex point, it is important to take into consideration the conflicting claims of those who favour a translation bearing the maximum impact of LC1, and those who plead for a maximum normalization, or the disappearance of all LC1-related traits.

SOURCE-LANGUAGE INFLUENCES V. TARGET-LANGUAGE INFLUENCES

The debate about LC1 and LC2 influences is both a historic one and part of the present-day discussion about translation theory. It stems, of course, from the undeniable fact that a translation is not the original,[20] and many, if not all, of the language- and culture-specific features of the ST must disappear. It would be a little unfair to say that the debate is animated by two sets of equally lucid purists – those who cannot bear to see the LC1 disappear, those who cannot tolerate the slightest foreign intrusion into LC2 – with, in between, a rather vague compromise position; but as, from a certain point of view, both sets of purists are right, and it is the compromise position that is so often practised, it is better to examine the complexity of the situation and to pay tribute to their respective demands while at the same time attempting to go beyond what appears to be yet another of the aporia surrounding the whole subject of translation.

LC1 influences

Arguments in favour of the *LC1 influence* tend to lay the stress on certain LC1-related elements which are seen as fundamental to the essential message being conveyed by a text. The oldest of these undoubtedly concerns the religious or esoteric message, where the message – the word of God – is either seen to be intimately bound up with a form, or with a phonetic sequence.[21] The ideological stance adopted is that translation is tantamount to heresy, because what is perceived – by the TI or TO – as the fundamental message will disappear. The only type of translation conceivable is the LC1-dominated one, where a maximum number of LC1 structures and words are 'borrowed' and introduced into the LC2.

Writers on literary translation often make similar claims, couched in terms of praise for LC1 (its purity, expressive nature, etc.) and frustration at the apparent lack of expressiveness, purity, etc., of LC2. The 'genius' of the original has to be maintained at any cost – the highest cost being the non-comprehension of the LC2-reader. This 'genius', as we will see below, is nothing more than culture-specific references intertwined with LC1-specific linguistic and rhetorical devices.

We should note, then, at this point that there is inevitably a subjective value judgement involved in statements of this kind as to the precise nature of the unique LC1 elements present in the Source Text. Two problems can be identified here: the first concerns the terminology used to describe the ST and the LC1 – the specific 'flavour' of a text, the 'genius' of a language, the 'richness' of a culture are, in fact, ideologically charged labels which prevent one from analysing the specific ST characteristics, and lead inevitably to the conclusion of 'untranslatability'; the second stems from the very *general* nature of such statements, which, in our view, have always to be related to the discourse family in question. There follows, therefore, a classification in which we look at the sort of categories one can use to analyse the 'genius' of the ST; these general remarks have always to be modulated to take into account the type of text under consideration.

The Cultural Equation

Cultural elements mirroring the unique structure of each SR

As virtually all texts are in some way culture-specific, this constitutes – in varying degrees – the first and most important problem for the translator. Although on one level culture-specific references 'disappear' in translation, it is not enough simply to deplore this state of affairs, which assumes total ignorance of LC1 on the part of the LC2 readership. One can look at the example quoted by Duff (1981: 112) in this light, where he examines a translation of E.M. Forster's *Passage to India* in Serbo-Croat. The passage quoted mentions Ronny's 'sterilized Public School brand' religion, which is translated as 'Ronnyeva je religija bila steriliziranog srednjoškolskog' – the Public School has been replaced by the secondary school, with all the loss (and in fact gain[22]) that that entails. One should distinguish here two distinct levels of potential 'untranslatability': (1) the literal one, where 'Public School' produces the opposite image when translated (cf. 'école publique' in France), and (2) the LC2 readership level, where an assumption is made of knowledge about LC1 culture. It is probably true here to say that the majority of LC2 readers would not have the necessary LC1 knowledge to understand an approximate translation of the type 'privatna škola' – which would be understood in relation to *LC2* values where the 'private school' does not exist.[23] In all events, the choice of translation will be made according both to the Translation order made by the TI and to the definition of the LC2 public; if such information is taken to be vital for a correct understanding of the book, and an element of explanation to be necessary for the LC2 public, this will have to be incorporated into the Translator's Introduction, into the notes accompanying the translation,[24] or indeed as an addition within the text itself.

The above discussion concerns a recognizable LC1 element which can be said to belong to 'the British culture'. But it would, of course, be wrong to assume that there exists a homogeneous and defined 'British' culture to which we could unfalteringly refer on all occasions. Distinctions must be drawn on every possible level, whether it be regional, social class, professional, political, sexual, etc. The lexical item 'tea' designates different realities depending on geographical area (a beverage, a light meal, dinner, or supper), social class (with all the different qualities and blends of tea available), etc. It would appear, then, that *the very general statements about the genius, etc. of a culture need to be finely tuned in relation to each text translated*. In other words, 'culture' is not some homogeneous and eternal truth, but a specific collection of features which have to be minutely examined in each Translation situation.

But it is not enough just to state that culture itself is a problem concept in Translation Studies. If, on the one hand 'British culture' is seen as a fundamentally heterogeneous entity, it can be argued on another level that certain cultures (or cultural traits) go beyond national borders, as in the case of similar languages (e.g. Anglo-Saxon, Francophone) or related languages (e.g. Slav). This can, by stretching the imagination, be extended to comparable political and economic systems, enabling 'direct' transfers to be made in certain contexts.[25] This is further complicated by multilingual and multicultural countries such as Yugoslavia, in which there is – or was until recently – a shared politico-economic federal structure (allowing for direct translation), but marked cultural and religious differences.[26]

One should finally also add that certain specific supracultural structures exist (i.e. the EEC), and that the terminology in specialized texts referring to such structures no longer mirrors the particular LC1.

In short, 'culture' is of little interest to us as a general concept, but must always be related to the Translation situation under study, that is the global communication process.

Lexical items reflecting a specific plane of extralinguistic reality

This second category is in reality a subcategory of the first one, given that lexical items necessarily belong to the SR they stem from, and reflect the socio-economic basis designated as 'reality' – thus, 'equivalents' between different languages can only at best be approximate. It is, however, useful to analyse texts at this level not to discover, as above, that items within cultures cannot (necessarily) be compared, but to look at the way extralinguistic reality is segmented by a language. This approach helps to counter the 'universalist' argument used by Mounin and others (see Chapter 1) as a basis for establishing 'equivalence' between LCs. In fact, examples abound in the literature of the different segmentations of extralinguistic reality, with the most famous one perhaps being the colour spectrum.[27] Lists are drawn up of *faux-amis*, or false friends, which seem to imply that there are a large number of *true* friends. Our starting point, to stretch the metaphor a little, is that one not only has to be wary of 'true' friends, but even 'good' friends tend to be highly unreliable – thus necessitating the work on homologies which we have developed in such detail. But it is not enough just to advocate caution when considering one-to-one lexical 'equivalents' between languages; to this one must add a comparison between predominant lexical features of different discourse families and their subclasses. One can note, for example, different usages of technical language in specialized domains. This is the case when one compares French and

English medical discourse aimed at the general public, which, as we pointed out in relation to the Delisle text, clearly function on different levels.

Culturally identifiable and stable connotations

This is, again, another subcategory of the first one. If examples abound in the literature (see, for example, Ladmiral 1979), one should again stress the need of referring to each particular Translation situation, rather than making general statements about the problem of connotations. Our analyses of Sillitoe (above, pp. 79ff.) and Pinter (below, p. 128) show that the problem should not be treated on a word-to-word basis, but on a text-to-text basis. In all events, if connotations are thought by some to belong to the 'genius' of a language, then it should be said (1) that their stability is only at best relative, and each text will 'vibrate' in a specific way according to the communication situation in which it is being made to function; and (2) each language possesses its own 'genius', which the TO can exploit at will.

Syntactic or grammatical structures recognized as LC1-specific

When discussing different languages on a general level, it is difficult to go beyond observations of the most simplistic kind, such as the different grammatical structures, or different rules governing word order, etc. To say that the end-position of the verb in a subordinate clause starting with *wenn, daß*, etc., in German is LC1-specific is hardly very useful as it is both 100 per cent predictable and inimitable in most other languages (at that degree of predictability). We have found that it is more profitable to look at rules and trends governing different discourse families. One might note, for example, the recurrent placing of the time adverbial after the verb in main clauses in French journalism. Or when one compares rhetorical structures in different languages, one has to conclude, quite simply, that they are different. On arriving at the scene of a terrorist bomb explosion before becoming prime minister for the second time, Jacques Chirac was asked what security measures should be taken, to which he replied: 'Ecoutez! Il faut prendre les mesures qui s'imposent.' His 'Ecoutez!' is a typical (and therefore predictable) rhetorical device used by politicians in France, partly to gain time and/or to gain attention (and to express determination). As such, it announces simply 'I am going to speak (seriously)'. The LC1-influenced translation 'Listen!' may inform bilingual listeners that a translation from French is underway, but does not translate the rhetorical device itself which constitutes the

126   Redefining Translation

essence of this first part of his message. The second part of his statement hardly lends itself to a literal translation either, but could be variously interpreted as 'what a politician will say when put on the spot', or 'saying nothing when appearing to say everything'; the TO would have to examine the possible rhetorical devices available in LC2.[28]

LC2 influences

Coming now to LC2, one can say that those in favour of *LC2-influenced translations* tend to bring out the 'communicative' aspect of language and translation.[29] The ideological viewpoint is what might be termed universalist, or, following Wilss,[30] non-racist, whereby every language can equally express (more or less – and the qualification can prove to be vital) everything; the greatest possible effort is made for the reader, who must not be put off by a text perceived in any way as 'foreign'. The result is a greater or lesser degree of 'normalization', where all the LC1-specific traces are made to disappear. This naturally involves a standardized view of lexis, grammar, and syntax, a value judgement of the type 'what the writer would have said, had he been French, English, etc.' One of the fundamental problems is to judge what is 'normal' – and this seems to be one of the stumbling blocks of comparative grammars or studies of comparative syntax, which tend to create a *context-free* norm.

In the LC2-influenced text, then, the essential foreignness of the original, as perceived from the standpoint of LC2, has disappeared.[31] For non-literary texts, this requires a degree of adaptation and 'localization' of the original, the first term covering all changes which standardize usage according to the prevalent LC2 norm (e.g. 'miles per gallon' becomes 'litres per 100 kilometres'), the second involving changes in the referential structure of the text (see Chapter 8, pp. 179ff.). For a literary text, not only are the different categories mentioned under the title 'LC1 influences' normalized, but there is often a partial or total assimilation with a recognizable LC2 style of writing. This would appear to be the case with Vialatte's translation[32] of Kafka's *Die Verwandlung* into French where numerous constructions have been 'embellished' to produced a pseudo-literary (and culturally identifiable) effect, as can be seen in the highlighted passages in the example quoted below:

Gregor sah ein, daß er den Prokuristen in dieser Stimmung auf keinen Fall weggehen lassen dürfte . . . . Die Eltern verstanden das	Grégoire comprit qu'il ne fallait à aucun prix le laisser partir dans cet état . . . . Malheureusement ses parents voyaient moins clair dans

alles nicht so gut ... (sie) hatten außerdem jetzt mit den augenblicklichen Sorgen so viel zu tun, daß ihnen jede Voraussicht abhanden gekommen war. Aber Gregor hatte diese Voraussicht. Der Prokurist mußte gehalten, beruhigt, überzeugt und schließlich gewonnen werden; die Zukunft Gregors und seiner Familie hing doch davon ab! Wäre doch die Schwester hier gewesen! Sie war klug; sie hatte schon geweint, als Gregor noch ruhig auf dem Rücken lag. ... Aber die Schwester war eben nicht da, Gregor selbst mußte handeln. Und ohne daran zu denken, daß er seine gegenwärtigen Fähigkeiten, sich zu bewegen, noch gar nicht kannte, ohne auch daran zu denken, daß seine Rede möglicher – ja wahrscheinlicherweise wieder nicht verstanden worden war, verließ er den Türflügel; schob sich durch die Öffnung; wollte zum Prokuristen hingehen. (*Die Verwandlung*, p. 20)	la situation ... et leurs soucis présents *absorbaient trop leur âme pour qu'ils trouvassent encore la force de prévoir*. Mais *un pressentiment habitait le cœur de Grégoire*. Il fallait arrêter, calmer, convaincre et finalement conquérir le gérant, il y allait de l'avenir de Grégoire et de sa famille. Ah! si sa sœur avait été là! Elle comprenait, celle-là, elle qui avait déjà commencé à pleurer quand il n'était encore que couché sur le dos *plein d'insouciance*! ... Mais voilà, elle n'était justement pas là; *toutes les négociations incombaient à Grégoire*. Et sans même s'inquiéter de savoir s'il pourrait aller bien loin ni si son discours avait été compris – ce qui semblait peu vraisemblable – il abandonna son battant de porte, passa par l'ouverture pour rattraper le gérant. (*La Métamorphose*, pp. 28f.)

One of the characteristics of this type of translation is the *addition*.[33] Not only does the TO somehow find it necessary to 'improve' the ST, but he also fills in the 'gaps' that he perceives, or foresees for the LC2 reader. It is as if a TT must correspond to a series of unwritten norms of 'readability': any potential ambiguity must be explained, every reference must be spelt out, even if the translation becomes more of a commentary. We find ourselves here in the very heart of the ideological struggle concerning the translation of literary texts. When one studies certain published translations,[34] one begins to understand why theorists such as Meschonnic (1973) and Berman (1984) devote such energy to condemning the 'annexing' of works of art in another culture. Our aim here is not to come down in favour of one or the other, but to consider the possible intermediate positions between LC1 and LC2 which the TO can explore.

Between LC1 and LC2

It should be clear from the outset that there can be no one stable and defined midway position between two LCs where, miraculously, the LC1 'flavour' would be maintained in a LC2-accessible context. At best, a TT will oscillate between the two poles. But in the light of what has been said above concerning the problematical status of the very concept of 'culture', it should be clear that Translation – by the very 'unnatural' influence that it exercises – works on, bends, and even deforms the LC2. This, in all events, is how we see the notion of 'decentring', introduced by Meschonnic (1973: 307ff.). In this very important book, Meschonnic shows how translation first 'decentres' an LC (i.e. pulls it towards LC1) until LC2 develops and is redefined to include what were originally the foreign elements. One can see how, during different historical periods, translation has helped an LC to develop, rather than to become stultified in some splendid isolation. A diachronic perspective is essential here, for, as Foucault never tired of pointing out, all cannot be said at any one time in any one culture. The point here is then that translation can be an *enriching* factor in the development of a culture – and not, as is often maintained, a dangerous external influence 'polluting' the LC.[35] However, it is necessary to move from this very theoretical aspect to a more practical consideration of the terrain between two LCs. We will illustrate this with an example taken from Harold Pinter's *No Man's Land*.

The passage comes from the first act. Hirst and Spooner (who apparently do not know each other) have started up a conversation in a pub and then gone back to Hirst's house for another drink. Spooner has been highly loquacious, and has started to try to find out details about Hirst; Hirst has said little.

SPOONER: Tell me then about your wife.
HIRST: What wife?
SPOONER: How beautiful she was, how tender and how true. Tell me with what speed she swung in the air, with what velocity she came off the wicket, whether she was responsive to finger spin, whether you could bowl a shooter with her, or an offbreak with a legbreak action. In other words, did she google?

The Translation 'problem' here is obvious, given the culture-specific references which one could, on the face of it, hardly imagine in another language. Before tackling the problem, let us first consider the type of instructions we might expect to be given by the TI, and the sort of translation strategies that the TO might contemplate.

The Translation strategy instigated by the TI could be of several types: given that this is a play, one might expect first and foremost a request for a 'dramatic' text which is both possible to perform and likely to be a success on the French stage, with, naturally, an emphasis on the spoken word; the TO may be asked to preserve the maximum number of cultural references (the play is set in London, with specific mention of pubs, street names, etc.[36]); the TI might insist on a 'comprehensible' (i.e. normalized) text (with a definition of the expectations and limitations of the LC2 public).

Before contemplating any translation strategies, the TO has to analyse the component parts of the message he or she is being asked to translate. It is clear that this passage is not 'about' cricket, but uses cricket as a metaphor to convey another message. His definition of the prime message will be the circumscribing factor in his production of LC2 paraphrastic sets. The 'subject', then, is Spooner's rather misplaced enquiry about Hirst's wife, with a sexual innuendo which is increased as this passage follows his long defence of himself as a 'betwixt twig peeper' (i.e. voyeur).[37] The description also stands in ironic contrast to that of Hirst's affair with Spooner's wife in Act 2.[38] Cricket, then, is 'grafted' on as a cultural metaphor which, in fact, has undeniable importance in the play as a whole.[39] Ideally, then, the TO would seek to reproduce Spooner's voyeuristic enquiry – bearing in mind his overall interpretation of Spooner's character (a weak man trying to insinuate himself into someone else's household; a sexual failure and/or (repressed?) homosexual) – while at the same time recreating this essential cultural element. In the light of the analyses made above, he would appear to be faced with three equally unsatisfactory options: (1) keeping the LC1 references but producing a virtually incomprehensible LC2 text (not because cricket itself is unknown, but because all the vocabulary associated with the game is technical and highly specialized); (2) finding 'equivalent' LC2 references, but losing the reference to cricket; (3) inserting a simple passing reference to cricket, which would mean losing the overall coherence of the image, and which might well fall on deaf ears anyway. We shall briefly explore the second and third points.

In this play, cricket functions not as the popular sport played at all levels and followed by all social classes, but as an element of the pre-war upper-class splendour evoked by both Spooner and Hirst in Act 2. It is part of the world of London clubs and connections in high places which Hirst apparently still enjoys, but which Spooner – who has fallen on hard times – has lost and is seeking to retrieve. It also mirrors the active and healthy life which both men have left behind. Finding an LC2 'equivalent' to replace all[40] the references to cricket therefore entails taking into account above all the 'position' of cricket in the play, rather than the sexual innuendo brought about by the description of a woman as an object to which one does certain things – one can justify this approach because the innuendo is relatively easy to reproduce the moment we have an 'enquiry about another man's wife'. The choice of sport or sporting activity is fairly delicate. We would propose horse-racing for a French translation (both as a sport and a sporting event one goes to) and hunting for a Serbo-Croat translation.[41]

As for the middle ground between two LCs, this is, paradoxically, both something which *already exists* and which *has to be created* for each translation undertaken. It exists to the extent that all published translations themselves constitute, as it were, a series of bridges or connections on which the TO can call.[42] It has to be created because each text is itself a reworking of the SR and cannot be transposed according to a predefined set of rules. References to the game of cricket have, of course, been made in texts in other languages, but is it possible both to 'decentre' a language here and to produce something which reflects the original? It would seem that in this instance such a translation – using, for example, the Anglicisms quoted by Harraps such as 'bôler'[43] – would put all the emphasis on the fact that cricket was being used as the image, rather than what is actually behind that image. If that is the case, then the TO would do better to concentrate on more general forms of decentring, whether these be on a linguistic level (such as the use of recognizable syntactic forms or lexical items) or on a different semiotic level (adapting the set, props, clothes, etc., to replace the connotation judged to be missing[44]).

Let us finally take a brief look at the strategies chosen by two translators of this play.

SPOONER: Alors parlez-moi de votre femme.
HIRST: Quelle femme?
SPOONER: Combien elle était belle, et combien tendre et combien fidèle. Parlez-moi de son jeu de jambes, dites-moi quel effet elle donnait sur son revers, si elle trouvait le lob aisé en fond de court, si elle renvoyait de volée l'amorti de l'adversaire, si ses boyaux résistaient à l'humidité du gazon, si elle n'était pas trop molle au second service. En d'autres termes, est-ce qu'elle servait bien?[45]

SPOONER: Pričajte mi onda o svojoj ženi.
HIRST: Kojoj ženi?
SPOONER: Kaka je bila lijepa, kako laka, kako pouzdana. Pričajte mi kako se spretno mogla nabijati, kako je glatko repetirala ili zvučno palila, je li bila osjetljiva pod prstom, kako su joj čudesne bile mušice, kako se lako na njoj napinjao kokot, jeste li mogli s njom kroz vatru i kroz vodu. Drugim riječima, je li trzala, je li zanosila?[46]

Both translators have, in fact, produced texts according to 'dramatic' criteria which read well and will have a certain effect on the LC2 public. In both cases, the effect is primarily comic, and brought out by emphasizing the sexual connotations of the passage. However, the effect in French is undoubtedly diluted, both by the transposition into the tennis metaphor, and by the fact that the wife is the (active) tennis player rather than the (passive) ball. The Serbo-Croat translator has chosen to portray the wife as a rifle[47] – which, incidentally, would be compatible with the hunting image suggested above. But even the approximate translation back into English given in note 47 is enough to show that the wife has become purely a sexual object and nothing else – to the extent that the audience may laugh at or be shocked by the crudity of the images.

One can see, then, that a wide variety of translation strategies are open to the TO, and that his final version will both reflect the overall prerogatives defined by the TI (in relation to the type of public aimed at) and the particular reading of the text adopted by the TO. We hope that this brief example has helped us to show both just how rich the 'middle ground' between LCs is, and types of approach that the TO can adopt.

CONCLUSION: THE CULTURAL EQUATION

We are now in a position to bring together the different material put forward in this chapter in order to make some final comments about what we have called the Cultural Equation. We have spoken in some detail about two apparently unrelated areas: on the one hand, the 'actors' in the Translation situation, on the other hand, LC1 and LC2 influences. In our view, the TO must bring together and fully define these two separate levels for each translation undertaken, in order not to fall into the trap of highlighting one particular element, and thus distorting the overall balance of factors to be taken into account. At this stage in our presentation, the Cultural Equation remains on the level of a concept; as our book proceeds, and further parameters in the Translation situation are defined, the practical applications of the concept will become clear, and in particular, we hope, in Chapter 9.

Thus we conclude this chapter by reiterating our claim that the Cultural Equation should be an essential part of Translation theory and practice alike. This claim is, in fact, the logical consequence to be drawn from our theoretical position which both seeks to understand the translation process in relation to the actors involved in it, and to account in particular for the idiosyncratic or individualized conception of Translation which any Translation Operator must necessarily have. The

TO will both occupy a specific position in relation to the LCs, and will bring his or her own conception of what translating is to bear on the operations that he or she carries out. We hope that we have shown that it is not enough just to think of a TO as being LC1- or LC2-influenced; the very richness of all the intermediate positions between the two is such that he must redefine his own position both for a text as a whole, and for each individual component of that text. This theoretical position obviously has important consequences for the teaching of translation, which we shall be exploring in Chapter 10.

As a final remark in this chapter we would like to come back to the point that the tension induced between two LCs in translation should not be considered in terms of an LC 'gap', but as *highly fertile ground to be reassessed by each TO for each translation*. We shall be exploring this ground further in the following chapter as we look more closely at the role of the translator as Cultural Operator.

7 The Translation Operator as a Cultural Operator

INTRODUCTION

In our previous chapter, we examined the tension that the act of translating induces between two cultures. Our task is now to look more closely at the Translation Operator himself and the unique position he occupies, and then at the different operations that the TO must carry out within each culture. Thus we shall be seeking to explore the particular characteristics of the TO in linguistic and cultural terms, and then to break down the different phases of his work. We shall thus be showing what reading, interpreting, and translating strategies the TO will tend to use, given his very particular position between two LCs. This will lead us to some concluding remarks on his potential role within the Variational approach.

This chapter is necessarily a development of some of the points that have already been made, if sometimes implicitly. When we looked at the short passage from *No Man's Land* in Chapter 6 (p. 128), we gave a cursory indication of the sort of work the TO might be expected to do in order to situate the text within its original culture. We thus made some brief remarks about the role of cricket, and how in this play cricket is used by the playwright to impart a certain flavour to the speeches of the two major characters. Similarly, our discussion of possible translations of 'Cette semaine on tue le cochon!' was centred around what is eventually a culture-based reading of the function of this particular utterance. The time has now come to give a more systematic and developed presentation of the range of exploratory movements that the TO can undertake within different cultures.

A certain number of remarks can be made from the outset. The operations that we are going to describe are necessarily of an extreme complexity. Furthermore, as on the one hand they are both interrelated and *ad hoc* operations,[1] and on the other hand they are ordered – if not sometimes conditioned – by the type of text chosen for study, our description should be taken to be indicative of the research strategies that the TO (and the theorist) can develop, rather than of a series of 'rules' governing the Translation operation. It would be more accurate, then, to describe the second part of this chapter as a series of research proposals, a kind of open workshop designed to clarify – if only partially – the vast process accounting for the 'interpretation' of the ST and the exploration of possibilities in LC2.

For the purposes of the following discussion, we shall both be resorting to the notion of the 'standard' TO that we described in the last chapter, and modulating this notion to take into account the potential work that an 'idealized' TO – i.e. working at the highest level – can carry out. Thus our TO is translating into his own mother tongue, with all that that implies when considering his interpretation of the ST and his ability to produce paraphrases in LC2. We shall also be considering some of the other 'positions' the TO can occupy in the following chapter.

THE NATURE OF THE TRANSLATION OPERATOR

We mentioned in Chapter 6 how writers on Translation seem to take the TO for granted, or to assume that his or her aims correspond to their own aims. We said that the TO is virtually absent from Translation theory and that we wished to restore him to his rightful place at the centre of the debate on translation. We thus made some preliminary remarks about his position in relation to LC1 and LC2 and the different strategies he may adopt as a consequence of this very position. We now consider his role as a mediator between two LCs and as a regulator of the conflicting forces that are necessarily induced by the bringing together of two cultural systems.

Perhaps the most obvious statement one can make about the TO is that he must be competent in two LCs. This means that, however he has acquired his languages, he must maintain and develop both a knowledge and a practice of two independently developing entities. This is, on close examination, a fairly extraordinary state of affairs, as the middle ground he seeks to occupy – in other words, a position from which he can compare and convert from one LC into the other – is never one fixed and 'comfortable' area, but an obscure no-man's-land whose boundaries, LC1 and LC2, seem constantly to draw nearer and to recede, to change shape and size, as the LCs evolve independently, and as the practice of Translation itself evolves *within and between LCs*, both influencing and being influenced by the independent development of the LCs. We illustrate this in Figure 7.1. One or two comments on this static figure: if

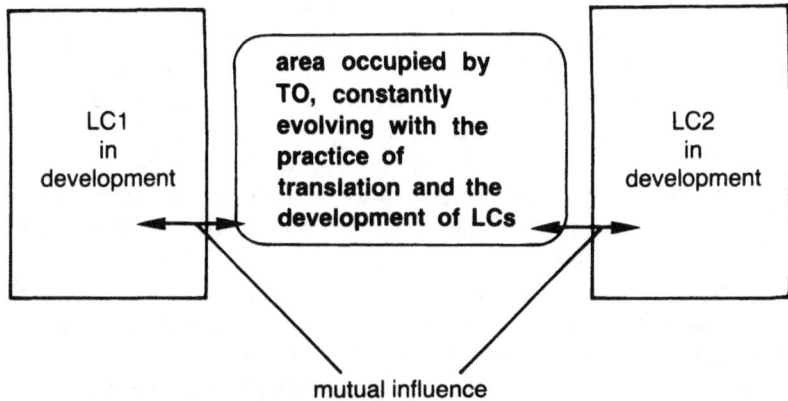

Figure 7.1 The 'area' occupied by the TO

the TO occupies the ground between LC1 and LC2, this does not mean that he is, somehow, a 'balanced' operator, midway between two entities. As we pointed out in the last chapter, he may seek to occupy this middle ground, but he is always anchored – to a greater or lesser extent – in one LC. Occupying the middle ground is an image which allows us to consider the idea of competence.

How, then, can one define the competence of the TO? For us, this is measured by his ability to analyse, compare, and convert cultural systems, while respecting both the conflicting forces within one LC, and the interplay of these forces as LCs are brought into contact. This means that the TO is constantly working both within the LCs taken separately, and on the comparison and conversion procedures which constitute his activity.

Thus the TO can never be secure in his position, and if he acquires competence, this competence is partly an ability to reflect and question his own role as a mediator. This means that he must be aware not just of developing LCs, of developing translation practices, but also of *the changes brought about in his competence as a result of repeated Translation operations*. This last point is vital both for the teaching of translation, and for the career translator – for the learner, it is important to see Translation as a dynamic process, and for the professional, there is nothing more stultifying than using 'pet' procedures because they have worked in the past.

After these initial comments about the nature of the TO, we come now to look at his role as a Cultural Operator. We begin by looking at the reading and interpreting strategies that will normally be employed by the TO translating into his own mother tongue. Our aim in exploring these strategies is (1) to help the translator to become more aware of the effect that his own position in the Cultural Equation will have on the operations he carries out, and (2) to prepare the ground for the fullest possible exploitation of the Variational approach, whose whole generation and homologizing processes, as we shall discuss at the end of the chapter, are carried out, as far as possible, in a cultural 'vacuum', but whose selection processes spring from the Cultural Equation. Thus the next section shows some of the limitations of the more traditional approach to Translation, and the 'natural' built-in bias the TO will have. The third section is an attempt to show the kind of exploratory strategies he can carry out as he puts the Variational approach into practice.

THE TO'S READING AND INTERPRETING STRATEGIES

One of the disadvantages of traditional theories on translation, as we have pointed out several times, is that the 'standard' TO is regarded as a culturally neutral operator. But as every translator knows, a TO does not put languages into watertight compartments and enter at will and exclusively into one or another linguistic universe. By his very activity, he is constantly going between LCs and creating/recreating links where no specific connection existed before. It follows, then, that the whole process of reading and interpreting the ST is a culture-bound activity which, as far as the TO is concerned, *is carried out in the perspective of the Target Language and of the forthcoming translation.* Indeed, so strong is the translation reflex that many people will begin a tentative translation as they begin reading a text for the first time, irrespective of the potential pitfalls of this procedure.[2] This means, in practice, (1) that a text is initially decoded – at least partially – from the LC2 perspective (before the LC1 context is fully simulated; see below); (2) that a degree of LC2-based explanation or commentary is immediately introduced; (3) that the TO simply cannot be blindly assimilated to the LC1 reader of the text; and (4) that the TO is not just any foreign reader of the ST, but a reader with a specific motivation. We shall illustrate each of these points separately in the following sections.

The LC2 perspective in decoding the LC1 text

It is very hard to prove that a reader will adopt one particular reading/interpreting strategy rather than another. There is nothing to stop one arguing that the 'virtually' bilingual speaker who has an extensive knowledge of the domain in question will decode the ST from 'within' the ST culture. But we would stress here that the whole perspective of translation brings a particular reading strategy to bear on a text and that the circulation of meaning both within the text, and of the text within the culture is profoundly modified as a result. The network of relations allowing a text to function within a culture becomes, as it were, loosened and slightly distorted as the magnetic effect of the second culture starts to exercise its influence. If one thinks of the SR as a series of points, each point is both defined by its relation to each other point, and maintained in a relatively stable place by the forces acting within the particular culture. The outside or LC2 vision has a loosening effect on the different points, by the very fact that a different network of relations and forces is operating for the LC2 native speaker, with the consequent pull that this induces.[3] Thus each cultural element is not simply seen in respect of LC1, but viewed as being the ground of a potential *difference, distinction,* or *tension*. One might even be tempted to conclude that a text does not 'mean' the same thing when seen through the eyes of a TO, when compared with a LC1 receiver; but rather than get caught in arguments of this type, it is more useful to confine oneself to underlining and developing the very particular reading strategies that the TO has, which are radically different from those of the 'normal' reader.[4]

The text quoted in Appendix 8, entitled 'Baillargues', provides one or two interesting examples of this phenomenon.[5] The text was chosen for several different reasons. It was felt first of all that, given the nature of the passage and the newspaper in which it appeared, very many LC1 readers would give only a cursory glance to the passage or simply would not read it through to the end.[6] Second, and as we shall see, this – in LC1 terms – bland and unremarkable text cannot fail to attract the attention of the LC2 reader/TO. Third it is the potential translation difficulties (and the SR-linked problems) which tend to catch the TO's attention as he or she goes through the passage. Finally, this is just the sort of text that one does *not* find in theories of translation, precisely because it is non-literary, and in most people's eyes, badly written and of little intrinsic interest. This last point is important, as we have taken some pains to stress that Translation theory should not be confined to one particular type of text, or be based on questionable value judgements. As many professional translators know only too well, STs are often hard to translate when they do not conform to received norms of 'textual beauty', 'acceptability', etc., and when they are obscure, poorly expressed, etc. It is only by integrating such passages into Translation theory that one can hope to reach an overview of Translation which is both more comprehensive and, in the final analysis, applicable.

138 *Redefining Translation*

Let us look, then, at the image the *LC1 reader* receives as he or she reads this passage. The overall impression that people have is of a lively and young town where plenty of things are happening, and therefore which is not just some dead dormitory town. Some readers point to the journalistic style, which, according to them, helps to underline the impression of liveliness and activity. Others assimilate the text to an advertisement for Baillargues, and feel put off by the 'sell' aspect they perceive. In all events, the text is not perceived as particularly 'interesting', and the average reader maintains he or she 'understands' everything. When questioned closely, certain passages are judged as 'obscure' or indeed as meaningless (e.g. 'Les arbres ouvrent des parenthèses . . .'), but they do not in themselves strike the reader as particularly significant or unusual.

LC2 readers, however, speak of a very different impression. Leaving aside the hotch-potch impression made by the mixing of different styles,[7] the TO's attention will inevitably be drawn to the LC1-specific elements of the text, as his reading is always situated at the level of *difference*. In very general terms, he will be aware that a journalistic passage praising the merits of a small town will not be couched in the same terms or use the same norms and cultural references.

Once again we must navigate between the more or less subjective impressions of the TO and the research which can be carried out on discourse families. Although detailed and statistically based research remains to be done, one can risk making some generalizations about 'tourist brochure' discourse, if one takes this text as a variant on this type of discourse family.[8] The predominant function of this type of discourse is, of course, a pragmatic one which one could define as 'awakening the tourist's interest in a town'. A double value judgement is automatically introduced: the writer of the text will (1) bring out what he or she considers to be the attractive elements of the town and (2) modulate this according to his or her vision of the groups of tourists likely to visit the area. As, in fact, such brochures are often written primarily with domestic tourists in mind, the value judgement is simply a reflection of the SR, whereby certain 'objects' are given a value rating and others are not. In the passage under consideration, the mention of the age of the church, and the fact that it is a listed building, is a case in point, plus the more localized reference to 'boules'. One often finds a fairly massive dose of pure ideology in such texts: for example, in the tourist brochure describing the island of Brioni off the Yugoslav coast:

Uz Brioni je vezano ime TITA, jugoslavenske socijalističke i nesvrstane misli. (*Pula Turistički informator*)	To Brioni is connected the name TITO, the Yugoslav socialist and non-aligned philosophy.

But if such an example is (from the LC2 point of view!) a fairly striking one, all texts contain SR-related elements (ideological stances) which tend to pass unnoticed. Some of these will be brought out in our 'Baillargues' text (see pp. 140–1).

Two major differences between French and English discourse can be pointed to, along the lines of the division made above. The focus of orientation in English is usually the tourist, who is both directly referred to as 'you', and identified according to the various pastimes he or she might enjoy ('Golfers can tee off from . . .'). He or she is, as it were, taken by the hand and shown around the various places. What is more, special care is taken of his or her needs and interests – it is a *personal* presentation in which the host town plays an active part, being identified as 'we'. Although one does find references to 'you' in French discourse, they are much less frequent and often simple imperatives/infinitives ('visitez'/'visiter'). The tourist is not so much being addressed directly as being introduced to a general historical and architectural presentation. The emphasis is usually placed on the object itself, which is made to vaunt its own merits.[9] Two brief examples will bring this out:

You can go walking across the nearby Downlands (. . .) which will take *you* to Downland summits . . . .Something for everyone, *we* think *you*'ll agree. (*Brighton Tourism and Resort Services,* 1988 brochure)	Montpellier *se rappelle* son histoire prestigieuse, pour mieux *se projeter* dans l'avenir en *créant* de nouveaux pôles de développement. (*Guide Touristique du Comité départemental du tourisme de l'Hérault,* 1989 brochure)

Needless to say that in the vast majority of cases such differences are only rarely taken into account in published translations, much to the amusement of the itinerant tourist.

The TO's attention will thus be drawn to certain elements which take on a particular importance *when considering the text from the LC2 perspective*. The first of these is the technical or semi-specialized terms ('paramètres solides', 'équipements structurants', 'démographie', 'la vie active,' etc.): these constitute a kind of jargon which one can encounter in several different types of text.[10] The important point here is that one would only be likely to find the equivalent terms (if one finds them at all) in specialized contexts in English. 'Démographie' is a case in point here: it is a commonly used word in French, but 'demography' is extremely rare in everyday English. These terms impart a distinct flavour to the text which, *from the point of view of the LC1 alone*, is absent. Moreover, certain LC2 readers will immediately attempt to translate such terms, despite the fact that the passage is read in the original language without being translated. This confirms the impression given by some readers that such terms are in fact 'incomprehensible' – simply because they cannot find LC2 equivalents to help them understand what the original means.[11]

Second, the TO will undoubtedly be struck by the types of images used: 'une épine dorsale dans le plus pur style patrimoine vivant', 'une ruelle rêveuse', 'quelques jets de boules plus loin', 'les arbres ouvrent des parenthèses', 'des brochettes d'hommes', etc. It is not that such images are impossible in English in general or in tourist-brochure discourse in particular; but they would constitute something of an exception, whereas this type of image – even if the present examples do 'go over the top' somewhat – is common in French in this type of discourse.

This differential reading therefore allows the text to function on a double plane: as something which belongs within its LC and as a series of differences seen from LC2. As the differences constitute 'what one does not expect to find', the TO's task will be to develop his or her reading into a LC2-based explanation or commentary.

LC2-based explanation or commentary

The whole question of explanation and commentary in translation is a very delicate one. In fact, it brings us back to the LC1-/LC2-influenced translation strategies evoked in the last chapter. More specifically here, the question posed is 'how far a reader should be led by the hand', or conversely 'how much a reader should work out for himself'. As is now, we hope, clear, such decisions can only be made in the light of the whole series of parameters operating for any one translation (and thus are dealt with more fully in the next chapter). We limit ourselves here to spelling out the second stage of the TO's reading of the ST, as he foresees the problems his text is likely to cause in an LC2 environment.

Our starting point here is once again the fundamental non-comparability of SRs. If, coming back to the 'Baillargues' passage, one takes English as one's LC2, one might be tempted to say that there is enough that is directly comparable between the two LCs to make direct transfer both possible and comprehensible, that, after all, we are talking about small towns which are conscious of their own identities and which do not wish to be assimilated to dormitory towns. One might point to the value attributed to old buildings and the cultural heritage in both LCs, and indeed to many shared characteristics. But these superficial resemblances hide profound differences which will be of greater or lesser importance, depending on the passage under consideration.

Two examples will serve to illustrate the type of commentary which could be extended to include the whole of the text. One can look, first of all, at the different *political* realities embodied by the terms 'délégué aux affaires économiques' and 'District' (when compared with LC2 local government equivalents). One immediately comes up against contrasting structures, attributions, powers, etc., which represent potential grounds for commentary or explanation. There is, of course, a whole language which accompanies such structures (in this case: 's'appuyer sur', 'développement harmonieux', 'jouer les cartes de', 'volonté',[12] 'entreprenant', etc.) which cannot be divorced from the way the structures reflect and are reflected by the SR. The TO will have to envisage pointing to the salient differences, in accordance with the instructions received from the TI. The second example seems even simpler on the face of it – we learn that 'sporting activities' (or to normalize, 'sports') are part and parcel of the development of the town. But the TO may have to take into consideration the enormous differences in the functioning of 'sport' in the two LCs – not here as professional activities, but as playing a part in the substructure of the culture. People conversant with the two educational systems, for example, will know that sport not only occupies different positions in school timetables, but is given a different rating and value, to the extent that the term (rather than the reality it describes) functions quite differently.[13] Thus the innocent looking 'activités sportives' conceals a whole network of positive ideological images unconsciously picked up by the LC1 reader, but which might need to be spelt out in the TT.

In comparison with the points made above, certain features will always strike one as being obvious 'problem points'. One can cite here the image 'quelques jets de boules plus loin', which has the function of producing a connotation of the south of France. One is, of course, reminded of the 'cricket' problem considered in the last chapter, where both keeping the image and modifying it appear to be unsatisfactory solutions. The TO has here both to weigh up the Translation order given by the TI and consider the LC2 public before putting forward possible translations – which will certainly include keeping the LC1 term. (If the LC2 reader is thought to understand the reference, an expansion might read:, 'A stone's throw further on – or a *boule*'s throw'.)

TO v. LC1 reader

If we have concluded that the TO and the LC1 reader have very different reading and interpreting strategies, this has been on the basis of extensive enquiries amongst different categories of people. The overall pattern observed shows the highly motivated attitude of the TO compared to the rather passive reading habits of the LC1 reader.[14] When an LC1 reader is incited to explore a text, he or she tends – naturally enough – to be insensitive to the particular characteristics cited above, especially those one can define as belonging to a norm operating in a discourse family or as being (more or less) predictable. The TO, on the other hand, is automatically sensitive to all the potential problem areas. The conclusion that must be drawn from this is that not only must one fully explore the role of the TO in decoding the ST, but one must also see this act of reading/interpretation as a specific act geared to the future translation, and therefore not directly comparable with normal LC1 reading habits. As one might expect, one tends to find two contrasting attitudes in the literature on translation. On the one hand, the translation theorist speaks from his highly privileged position of access to two LCs, with the comparative basis that this gives him; on the other hand, the LC1 specialist denigrates translation as being a 'betrayal' of LC1 cultural and linguistic values – and we are back to the ideological images of translation that we explored in Chapter 2. The moment one concentrates on the specific position and function of the TO, these problems do not disappear as such, but can be considered in a completely new light.

The specific motivation of the TO

We should now develop our statement that the TO reads the ST in the light of the translation he or she is to carry out. By starting from this very general statement, we have been able to show that the whole decoding process of the TO is particular and has to be examined in some detail. It is now necessary to add that the reading/interpretation of the text is not only conditioned by the fact that a text is to be translated, but also by the type of translation envisaged, as defined by the TI. In other words, the TO will not normally make an exhaustive reading of each text he is confronted with, but will allow his vision of the text to be coloured – or predetermined – in advance. Indeed, how else can one account for the extraordinary gaps one discovers in certain published translations, where words, sentences, and even paragraphs are missing? A short example from the French translation of Golding's *Lord of the Flies* can serve to illustrate this point:

He had just time to realize that the age-long nightmares of falling and death were past and that the morning was come, when he heard the sound again. It was an ululation over by the seashore – and now the next savage answered and the next. The cry swept by him across the narrow end of the island.[15]	Il eut juste le temps de comprendre que les éternels cauchemars de chute et de mort étaient passés et que le matin était là quand le son se répéta. Le rideau de cris se déplaça comme un vol d'oiseaux.[16]

Half of the ST has been amputated, and, of course, the LC2 reader who has no access to the ST has no way of knowing this. The motivations behind such translations would appear to be either economic ones or the amount of time available (which often come down to one and the same thing). Conversely, certain texts have been subjected to what one might call an intense and loving scrutiny, producing what Ladmiral calls a 'hyper-reading' of the original – to the extent that people might well consult a translation in order to have a better (or more complete) understanding of the original.[17] As one can see, therefore, there is no one reading strategy practised by a hypothetical TO, but an *ad hoc* situation which has to be defined in relation to the parameters governing it.

Having spent some time discussing the typical reading and interpreting strategies of the TO, we now change our perspective to consider some of exploratory strategies he may employ as a Cultural Operator. We illustrate work at the LC1 level by reference to newspaper discourse and look at some problems of literary discourse in relation to LC2 choices.

EXPANDING READING AND INTERPRETING STRATEGIES
Exploring the ST within LC1

Having pointed to the particular reading strategies the TO is likely to employ in the previous section, we now turn our attention to what we feel to be more productive strategies in decoding the Source Text and situating it within LC1 productions. What we are concerned with here is to prepare the TO for the final choices he or she will make when selecting among the different paraphrases produced during the stage of homological generation. The present analysis thus takes place on a very different level from those proposed in Chapters 4 and 5, and should be seen as part of a wider examination of all the different socio-cultural, economic, and other parameters which have to be borne in mind, and which will occupy the major part of Chapter 8. As a final introductory remark, we should point out that the following analyses are a development of those put forward Chapter 6, pages 117–21 ('The Source Text and the discourse family'), and anticipate Chapter 8, pages 173–83 ('Choosing the Target Text).

The approach which for us is the most satisfying from the theoretical point of view and the most practical in terms of potential applications is, following Foucault's terminology (e.g. 1969), an 'archaeological' one.

We present here our own interpretation of various areas of research, which have been developed in France and elsewhere. As there is not enough space here to give a detailed presentation of each area, the reader is invited to follow up some of the bibliographical references given below. These approaches include more historically oriented ones (see Robin, 1973), Marxist (e.g. Althusser, 1976), socio-critical (e.g. Angenot and Robin, 1985), to which one can add the work of Foucault (1969, 1971). An introduction to some of the main ideas of Althusser and Foucault (together with details of English texts available) can be found in Macdonell (1986).

Using such an approach, a text is seen to be the result of the conditions of production – whether these be mere material conditions, or the ideological and cultural 'frame' (SR) operating in any LC. At any one time, there are limits to what can and must be said, and consequently, what is said is a consequence of the 'frame' surrounding it, and thus in a certain manner predetermined, and to varying degrees predictable. In certain types of discourse, the number of forms and lexical items available is so restricted, that given the particular circumstances of an utterance, one can foresee what that utterance will be.[18] As one moves towards a more creative type of discourse, the possibilities and combinations multiply, paradoxically reflecting the SR while helping to redefine it.

Two examples will help to clarify these points, and to show how such an approach can aid and abet the TO in his or her work as a Cultural Operator. In the first of these – one segment of the written press – analysing the conditions of production of a newspaper article can help both to understand the choices made by the journalist and to choose amongst LC2 alternatives; in the second – literature – we will show how the TO can work with a certain number of perceived norms which allow him or her to 'situate' a ST, and again to judge the qualities of 'rival' LC2 forms.

Approaching newspaper discourse

Journalistic discourse presents several interesting features from the point of view of Translation Studies. As has often been noted, a newspaper is the reflection of a certain number of choices, among which the most important are ideological and economic ones.[19] The ideological ground occupied by a newspaper is rarely a stable and fully identifiable one. The specific policy of a newspaper can be to include conflicting ideological viewpoints – as is the case of *Le Monde*, where one finds commentaries published by well-known people from a wide variety of political backgrounds. More generally, a certain 'floating' can be observed, as has been noted in a recent study of the British and American press:

> No paper is unchanging or totally consistent. Changes can actually be perceived from day to day: each issue is a highly individualized product resulting from a complex process which involves a *sui generis* team-effort and a non-recurring economic, political and cultural context. Such changes can be either piecemeal or quite sweeping. After Rupert Murdoch took over the London *Sun* in 1969 and the *New York Post* in 1976, his initiatives set off a chain reaction which is still being felt . . . . Each article one reads must be put in the proper perspective and linked to the particular time of its writing. A newspaper is never quite what the reader thought it was the day before.[20]

Each article results from, and can be analysed according to certain variables. We have a look at some of the most important of these in the following paragraphs, beginning with the dominant category of ideology.

The ideology 'behind' the newspaper article and the illusion of objectivity

We look here briefly at the interaction between the specific ideology of the newspaper and the SR. This will take the form of conforming to (and therefore confirming) the major ideological positions, or of producing counterpositions (in relation to the major ones, thus again confirming their predominance). Each article can be placed in relation to the reigning ideological battles of the time and can be classified in terms of conformity or revolt. Such analyses help to dispel the illusion of 'objective' journalism or that of the newspaper 'mirroring' reality, even though most newspapers are at such pains to present their own objectivity.[21] Needless to say, the 'image' of the newspaper is a crucial aspect, and vital for its survival, and it is not hard to see how economic necessity prevails in the face of all other. In the final analysis, the consumer is king, and if one is to judge by the 'content' of tabloid newspapers – which in Britain at present account for about some

12 million copies sold on a daily basis (or 82 per cent of the total)[22] – he or she is only too happy to find confirmation of everything he or she 'believes' to be true and right. This is, of course, not to say that the 'quality' papers, on the other hand, are paragons of objectivity, despite the fact that they often appear to be simply relaying information received from a variety of sources. A case in point, which can be found in Appendix 9 – it is an article from the *Guardian* entitled 'Mystery dash of Ivan the Terrified' – will be analysed below[23] in order to show how important it is for the TO to go beyond the received image one has of certain sources of information.

The illusion of objectivity is given in this article by the different sources cited – in order to narrate an 'event' the journalist quotes the residents/witnesses and also the Scotland Yard spokesman, giving the impression that his job is simply to collect and present all the material available. The journalist is highly prudent about the affirmations he makes, each time letting the reader know that the information is not confirmed, which again strengthens the illusion of objectivity. So he is careful about the very identity of the man ('is *understood* to be') and says that the man 'was *believed* to be inside the Soviet Embassy' (it is only when one's suspicions about the ideological bias of the article have been aroused that one starts to question the use of such words as 'inside' – why not simply 'in'?). He 'lets the residents speak', maintaining the slightly obscure points and minor contradictions, which all add to the 'slice of life' impression being created. When one comes to analyse the passage more closely, the ethnocentric bias and political prejudice become much clearer, both in the choice of title, with the use of the Ivan stereotype, associated with mystery, fear, and fleeing, and in the choice of key words, which all contribute to stressing the Gulag feeling lurking behind the presentation of the facts. Only a close reading will reveal such details as the choice of tense in the second paragraph ('He *had* been in Britain since last September') suggesting that the man has already been absconded elsewhere.[24]

The above analysis does not, of course, allow us to conclude that the *Guardian* is (or was in 1977) a reactionary anti-Soviet newspaper. Nor does it allow us to make simplistic generalizations about a predominant ideological position prevalent in Britain at that time. The aim of such an approach is to 'open up' an article in such a way that the TO can fully measure the impact on the reader (whether it be conscious or unconscious) of ST terms and structures (regardless of whether they were deliberately chosen or not by the journalist) and hence, in the final analysis, choose between LC2 alternatives *both in accordance with LC1 choices and in relation to the kind of image aimed at and defined by the TI*.

The Translation Operator as a Cultural Operator

This will be demonstrated at greater length both in the next chapter, and in Chapter 10, where we give an example of a published translation which goes against the ideological presuppositions of the original.[25]

The type of article written: visual components

Leaving aside the actual 'event' deemed to be worthy of the status 'news',[26] it is important to consider the nature of the article in question (very broadly speaking, one can find four categories: 'news', survey-type articles, leaders, feature articles or columns). Each type of article corresponds to a different writing process and is based on different conditions (see below). Moreover, it is important to consider the newspaper as a whole, and not to take one single article as a generally valid example of some value being put forward. This is crucial when newspapers juxtapose articles in order to influence what might otherwise be a more 'neutral' piece of reporting:

> The juxtaposition of facts, sources and quotations inside an article creates associations that lead to new meaning. A specific piece of news tacked on to the end of a story may suddenly reveal the deeper meaning that has been sidestepped up to that point (cf. the effect produced by the list of deaths by fire which concludes a seemingly unbiased account in the *Daily Telegraph* of the 1978 firemen's strike). If, moreover, the article 'happens' to be located next to other stories with presumably similar topics (see, for example, articles on political violence next to articles on crime), a new layer of meaning is added which cannot be perceived if the original article is analysed separately.[27]

In a finer analysis, it is necessary to consider the actual newspaper in question, and relate each article to the article types used in that paper. This provides a discriminatory apparatus which can form the base of choices in LC2. Moreover, it is important to look at the presentation of the newspaper, the amount of space given to an article and its position on the page, accompanying material illustrating the article – photographs, cartoons, graphs, etc. This might seem to be an obvious point, but one can find many examples of articles which are either translated without the accompanying material, or whose accompanying material has been changed, thus changing the overall impact of the message.[28]

Sources, conditions of production

Mouillaud and Tétu (1989: 37ff.) have pointed to the important role played by the press agencies in the make-up of a newspaper. They point to a certain standardization of language, as agencies manage to have their wires reproduced with less and less alteration by the editing team. This, we believe, is at present only a minor trend, as one can see the need for 'personalizing' or rewriting the 'event' into a piece of news which can be decoded within the framework normally proposed by the paper. Nowadays, newspapers function primarily with second-hand items, as the 'news' given is already known through the almost instantaneous presentation on television and radio. Thus a degree of transformation is mandatory, together with an updating element to bring the reader the most recent information possible at the time of going to press.

The conditions of production of a newspaper – as opposed to a magazine – are well known. Newspapers work with fixed deadlines which impose limits both on the time available for (re)writing and on the space available. These conditions pose a particular problem for the TO. His or her translation will obviously appear after the original, and may be amended to take into account the most recent 'facts' bearing on the subject in question. Such an approach is clearly the policy of the translation team working for the *Guardian Weekly*, where one regularly sees both updates of current events and comments designed to inform LC2 readers about cultural elements they are presumed not to know. In fact, translation puts the whole functioning of a newspaper article into question. The 'unwritten contract' whereby the paper will give all the latest information is, by dint of the time gap, not operable any more, and one is left face to face with the extreme subjectivity of the ST. Hence the TO is often faced with an interesting series of choices in LC2 (see next chapter).

If all newspapers have to operate within the bounds of space available, what is not so clear is how that space is divided up amongst the different types of articles. Each newspaper reader undoubtedly has an expectation about the make-up of his or her daily reading matter, which will include the percentage of space allocated to each type of subject. Any change of this will change the overall weighting, and thus influence the interpretation of the text. Research is yet to be done to compare this distribution of space in newspapers in different countries.

Newspaper language

Every reader of a newspaper is aware that his or her paper has what can be loosely termed a 'style'. This is traditionally broken down into a series of features, such as a certain level of vocabulary, or certain recurring or predictable syntactic patterns. In comparing 'quality' newspapers and 'tabloids' in the British press, one can risk making a generalization that the latter are much simpler and more straightforward to read than the former; semi-specialized words and technical terms are not out of place in *The Times*, but they are totally absent from the *Daily Mirror*. Sentence lengths, and the complexity of structures are quite different.

On a more general level, certain stylistic traits characterize journalistic discourse as a whole in one country, and pose a translation problem if not identified as being stylistic – and thus predictable – rather than informational. This is the case with anaphoric reference to well-known figures in French life, particularly politicians. Once a politician has been named, common practice is to refer to him or her by their functions – or former functions – and the more they have, the better. François Mitterrand and Valéry Giscard d'Estaing are thus very rich subjects for journalists. The former is identified by his known functions ('le chef de l'Etat', 'le président de la République'), lesser-used functions ('le chef des Armées') and what one might call occasional functions, such as 'le co-prince' on a visit to Andorra (jointly ruled by France and Spain). Former functions also abound, such as 'l'ancien premier secrétaire du Parti Socialiste', 'l'ancien député de la Nièvre', etc. The TO may decide that such references exist in British newspaper discourse, but as they are statistically much rarer (Mrs Thatcher was referred to as 'the prime minister', but not as 'the member for Finchley', or 'the former education secretary', 'the Oxford graduate', 'the grocer's daughter', etc.[29]), he or she will therefore alternate between the usual couple of name, pronoun. But it is not enough for the TO to recognize these as stylistic features and to normalize them for, say, a British audience. The problem is to gauge whether they bring additional information which the LC2 readership needs, and which the LC1 readership is thought to possess. This is the case, for example, with the references to Valéry Giscard d'Estaing as 'l'ancien président de la République', or as 'le président de l'UDF', 'le député européen', etc. After his election defeat in 1981, Giscard kept a very low profile for a couple of years, and was therefore absent from the British press. When he started becoming politically active again, his status in France was such that nobody had to be reminded of this former position, but it can be argued that an English reader needed at this time to be reminded of his past function. The same holds for his current position as leader of the UDF: it can be assumed that the average English reader simply does not know this, transforming what is in French merely a stylistic variation into an element of information, which needs to be translated accordingly.[30]

It has also been noted that journalistic discourse in general both reflects and shapes current language trends, particularly by its use of vogue terms, clichés, etc. This is particularly noticeable in the French written press, which adapts very quickly to language trends. One sometimes has the impression that the newspaper 'writes itself', that language takes over, whatever the 'event' which is being reported. Such language needs therefore to be identified for its cliché and predictable value, enabling the TO to explore the potential LC2 forms available. This does not, of course, necessarily mean replacing cliché by cliché, but looking at the general function of such language within the discourse family. One of these functions is to sound modern and up to date, giving the reader the impression of belonging and 'feeling at home'. The TO may decide that such functions are fulfilled at different levels in the British press: for example, by the use of first names in the tabloids. It is only by situating the ST within its production situation and by exploring LC2 possibilities that the whole range of translation possibilities can be evaluated.

The aim of this section has been to show some of the strategies the TO can adopt in order to have the widest possible basis for analysing the ST. Our analysis will finally be completed in Chapter 8, when we come to consider in more detail the identity of the LC1 senders and receivers. We now move on to look at strategies which can be used to explore the LC2.

Exploring the potential of LC2

Earlier in this chapter (pp. 136–43), when we looked at the reading strategies the TO will normally tend to adopt, we saw how the ST is decoded in the LC2 perspective. The change of perspective in our current development is that the TO will explore the ST as fully as possible (and as far as is possible) in the LC1 context before coming to consider the potential of the second Language Culture. Thus he comes to LC2 with detailed knowledge both of his ST and its conditions of production and reception, and therefore has already limited the scope of his enquiry in LC2.

It would seem at first sight that the TO explores LC2 with the aim of finding the 'equivalent' to what he has discovered in LC1. As we have already discussed, this notion of equivalence has been at the basis of very many theories of translation, and although it does have a certain use, it also prevents one from seeing clearly just what the operations involved in translation are. The point we would like to stress here and which we will come back to later is that work at the LC2 level cannot be assimilated to 'normal' creative production in LC2[31] because *the overall context remains the LC1 one*. This means that work at the LC2 level is necessarily undertaken in conditions of extreme tension as the TO seeks to 'bend' the second culture in order to accommodate a reality which is normally beyond its fields of reference. We look below at the different aspects of research that the TO can expect to carry out.

Limitations imposed by the exploration of LC1

It should be clear from all that has preceded that a TO will approach LC2 with a specific aim in mind, resulting from his detailed analysis of the ST. As a Cultural Operator, the TO must explore LC2 keeping in mind the required effect of his translation. Having said this, it is important to point out the danger of working at a micro-textual level. The temptation is to divide the ST up into very small units and to look for 'equivalents' for each and every unit. This is particularly dangerous for students who tend to work at the level of the word anyway. One can briefly illustrate this point with one of Ladmiral's examples (1979: xff.), where he discusses the problems of translating the French slang word 'bagnole'. It is the most common of the many slang words used to designate a car, and the problem is the lack of such words in English. The first reaction of the TO is to translate slang by slang (applying the immediate LC1 criterion), but this is precisely the sort of limitation we are trying to go beyond. In fact, 'bagnole' says little about the *object* referred to – except to identify it as the same object in extra-linguistic reality as 'voiture' or 'automobile'[32] – but plenty about the speaker using the word – and with this being the case, the TO would hope to compensate for the paucity of LC2 words by introducing a slang connotation at a different point in his text.

The problem posed by slang is, in fact, a highly complex one and can rarely be solved by applying a vague 'slang becomes slang' condition. People tend to differ widely on what slang 'means' or what it 'adds' to a meaning. In a British context, this might depend, among other things, on social background and age, but such categories tend to be less relevant in France, and in any case, different words possess slang equivalents used with different frequencies. The only option open to the TO is to try to judge the *overall* effect of the use of such words – and thus to solve the problem at a macro-textual level.

The LC1 context in the LC2

However much one believes in the 'virtues' of LC2-influenced translation, it is the LC1 context which usually prevails in any translation. The reality being described is an LC1 reality, and its description has been encoded in the LC1 System of Representation. The play *No Man's Land* continues to be set in London, and not Paris, the main characters keep their names,[33] and the cultural references are usually maintained.[34] This being the case, one cannot simply convert LC1 references into LC2, but one has to 'bend' the LC2 in order to encompass such references. We shall illustrate this by referring to Cavanna's *Les Ritals* (1978: 35). The narrator of this novel is a lower-class boy living in a Paris suburb whose father is an illiterate Italian immigrant. The story is set some fifty years ago during the thirties' recession, when immigrants were regarded in a particularly bad light. The narrator is caught between two worlds and identifies himself at times with the immigrant camp and at times with the French one.

This novel is a highly complex one to translate. The young narrator speaks the child's slang of the Parisian suburbs, while at the same time innocently repeating adults' ethnocentric or racist comments on immigrants in general and Italians in particular. The effect is both to underline the precise geographical and social location of the book, and to reflect the socio-economic and cultural reality of the period. The immediate problem of the TO is how to maintain this effect in translation.

Our starting point is the assumption that an English translation of this novel would seek to maintain the major cultural references on which the work rests. There would, therefore, be no attempt to 'transpose' the setting to Britain, with, say, West Indian or Pakistani immigrants. Now this assumption means that the TO is not looking for an 'equivalent' – and the West Indian in Britain might well fulfil this role at certain restricted levels – but seeking to express the 'same' reality (Italian immigrants in Paris) through the LC2 SR. Since a 'full' cultural context is being replaced by one which is virtually empty, and differently structured anyway,[35] there is obviously no immediately identifiable translation strategy available for the TO, who is forced to consider a wide range of potential translations for each and every element considered.

The TO's aim is to analyse as minutely as possible the various elements which go to make up the overall effect of the novel, such as he comes to interpret it (some of which we have outlined above). Once this analysis has been done, he is faced with what one might call the concave-mirror effect of trying to express such elements through another culture. This can be explained (1) by the distorting effect that changing cultures produces, and (2) by the automatic series of connections which are made within the second culture, and which interfere with the network of connections originally operating in LC1. The example of the slang used in the book shows this very clearly. English slang has a distorting effect on the ST as the original intracultural connections cease to operate ('localizing' the speaker very firmly in LC2), and general LC2 connections inevitably come into operation. The fourth chapter of Cavanna's novel begins: 'Les Ritals, on est mal piffés'. By placing 'Les Ritals' at the beginning of the sentence, all the ethnocentric reverberations of the word are set in motion, then causing a tragi-comic effect when the connection is made 'Les Ritals' = 'on'. Such an anteposition would be most unusual in English, and the TO would have to consider adding 'we' or 'us'. The slang element 'être mal piffés' would normally require a slang translation (such as 'get on people's wicks'), but the overall result is precisely the connotation of British slang, which is, in the final analysis, proper to certain segments of the British middle classes.[36] To which one has to add the fact that some of the slang used by Cavanna is outdated, posing yet another problem for the TO.

When faced with problems of this type, the TO may have to make fairly radical choices about the different elements of information he wishes to preserve at all costs. As he explores the LC2, he may feel obliged to envisage certain compensatory strategies to reinforce the translated image of the cultural elements proper to the LC1. These will include additions of various types, the use of LC1 words, certain explanatory details, etc. Above all, he will have to see how far the LC2 can be 'bent' to accommodate the original, and how the TT will find its place in an LC itself in a state of permanent flux. The series of choices that he makes will be an *interconnected* one, necessitating a certain line to be adopted – for example, whether the slang element will be maintained throughout, and what degree of slang will be used.[37] The decision to maintain the slang, for example, might mean compensating elsewhere for the strong LC2 connotations produced – i.e. strengthening the LC1 cultural context with additions, as we have already suggested.

THE TO AS A CULTURAL OPERATOR

We conclude this chapter by making some final remarks about the TO as a Cultural Operator. We have spent some time looking at two contrasting approaches which the TO might adopt. The first, corresponding to a more spontaneous, or non-systematized approach, entails reading and interpreting the ST in the light of the translation to be undertaken. The second, developed in the light of the Variational approach, requires an extensive examination of the ST in the LC1 context before the second LC is taken into consideration. But however much the TO seeks to broaden his approach to his work, he is limited by certain factors inherent in the Translation operation. We should come back to these now to underline the confines of the TO's work as a Cultural Operator.

In the interplay of cultural systems, the TO is entrusted with monitoring, organizing, or negotiating the comparative statuses of each system. The tensions that exist between them *can never be suppressed, only channelled or reconverted into various options*. The options open to the TO can be described as follows:

1 A system, because of its relative dominance, can absorb and so neutralize the values of another system. This process could be called *reduction*. In its most extreme form, one of the two systems is eliminated or integrated within the dominant structure. As opposed to reduction, *marginalization* is a situation in which a system is perceived as unconvertible into any other and so completely subtracted from the cultural interplay. This is what is commonly meant when people refer to the untranslatability of poetry. Working on the contrary on a case of reduction, a novelist like T. Morrison (1989) has shown how Afro-American cultural values were not only converted into mainstream white literary constructions such as Moby Dick, 'an idea of civilisation that he [Melville] renounces and an idea of savagery he must annihilate' (Morrison 1989: 16), but also completely reconverted and thus occulted. In both cases, the process of radical neutralization of one of the systems exceeds our immediate preoccupations and must be studied in its political, social, and cultural consequences.

2 A system can acclimatize the values of another system within its own frame of reference, that is to say interiorize the tensions regulating the two systems. The problem in the case of *insertion* consists in evaluating the patterns of relationships established by these multilayered constructions such as in *Les Ritals*, for example, the Italian *patois* coexisting with 'ordinary' French speech. More generally, all idiolects or sociolects can be perceived as inclusions of different systems within the mainstream culture in various degrees of convertibilty.

3 Finally, the two systems can freely convert into each other through the process of homological production and other similar procedures. In *conversion*, the two systems become permeable to each other in a state of both coexistence and rivalry. In this case, the specificity of each system is at the same time safeguarded and redefined. This type of relationship can be described as interactional. To take an example covering the difference between points 2 and 3, we could compare the way the two words 'fair-play' and 'glasnost' have been integrated within the French culture. If we disregard the difference in the dates of introduction, 'glasnost' is to be considered as imported and specifically relevant to another culture whereas 'fair-play' has been acclimatized. It is accepted as describing some particular attitude to games and contracts but also conceived as

extraneous and so in some form of deviance with the already existing values.

It should by now be clear that it is the conversion procedures which particularly interest us, and which we consider to have the greatest possible potential. None the less, these procedures are themselves subjected to other external constraints which must now be taken into account, in other words the most general socio-cultural parameters that form the subject-matter of Chapter 8.

8 Socio-cultural parameters and norms

INTRODUCTION

Socio-cultural parameters and norms are of prime importance in Translation theory. They constitute the final guidelines enabling the TO to choose between the different paraphrastic possibilities generated during the first stage of the Translation operation. And yet in translation theory, these parameters and norms tend to be either ignored or taken for granted, and when they are brought into a theory, they are given little more than a paragraph or two of comment. Our aim in this chapter is twofold: (1) to give as wide a description of the Translation situation as possible, integrating the maximum number of socio-cultural and other parameters; and (2) to give a working demonstration of the model as it is built up, using concrete examples. We begin by concentrating our attention on the two indispensable 'actors' who set in motion the Translation operation – the Translation Initiator and Translation Operator – and then consider the possible nature of the Translation order. Once these 'upstream' parameters have been explored, we develop some of the analyses briefly mentioned in Chapters 6 and 7 by looking at the importance of the LC1 environment of the ST and the whole range of options which can be considered in the LC2. Finally, we come to consider the importance and weighting of all the different elements which go to make the choice of the final TT.

THE IDENTITY AND MOTIVATIONS OF THE TRANSLATION INITIATOR

In Chapter 6, we looked in some detail at the Translation Initiator and at the importance of the order he or she gives to the TO. We now examine more closely the socio-cultural identity of the TI, and the motivations which may lie behind what was previously described as his or her need to convert a ST into a TT.

We mentioned briefly that the TI may belong to LC1, LC2, or indeed to another LC. This position will normally determine his access to the ST and his comprehension (and potential criticism) of the TT. In addition to this, we have to consider his 'position' in both economic and socio-cultural terms. In the vast majority of cases, the TI and the TO are linked by some form of contract[1] remunerating the translation work done. This contract will normally reflect both the economic capacities of the TI and the importance he accords to the translation to be carried out. Ideally one would think that a strong TI (in economic terms) would be willing to pay the price for a high-quality translation. And although this is undoubtedly the case with certain governmental or international organizations, one is forced to conclude that translation is still often considered as a costly extra which is better done cheaply and badly, rather than paying the price. Much comment has recently been made in France about small companies who lose their export markets because they are unwilling to invest the necessary money in speakers of the foreign language – how much cheaper, they argue, to give the task to someone who 'knows a bit of English' – with all the disastrous consequences that this entails. The economic factor obviously has a great influence on the work done, with repercussions at every possible level.

How, then, can one integrate this economic element into translation theory? As far as the TI is concerned, economic considerations tend to reflect the general image that the translating profession has in any society. Many people have commented on the difficult economic conditions in which the translator is expected to work. Although there is evidence that this is now changing for the better, the fate of the profession would still seem to rest on a naive or prescientific conception of what translation actually involves. In other words, the economic element tends to weigh very heavily as, from the translator's point of view, his or her work is constantly underrated, and thus subject to extreme pressures coming from the outside.

It would be wrong, however, just to think of economic considerations, however important they are perceived to be. The TI may be influenced by *all* the different motivations which can be behind a desire to communicate – or, in the case of translation, to re-establish communication. Although one might be tempted to think that translating necessarily means reconstituting all the perceived elements belonging to the ST, the TI tends either to work within a highly defined framework – concentrating on one particular aspect of a message – or to give a very general translation order to the TO. We look at this point more fully in a later section (pp. 165–73).

When one looks at the different forces acting on the TI, one comes to see that he or she often represents a *conflict of interests*, and that the Translation order given to the TO to some extent reflects this state of affairs. In other words, the TI is subject to different and sometimes contradictory forces which are a reflection of his or her position in society. The case of a publisher can be taken to illustrate this situation. If a decision is taken to publish a foreign work of literature, and thus a translation is ordered, this is normally taken primarily on economic grounds. But the contract linking publisher and translator will both reflect an economic reality and more or less explicitly reflect a desire to reproduce a literary text, thus to concentrate on the aesthetic aspects of the work, with all the investment in terms of time that this implies. Although these two elements may not necessarily be in conflict, they will be joined by other considerations *which may ultimately bear more weight in the choice of the final text*. These will include the perceived nature of the readership and ultimately the ideological and political framework underpinning LC2. Thus whatever the (say) aesthetic preoccupations of the TO, other factors might have considerably more force when the final text is being chosen. When one reads at the beginning of the English translation of Günter Grass's *Aus dem Tagebuch einer Schnecke* the following remark, 'The author and the publisher regret that certain passages have been omitted for British legal reasons' (Grass, 1976: 5), one begins to wonder just what the role of censorship in Britain (in this case) is,[2] and indeed, one comes to discover that some books can be said hardly to resemble the original texts at all. We shall take as an example of this the French translation of Forsyth's *The Day of the Jackal* (Forsyth, 1971).

As many people know, this novel is a fictional work centred around an attempt to assassinate General De Gaulle in the early 1960s. Because the action is for the most part centred in France and has a French socio-cultural background (with, for example, detailed descriptions of the functioning of the different police forces in France and certain assumptions made about French institutions), it would appear to be the ideal novel to translate into French, with very few of the typical problems we looked at in relation to the Cultural Equation. The translation is extremely interesting in our perspective, because the number of changes introduced are so many and varied that the TT can hardly be called a 'translation' at all, if one takes the normal criteria of judgement (see Chapter 10). Modifications are made to the form of the novel (the second chapter is divided up into two chapters), the names of some of the characters are changed, and most importantly, the narration of the story – which is extremely well organized in the ST in terms of detail, the build-up of suspense, etc. – is dramatically reduced, for no apparent reason. A brief example will serve to illustrate this, taken from the passage where the hero is interviewed and recruited for the assassination by the top members of the OAS:

Rodin ushered him inside the bedroom. It had been arranged like an office for a recruiting board. The escritoire served for the chairman's desk and was littered with papers. Behind it was the single upright chair in the room. But two other uprights brought in from adjacent rooms flanked the central chair, and these were occupied by Montclair and Casson, who eyed the visitor curiously. There was no chair in front of the desk. The Englishman cast an eye around, selected one of the two easy chairs and spun it round to face the desk. By the time Rodin had given fresh instructions to Viktor and closed the door, the Englishman was comfortably seated and staring back at Casson and Montclair. Rodin took his seat behind the desk. (pp. 48f.)	Chazanet le fit entrer dans la chambre. Elle avait été transformée en bureau de recrutement. De part et d'autre d'une table jonchée de papiers étaient assis sur des chaises droites Montclair et Casson. Derrière la table se trouvait la troisième et dernière chaise. Tandis que les deux assesseurs de Chazanet l'examinaient avec curiosité, l'Anglais regarda autour de lui, tira un fauteuil et le fit pivoter pour le placer face au bureau. Chazanet, en ayant fini avec Viktor, alla s'asseoir à la table et, sans quitter des yeux le visiteur, alluma lentement une cigarette. (p. 64)

There are clearly numerous differences between the ST and the TT. Some of these appear a little insignificant at first sight: for example, the details concerning the furniture, the new orders given by Rodin/Chazanet, the fact that he closes the door. But as Forsyth pays meticulous attention to detail, and draws very precise portraits of his characters, one begins to feel that the very essence of the book is altered. Forsyth takes particular trouble when describing the psychology of his hero. In this scene, the Jackal is the only one to smoke, thus emphasizing his calm and slightly insolent attitude; not only has the translator changed this by making Chazanet smoke, but he adds the adverb 'lentement', thus destroying the whole psychological balance which the author has built up in favour of the Jackal. When, in the ST, the hero 'selects' an easy chair, he is showing his unhurried and reasoned actions in even the most tense of situations; when he 'stares' at Montclair and Casson, he is not only showing how unimpressed he is, but emphasizes all the strength that he, as the world's best hired gun, has. Whereas in the ST, the man impresses by his quiet strength, in the TT he makes virtually no impact at all.

Radical changes are also made in less important passages (from the point of view of the plot). When the hero meets and subsequently seduces the Baronness de la Chalonnière,[3] the author devotes a page to describing how the Baronness yields to him. Not only is the passage reduced by two-thirds (virtually censoring its erotic nature), but again details are switched around, distorting the overall image we have of the hero. Now there are clearly no language or apparent cultural difficulties preventing a fairly straightforward translation of the novel. The Translation order would therefore appear to reflect the particular identity and motivation of the TI, who, in this case, is handling fairly 'sensitive' material, with the date of publication being only eight years after the 'events' purportedly described. Although we are not in a position to explain away all the changes, we would be tempted to suggest that a certain ideological stance and certain preconceptions (in terms of political perceptions) are behind the transformation of the blond Anglo-Saxon killer who almost succeeds into a rather watered-down and less effective version of the same. Or one might argue that the TI was motivated by his perception of the reading public's taste, in this case emphasizing the 'historical' perspective *seen from the angle of French readers* at the expense of the glorification of the 'exceptional' qualities of the foreign (perceived as anti-French) hero – whether as a killer or a seducer. In this latter case, it may well appear that economic considerations were also behind the Translation order, with the TI wishing to ensure maximum sales, and thus making what were felt to be the necessary adaptations. In all events, it seems highly unlikely that the TO was entirely responsible for the final text, thus illustrating *the preponderant role that the TI can play in the choice of a final text.*

THE IDENTITY AND MOTIVATIONS OF THE TRANSLATION OPERATOR

Having looked at the identity and motivations of the TI, we now turn our attention to the TO. It may seem a little strange in Translation theory to be looking at the 'identity' of the TO, as, after all, anybody can undertake a translation, thus making formalization or generalization very difficult. Our aim is simply to underline once again the TO's socio-cultural identity as being one of the many factors which account for translation being what it is. Not only – as we discussed in Chapter 7, pages 134–5 – will the TO have a greater or lesser degree of competence, but his or her work will also reflect an inevitable element of *subjectivity*. This encompasses what is often called the 'style' of the translator, which can be recognized by the constant recourse to certain lexical usages or syntactic forms, by the development of mannerisms, and more generally by a certain approach to translating. For example, Guillemin-Flescher (1981: 65ff.) notes a large number of markers of inchoativeness in the English translation of Mauriac's *Thérèse Desqueyroux*.[4] Among the supporting quotations, she uses – among other texts – the same translator's version of *Mme Bovary*. When one compares Hopkins' translations with other published ones, or indeed with other paraphrastic possibilities, one recognises a certain style of writing which can be attributed to this particular TO rather than to any 'rule' governing translation from French to English.[5] In other words, the subjectivity of the TO must be taken into account as one of the many factors operating within the Translation operation, and particularly when one considers Translation Criticism (Chapter 10).

Coming now to the motivations of the TO and the conditions in which he or she works, we would begin by stressing the point made in Chapter 6 that a rigorous distinction must be made between the TO who is his own Translation Initiator, and the TO who is dependent on a TI. Although it is the latter who will mainly concern us in the following paragraphs, we begin by making one or two observations about the former (abbreviated to 'TI–TO').

The TO who is his or her own Translation Initiator

It is interesting to consider in the first instance a totally 'free' TI–TO, by which we mean a translator who is bound to no one. Although such a TO must be something of a rarity, at least in our day and age, his or her situation constitutes an interesting point of departure when viewed in relation to the limits which normally bind a TO. The most unhampered translator would not only be translating at his own instigation (i.e. he chooses his own text, with all that that implies), but also for himself and in conditions which he himself sets. In fact, he can do precisely what he likes and how he likes, and his work is thus virtually unparametrable. But the moment one begins to simulate a 'real' (or probable) Translation situation, one begins to appreciate the weight of the economic and socio-cultural environment in which the TO normally operates and the extent of the influence that this can have.

The first 'weight' to be added to the TI–TO is that of his receivers in LC2. To change images, one might say that the receivers act as a focusing apparatus clarifying the various choices of TTs which have been generated. If a particular readership has been identified (in terms of age, sex, social class, etc.), this will enable, for example, certain forms of language to be exploited, or on the contrary eliminated. The TO might feel the need to play on a certain socio-linguistic register, to avoid specialized vocabulary, to adopt a certain style.

A typical example of this type of problem occurred during the translation of a short story[6] describing the relationships between a brother, sister, and half-sister. It became apparent that 'elles' had to be translated with particular care. The unmarked English 'they' was, in this case, particularly unsuitable, as 'elles' specifically excludes males. The TO took particular care to spell out this distinction in English by substituting nouns for pronouns, despite the problems of complexification and reformulation involved, because it was felt that the readership of the short story would be primarily feminine, and thus particularly sensitive to the male–female conflicts (and female solidarity) being exposed.

One can also consider the case of the TI–TO translating with the aim of selling his or her translation to a publisher. Although economic and time considerations might begin to play a part, they will not have the major function that they have when there is a contract, and when certain parameters are predefined. This type of work will normally be undertaken by a translator of literature, and his or her main concern will be to make the work of art available to people who would not normally have access to it. One might, again, think of the comparative freedom of such a TO, but, as we hope to show in a later section (pp. 173–83) below, there are certain variables which must be taken into account before the choice of a final TT is made.

The TO who is dependent on a Translation Initiator

When one looks at the TO who is dependent on an external TI, one is immediately aware of two constraining factors: the TI both chooses the ST and sets the general framework in which the Translation operation is to take place. This usually means that a certain type of TT is being asked for, to be produced in certain limiting and predefined conditions. For example, translating a computer software program may mean respecting certain material conditions, such as the maximum number of characters available per instruction (limited by the amount of space available on the screen). Such a limitation can become the most important specific criterion, following the general instruction to produce the 'same' program. Conversely, one of the problems commonly found in the teaching of translation is the fact that the TI often has very definite criteria in mind when setting a text to be translated, but these are simply not spelt out, or are mentioned in the vaguest possible terms ('respecting the beauty of a ST', etc.). The result is discouraging for the student, who understands when he or she makes grammatical errors, but not the wider parameters which come into play when choosing between rival grammatically correct sentences.

We shall be looking at the nature of the Translation order produced by the TI in a later section (pp. 165–73). Our concern at this point is to reconsider the approach of the TO when working within the predefined type of framework that we have envisaged. The important point here is again to measure the 'weight' of the contract between TI and TO, and thus to see just how far the whole Translation operation can be subordinate to this contract. Although it is not possible to give an exhaustive list of all the conditions which might come to bear on the TO, it is helpful to try to envisage some of these and briefly to image the likely consequences they may have.

1 *Material conditions* are often ignored or taken for granted but are always of great importance. Every professional freelance translator is acutely aware of the economic and time conditions in which they work. Each text is consequently given a definition and a value which has little to do with its nature, content, or communication purpose and which reflects the material conditions in which the translation will have to be carried out. This may ultimately induce in the TO a certain attitude towards a text, giving rise to a certain type of translation. Given the competition between translators, and the ever-increasing amount of material which needs to be translated, it is not hard to see that certain work is done in the worst possible conditions – i.e. poorly paid and finished quickly. But we feel it would be wrong to see a direct or necessary correlation between material conditions of this type and the finished product. Certain professionals maintain the highest standards even in the most exacting of circumstances, whereas others are too often content with what is at best an approximate TT. What is important for translation theory is to take these conditions into account when considering the work of the TO, the TT, and the Translation situation as a whole. In this way, translation can be placed within a socio-economic framework which at times can be the determining factor in the production of a TT.

The amount of *space available* to the TO can also have a greater or lesser influence on the whole approach to translation. This is the case, for example, for cartoon stories with predefined 'balloons' for the characters' comments (e.g. Tintin or Astérix). In the *Guardian Weekly*, one sometimes finds articles translated from *Le Monde* that have been cut; this can have serious consequences on the overall message being produced (see Chapter 10). In certain cases, the TO will have to make decisions about what to leave out, which entails redefining *with the TI* the overall aim of communication. As we will see below, the TI can become an active partner in the Translation operation.

2 *The TI's purposes of communication* are sometimes defined in very precise terms. By taking these into account as one of the parameters influencing the TO's work, one can free oneself from the naive perception that 'text' necessarily becomes 'text'. As we pointed out in Chapter 5, translating may imply operating on all the semiotic codes present in a message, including modifying illustrations, adding diagrams, or undertaking whatever adaptations are felt necessary in order to respect the Translation order. Some of these modifications can be grouped together under the title 'Translation Localization' – we give some examples on pages 179–80. Other changes may be necessary to take into account the particular identity of the LC2 receivers. One tends to assume that the LC2 receivers are native speakers of the Target Language, and therefore have immediate and wide-ranging access to all but the most specialized of discourses in that language. But cases do arise where the receivers are not TL native speakers, and certain modifications have to be made when generating different TTs. When a paper originally written in French had to be read in English at a symposium in South America, the TI required not only a simplification of terminology to take into account the fact that the majority of speakers were not fluent TL speakers, but also certain modifications to the original to render it more suitable for a (spoken) lecture, rather than the article form in which is was written. In this case, the TO was therefore working in very strict predefined conditions which automatically limited many of the potential TT choices that could have been generated.

3 *Technical terms* may prove to be problematical at both LC1 and LC2 levels. Although we look at some of the problems in greater detail below, it is useful here to point to the predominant role that the TI may play if he requires certain technical terms to be used which go against LC2 norms, at whatever level they are defined. Needless to say, the TI is normally the final arbitrator in such cases, and the TO's work will be

subject to all the special conditions he defines. Some TIs will provide the TO with obligatory transfer techniques based on texts already produced in the Target Language. As we discuss on pages 180–3, both TI and TO may be highly influenced by the weight of existing translations.

4 *The identity of the TI* may in itself prove to be a determining factor in the choice of a TT. In other words, the TO will tailor his work to correspond to the particular needs of his TI. Although in some cases the Translation order is very clear, the TO will normally have to adapt his work according to his perception of the TI's needs. If, for example, the TI is a French government organization, certain forms of language – such as words borrowed from English – would be avoided, even if they are used with other TIs. We looked at this point in Chapter 6 in relation to LC2 receivers, where we gave the example of one of the official translations of a 'VDU' (visual display unit) as 'la visu'. Computer terminology in French tends to be peppered with words taken directly from the original American terms; these words tend to predominate in the majority of the literature available (specialized magazines, instruction booklets, etc.) but not in official documents.

One must also envisage the possible positions that the TI can occupy in socio-cultural, political, ideological, etc., terms. Translation can become an ideological tool being used to 'prove' the superiority of one thesis over another. Indeed, the same ST could be used to prove opposite theories, with the appropriate choice of TT terms in each case. Or a text can be given a weighting and value which is very different from that accorded to the ST, thus changing not only its status in LC2, but the whole approach the TO will adopt when translating it.

THE TRANSLATION ORDER

We must now return to the Translation order as the natural starting point of all the operations to be carried out, and we will begin by questioning the assumption we made that the Translation order corresponds to a need felt by the TI who is faced with a foreseen or actual breakdown in communication. As professional translators quickly discover when contacted by clients, the Translation order often reflects the somewhat naive perception of what translation is – that a TT somehow 'automatically' results from a ST. Very often the TO will have to reformulate or explicate the order in terms of what the TI really does need. On a one-off basis, this is not hard to do, but what interests us is, of course, a more general framework which can be applied to the maximum number of situations. To produce this framework, it is necessary to look in some

166 *Redefining Translation*

detail at what we have called the TI's need, which we break down into the possible relationships first between the TI and the Source Text, then adding the parameter of the TT receivers.

The TI–ST relationship

A ST can never be regarded as an 'innocent' document. As it has been chosen to be translated, it is thought of in most cases as a read document whose purpose of communication has already been defined. Students of translation tend to think of the ST as a definitive and somehow untouchable entity which must be preserved in translation at all costs. This is, of course, the result of certain attitudes taught in translation classes, particularly at university level when the ST is taken from a work of literature. It is quite understandable that the 'beauty' of the ST is often evoked, but again the reality of the translating profession suggests a very different attitude towards the ST. This is not to say that there are 'literary' (and untouchable) texts in one group, and 'other' (somehow inferior) texts in another group, but quite simply that the teaching of translation does tend to exploit certain values which the professional will rarely find of use. For, leaving aside the case of an aesthetic text, the professional will often have to deal with a document *produced by the TI himself or herself*. As we will show, this instigates a very special relationship between the TI and the TO. This, then, is the first of four parameters linking the TI and the ST. For the purposes of the following discussion, we will assume that the TI belongs to LC1 – other possibilities will be explored later.

The TI has written the ST

It is not hard to see that, in this particular case, the TI has a very definite attitude towards the ST. As he has produced it with a specific communication purpose in mind, he will be looking to have *his* message reproduced, regardless of the interpretation of the TO. And one very often finds that the message encoded by the TI does not correspond to the one decoded by the TO. One can take a technical document as a case in point. Recent research on ESP texts has concentrated on the different possible levels of technicality of a text. The writer of the text may take certain things for granted which the TO will wish to reintroduce. The story goes that there was a person who decided to service his own car. He 'understood' the explanation about changing the sparking plugs but, unfortunately, as the manual omitted to say that the bonnet of the car had to be opened, he was at a loss to discover where the plugs might be located. If, in such cases, the TO might foresee a need which was not apparent to the TI, there are undoubtedly many more serious problems which the professional has to face on a day-to-day basis. These range from problems of comprehension via unintentionally ambiguous texts to basic errors in the original formulation. It is not uncommon for the TI who understands the second language to complain that the translation says the opposite of what he intended – and then be forced to see the shortcomings of his own writing and carry out the necessary modifications.

Whatever the problems of this type may be, it is important to point to the control which the TI exercises over the Translation operation. By his privileged position, he can intervene at any moment to modify the ST in order to produce a TT which corresponds to his communication need. Clearly, in such cases one can no longer think along the traditional lines of an ST transformed by a translator into a TT, but of a *partnership* between two complementary forces who collaborate to produce a highly defined message.[7]

The TI has read the ST

It may seem a little strange at first sight to produce a category where the TI has read the ST, which is probably the most frequent case one comes across. But the fact of creating this category highlights what is not so obvious, i.e. that there are cases of Translation orders made without knowledge of the ST. So despite the relative 'banality' of this situation, we should point to the fact that the TI will formulate his Translation order in relation to specific criteria connected to the ST, and with knowledge of the particular problems related to that text. Thus the TI will be able to dictate certain conditions in the Translation order, and intervene knowledgeably and critically when the final TT is selected.

The TI has not read the ST

It thus becomes apparent that the TI who has not read the ST will be able to give little more than a very general Translation order, thus diminishing his impact and influence both on the Translation operation and on the final choice of a TT. This will often be the case for documents which are not given much value by the TI, *where the whole responsibility for the TT is given to the TO*.

The ST has not been written at the time of the Translation order

This is the most extreme case of all, where the responsibility of the TI is reduced to the lowest possible level. One may wonder why a distinction

168 *Redefining Translation*

between the previous category and this one is necessary; in our view, each possible determining factor in the Translation operation has to be taken into account. With the previous category the ST already belongs to a communication circuit, with its LC1 sender and receivers. The TI's order can explicitly refer to this by, for example, bringing out certain elements to be maintained or suppressed. The present category, however, functions totally by anticipation. It will normally be covered by a generalized Translation order, for example given to a company employee who has to translate all mail arriving from foreign countries. In such an example, the subject-matter in question is probably highly predictable and of a limited nature. It is, however, not hard to imagine cases where the TI's role is extremely limited in the whole Translation operation.

We can illustrate the four categories developed above with the aid of a simplified figure (see Figure 8.1). The four numbers correspond to the four situations envisaged above. By adding the letter A in front of the four numbers, we signify that the TI belongs to LC1. The figure is enclosed in a large square, which itself represents the LC1 as a closed entity.

In this figure the relationship on the one hand between the sender of the message and the message itself (the ST) and that between the message

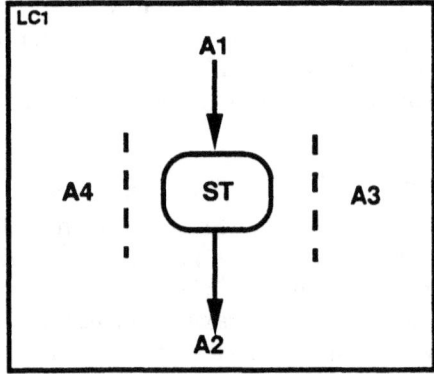

Figure 8.1 The four possible positions of the TI who belongs to LC1

Socio-cultural parameters and norms 169

and its receiver is represented by the arrow going from the sender (A1, i.e. the TI who has written his or her own text to be translated) to the ST, and from the ST to the TI-receiver (A2). The two dotted lines on either side of the ST show that A3 and A4 are excluded from the communication circuit, either because, in A3's case, the ST has not been read, representing the non-specific translation order envisaged in the third category above, or because it does not exist at the time of the Translation order (A4).

The time has now come to return to the parameter mentioned at the beginning of this section concerning the LC identity of the TI. When the TI belongs to LC1, the situation is relatively clear as one can suppose there is a good knowledge of the ST as either the producer or receiver of the message. If the same figure is reproduced to include other TIs, their relative isolation is clear from their position *outside* the square representing LC1. In Figure 8.2 we have coded the LC2 TI as the letter B, and members of a third LC by the letter C.

Whether TIs B/C 1–4 are producers or receivers of the ST, it is necessary to introduce a supplementary variable which is their knowledge of LC1. One might think that the TI who produces his or her own text will have a very good knowledge of the LC in question. But when

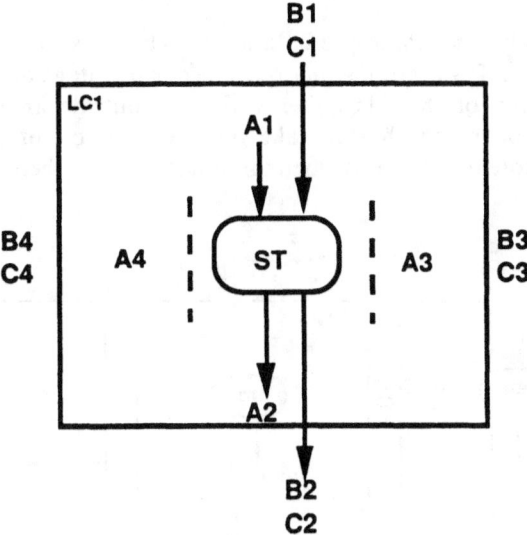

Figure 8.2 Comparison between the TI belonging to LC1 and the TI belonging to LC2 or LC3

170   Redefining Translation

one knows the difficulties that translators have when trying to understand some texts written by native speakers, one must bear in mind the possible deficiencies of any ST, and particularly one written in such conditions. Now this very fact brings us back to the point raised at the beginning of this section (pp. 165–6), i.e. that there may not be a one-to-one correspondence between the need of the TI and the Translation order given. When, for example, the TI B2 or C2 asks for a translation, this may well be a request based on total non-comprehension of the ST. But one also cannot rule out the TI's biased reading and comprehension of the ST, and consequently displaced Translation order.

At this stage, then, it can be said that a very close analysis of the position and role of the TI is essential in order to understand some of the variables which come in to play during the Translation operation. Up to now, our presentation has concentrated on the LC1 and the ST. We now propose to extend our figures to include the LC2 and the hypothetical third LC, again to illustrate the potential complexity of the Translation situation, and the need for exhaustive analysis (see Figure 8.3). One further variable must immediately be introduced in order to make our presentation clear. This concerns the nature of the *receiver* of the Translated Text. Rather than consider all the cases possible, our aim here is to limit the possibilities to the TI, and just consider the Translation order given by the TI who is himself the receiver of the final TT.

Figure 8.3 is a general representation which needs to be adapted to each particular Translation situation. The disadvantage of the figure is the positioning of the TIs either within or outside an LC. As we mentioned above, one has to take into account bi- or plurilingual speakers as potential TIs. But when this is not the case, there are very big

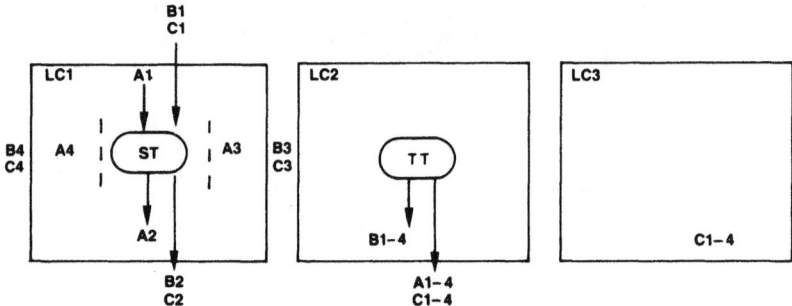

Figure 8.3 Positions occupied by different TIs as givers of the Translation order and receivers of the TT

Socio-cultural parameters and norms 171

differences between the different TIs, and that much is quite clear in the figure. In particular one can see A2's access to the ST but his position outside the LC2 as receiver of the TT. According to the hypothesis we are developing, this particular TI is also the receiver of the message, and thus will understand the second language. But the very fact that he does not belong to that LC group is in itself of great importance, as we have had several occasions to mention. Conversely, B2 has limited, if any, access to the ST, but total comprehension of the TT, with all that that implies when it comes to his attitude towards the TT which is submitted to him. As for C2, he is outside both LC1 and LC2, and thus presumably not in a position greatly to influence the Translation operation, at least on a purely linguistic level.

Figure 8.3 also helps one to understand better some of the complexities of 'real' translation situations. The example mentioned on page 164 above of a Translation order for a symposium taking place in English in South America illustrates both the role of A1 and of C4: A1 has produced the text and ordered the translation at the behest of C4, representing the organizers of the symposium requiring a paper to be read in English before the paper was actually written. Once these parameters have been spelt out, the role of the TO is in fact considerably simplified when it comes to choosing between the different TT forms available.

If the above section does appear to be both somewhat theoretical and complicated, it should be pointed out that the 'hidden' factors in the Translation operation are much more important than is often imagined. Indeed, the LC2 public tends to imagine that the TT has a direct one-to-one relationship with the ST, but, as professional translators often point out, the factors intervening, and in particular the requirements of the TI, can be extremely complicated. When one considers the case of certain TTs which are produced not from an ST, but from a TT in a more 'accessible' language[8] – and when one thinks of the multitude of complications that this can produce, one begins to see that a full consideration of all the parameters not only aids the TO in his task, but also enables the translation critic to evaluate the TT produced in a more objective light.

In the final part of this section, we look at the relationship between the TI and the LC2 receivers.

The TI–LC2 receiver relationship

One of the new perspectives introduced into Translation Studies by considering the TI is the relationship between the TI and the LC2 receivers. The LC2 receivers have very often been taken for granted in previous theories, or at best seen as a parameter to be taken into account by the TO. But in our view, it is wrong to overlook this 'framing' relation between these two actors in any Translation situation. This relation can be present to a greater or lesser extent in the Translation order. Having considered the case of the TI being his own receiver, we now extend this to include other possibilities.

A Translation order can be characterized by the degree of definition of the LC2 receivers. A detailed definition will usually have the effect of reducing the range of acceptable TTs; if, however, there is no mention of the receiver, the TO will have a great degree of latitude in his choice of TT, which in some cases can produce an unfocused or poorly adapted text. A brief example will illustrate this point. If a TO is asked to translate into English the text accompanying a French pharmaceutical product, he will be faced with a problem of finding the right level of technicality if there is no indication of the receiver. He may be tempted to 'play it safe' by maintaining the same level as in the ST, but if the TT is aimed at the general public, this will produce a text which is much more detailed and technical than the majority of equivalent texts produced in LC2.[9] In this case, then, if no receiver is stipulated, an inappropriate text may be the result, but the identification of the receiver will encourage the TO profoundly to modify his TT.

A second point we should consider is the probable ignorance of the TI regarding the problems which all translators face. Given the size of the translation 'industry' and the publicity made for 'instant' translation techniques,[10] people tend to think that a TT is immediately and automatically available and that it will exactly correspond to the desired communication aim. This may lead the TI to make totally unrealistic demands on the TO, based on his comprehension of the ST and either his knowledge of the LC2 receivers' needs, or his assumption that LC2 needs will be the same as LC1 receivers' needs. The most common case arises when the LC1 TI has no knowledge of the LC2, and requires 'the same using the same'. Translating a pun, for example, using the same elements as in the ST is often virtually impossible, and when the TO is given no latitude, this can lead to an unsatisfactory TT from every point of view. As for the naive assumption equating LC1 and LC2 receivers' needs, this can lead to a totally unrealistic Translation order. If the TO is asked to maintain certain LC1-specific elements, this can not only change the message, but even produce the opposite effect of the required one. One only has to think of the literal translations of our example from Chapter 6 – 'Cette semaine on tue le cochon!' – to see this.

Before moving on to consider the ST in its LC1 surroundings, we would conclude this section by underlining both the importance of the TI and the large number of ways in which he can come to bear on the Translation operation. Our analyses of this phenomenon are necessarily incomplete, but we hope that our approach lays the foundation for a more comprehensive vision of this most important parameter.

CHOOSING THE TARGET TEXT

We have been at some pains to stress that the choice of a TT depends on a very large number of different factors, or parameters in our terminology. During the first sections of this chapter, we explored two of these in some detail: the Translation Initiator and the Translation order. We now take a second look at some of the material we considered in Chapters 6 and 7 regarding the Cultural Equation, in particular LC1 and LC2 influences, and the role of the Translation Operator. We also introduce another key parameter intervening at this stage, constituted by the influence of existing translations.

The Source Text in its LC1 surroundings

When we discussed the TO as a Cultural Operator in Chapter 7, we looked in some detail at the very special 'position' which the TO occupies when compared with the normal LC1 receiver of a text. We pointed in particular to the influence that the second Language Culture can have when the ST is read, and to the mental operations which are undertaken in anticipation of the translation about to be accomplished. Our purpose in returning now to the ST in its LC1 surroundings is to try to map out certain research options which are open to the TO, and yet which tend to be ignored both in translation theory and in the everyday work of professionals. This is not to say that a TO will completely pass over all the LC1 aspects of a text, but one may wonder if these aspects are given sufficient weighting when the final TT is to be chosen. This aspect also forms part of our fundamental rethinking of Translation operations which we have developed as part and parcel of our Variational approach, whereby we try enlarge the whole Translation situation and hence to produce, ultimately, a more powerful and creative model.

Our starting point here is therefore to stress again that in the majority of cases, the TO is not a LC1 native speaker, and that by the TO's very position, the ST will be given a different force. When coming to consider the socio-cultural and economic parameters weighing on the choice of the TT, the Translation Operator can, as it were, substitute himself for the LC1 reader or class of readers most likely to be addressed by the ST. In other words, he reactivates the factor of co-significance which enables the text to function (see Chapter 2, p. 26). This means (1) identifying the sender of the text and (2) taking the place of the LC1 receivers.

Identifying the sender of a text may, on the face of it, appear a simple task. Many texts are signed or emanate from known sources. But, as recent research both on intertextuality and on the origin of discourse has shown, rather than thinking that the sender 'speaks through the SR', it may be more apposite to say that the SR 'speaks through the sender'. From our point of view, one can refer best to a *socio-culturally positioned sender* whose act of discourse can be assimilated to a purpose with specific reference to the receivers. The meaning will be jointly negotiated with reference to the common system (i.e. the SR). By reactivating a text (here the ST), the TO adds his voice to the multitude of voices which are constantly both reflecting and restructuring the SR. He participates in this joint construction of meaning activating the whole SR network of relations.

The advantages of our theoretical position are two-fold. Not only can the TO reconstruct the homology to which his ST belongs, but he can also reactivate the socio-cultural and economic network allowing the text to function. It is this reactivation and functioning of the text which will enable him to measure the impact of the ST in the LC1 environment.

We will illustrate the above points with a document taken from a hotel in Yugoslavia – the document is displayed in four languages in a prominent position in all the rooms of this particular hotel. We quote the original plus the English translation which is given. The document begins:

U ime naše hotelske kuće, kao i u svoje lično ime, želim Vam srdačnu dobrodošlicu. Nadamo se da ćete se kod nas ugodno osječati i da ćete nas još koji put posjetiti na čemu Vam se unaprijed zahvaljujemo. U slučaju eventualnih primjedbi na neku od naših usluga rado Vam stojimo na raspolaganju. Pri izlasku iz sobe zatvorite prozore i zaključajte vrata, jer će Osiguranje priznati samo provale, a ne običnu krađu.

Dear Guests, On behalf of the Hotel staff and myself I wish you a cordial welcome. We hope that you will find pleasant your stay with us, and that you will come again, for chich we thak you in advance. I am at your disposal for any complaint, you hove, regarding our services. Going out do shut the windows & lock the door, as only insurance against burglary is provided, and not against simple stealing.

Now the majority of readers of this book will, in all likelihood, go straight to the English to get an idea of what the original means. In other words, they will be decoding the message from the LC2 or LC3 perspective. But if the TO places himself within the original context of production, what does he discover? In the first instance, the communication circuit seems clear enough – between the hotel management and the guests. But this apparent simplicity hides a complexity which, although necessarily dependent on the particular situation and therefore unique, is symptomatic of complexity of relations and motivations one can discover when examining virtually any text. We will examine the different points one by one.

Who is, in reality, the *sender* of this text? The text itself announces that it is the manager who is speaking 'personally' ('u svoje lično ime') as if he were 'laying down the rules' of staying in the hotel (cf. the commands which occur later in the text – not to take out towels, not to make noise after 11 p.m., etc.). But the very fact that rules are being laid down and that the text corresponds to an *economic* necessity (doing everything possible to make the tourist welcome and to ensure that he or she will come back another year) means that we are being confronted with the SR in a highly predictable and therefore clichéd form. The SR speaks through the hotel manager as he produces a variation on the 'notices found in hotels' throughout the country.

If we think that the *receiver* of the ST is the LC1 tourist,[11] we run into a slight problem because there is only a very small percentage of Yugoslav nationals in the tourist hotels. These people, naturally enough, are very well off by local standards, and thus do not directly compare with (run of the mill) tourists coming from other countries. The ST would appear, then, to exist primarily to be translated, and thus to be aimed at all the different peoples who spend their holidays in this country. In this way, it belongs to the discourse family of 'tourist notices' which in Yugoslavia often totally ignore potential LC1 tourists.[12] This, in fact, reinforces our argument about the sender of the message, who, by reflecting the SR so accurately, has undertaken no concessions whatsoever to his foreign receivers.

By reactivating this text in the LC1 environment, the TO becomes infused with the socio-cultural and economic network allowing the text to function. In this case, it is a text which is both turned towards the LC2 (3, 4, etc.) and which reflects certain LC1 priorities. These priorities would probably be very important for the TI, and normally respected by the TO. They include the 'rules' of behaviour, the economic necessities mentioned above, and certain LC1-specific details such as the importance of locking one's room because of the particularities of the hotel's insurance policy. In maintaining such details, the TO might have to envisage going beyond a one-to-one translation in order quite simply for the message to be clear. In all events, the decision to respect the LC1 formulations would probably be to the detriment of the LC2 discourse family, at least if this is a European LC. For this text is very far from the typical notice found in, say, Italian or French hotels, which will mention the times one may have breakfast, the different services available, and generally have a more informative function.

The example we have taken is very far from the typical examples one finds in Translation theory when LC1 criteria are taken into account. People tend to think of the literary text as embodying the most important set of LC1 parameters. And although this may well be the case, we feel that Translation theory should pose the *general* problem of LC1 parameters, and not confine this to one particular type of text.

LC2 parameters

Many of the points made both in the previous sections and in the last two chapters can be applied under the general heading of 'LC2 parameters'. It should be noted from the outset that some professional translators in France talk of 'localization' to describe the general transposition into the LC2 context – we will be restricting this term to the geographical type of transposition which we look at below. From what has already been said, it should be clear both that LC2 parameters can be extremely varied, and thus can play an important role in the choice of the TT, but also that if, say, the TI has given definite and limiting instructions, these parameters may be completely ignored. If the TO has decided that a SL-influenced translation is the most apposite, he may simply choose not to incorporate what otherwise might be crucial elements. Our task here is to look at a cross-section of the elements that can be borne in mind once the totality of the Translation situation has been analysed. Our examples will be as wide as possible, in order to illustrate the extraordinary richness of LC2 parameters.

The first category we shall study consists of *socio-linguistic norms*. The TO will situate the ST in a socio-linguistic framework of production–reception and will then simulate what is felt to be the relevant LC2 framework. This can, perhaps, be best illustrated by using dialogue and general spoken exchanges. Cross-cultural comparison shows that certain situations will call for either a change of linguistic or of semiotic category. For example, the French 'bon appétit!' has no direct equivalent in English where one tends simply to find a silence.[13] The same is true when one compares everyday social intercourse in general when, quite simply, norms change from country to country. The different translations of the Albee text in Chapter 9 reflect this. If, in a spoken text, the TO is being asked to produce the equivalent socially determined text, he will often have to work with the largest possible Translation unit in order to account for general aims of communication, rather than translating, for example, expression by expression. This is obviously the case for different phatic devices used in everyday conversation. Research into levels of frequency and predictability would be of great use here. A homologon definition of 'You see' (e.g: 'So, *you see*, we got in the car . . .') would produce acceptable solutions in French and Serbo-Croat such as 'tu vois'/'tu comprends', 'razumiješ'/'kužiš'/'vidiš', but the whole problem would be to determine likely occurrences (and syntactic positioning). It would appear that there are fewer variants in English than in the other two languages, and a very much higher probability of use in Serbo-Croat, which might lead the TO to add or take away elements in accordance with this LC2 parameter.

Translating from Serbo-Croat into French or English therefore means either cutting down on the number of occurrences and/or changing the positioning in the sentence. 'Razumiješ'/'kužiš' can occur in end-position, which would produce an overaggressive 'Do you get/see what I mean?'/'Do you follow?', etc., in English, whereas the main force is not to check comprehension but to increase complicity between co-locutors. There is a more general translation problem associated with markers of complicity in this language, which tend to be very common – an ST such as 'Šta mi radiš?' may have to be glossed as 'What are you/ have you been doing (you are a person I feel concerned about)?'

This naturally brings us back to the remarks we made about discourse families in Chapter 6, (p. 117) and to LC2 parameters which go beyond the socio-linguistic level *to include the whole of the SR*. It may be felt that the general rules of a particular discourse family are such that a certain level of vocabulary or certain types of structures need to be used in order to produce an 'acceptable' text (according to the definition of the Translation situation). Part of the TO's function is to explore comparable LC2 texts in order precisely to identify such elements and to decide whether or not they should form a part of his TT. We have already noted several times (in Chapters 4 and 6, pp. 72 and 125 and in the present chapter) the difference in specialization and technicality in medical documents aimed at the general public in France and Britain. The different usages can lead to profound modifications being introduced during the Translation operation, with, say, extra technical material or the use of other semiotic codes (such as the addition of tables, diagrams, etc.).

Coming now to the SR in general, LC2 influences can be based on any of the constituent factors of the SR: for example the institutions at the most general level, the legal structures of the country, or the precise functions of different socio-professional categories of workers. Such parameters can intervene at many different levels. To take the last category first, one might be tempted to translate the American 'nurse' by the French 'infirmier'/'infirmière'. However, the TO would have to take into consideration the difference in professional qualifications and competence of the apparently 'equivalent' categories in order to produce an accurate translation. The American professional is, in fact, more qualified than the French counterpart, and thus performs duties which in France would only be carried out by a doctor. The decision not to translate the American term by the French one (or vice versa) would obviously have to be taken on contextual grounds, but is a clear example of the kind of trap learner-translators have to be informed of.

SR influences can come to bear at many different levels. 'Information printed on food packets', for example, is a fascinating category when one compares texts appearing in different languages on the same packets. The soya-milk drink marketed in France, Britain, The Netherlands and Germany under the name 'Soja Nature' is a case in point. The description and analysis of the product is printed in the four languages, and many of the details are maintained. Others, however, are not, and it is not because of a lack of space. For example:

Après ouverture, à conserver au froid et à consommer rapidement. Sans colorants ni conservateurs conformément à la législation en vigueur	Na openen koel bewaren. Darna is deze sojadrink nog minstens 3 dagen houdbaar in de koelkast. Zonder kleurstof of chemische toevoegingen bereid
Nach dem Öffnen im Kühlschrank aufbewahren und bald verbrauchen. Ohne Farbstoff und Konservierungsmittel	After opening, refrigerate and consume rapidly. Free of colouring and chemicals in accordance with the legislation in force

A cursory glance at these four texts is enough to see that certain details have been added, subtracted, or modified, according to the country in question. If one compares 'rapidement', 'minstens 3 dagen', 'bald', and 'rapidly', one is struck not just by the differences of time implied, but by the precision of the Dutch translation ('minstens 3 dagen'); similarly, the mention of legislation in French and English (with the rather surprising expression in the latter language) and the absence in the other two languages would appear to be dictated purely by LC2 priorities.[14] Such cases are clear examples of where the LC2 can be the predominant factor in the Translation operation. Official documents are a perfect reflection of the SR – whether it happens to reflect a legal, institutional, political, economic or other reality. The French parking ticket – to take a slightly improbable example – has a questionnaire to be filled in by people wishing to complain about the receipt of such an object (i.e. they contest the 'reality' of the offence). The questionnaire reflects the French legal notion of civil identity, in that one has to state one's nationality. It is highly improbable in an English LC2 context that the term would be kept in at all, as it is not part of the British concept of 'identity',[15] and would come to indicate some form of discrimination in parking fines according to country of origin.

One can begin to see how each SR-specific element can come to play a determining role. Our brief mention of the difference in legal systems can be extended to go beyond purely linguistic categories. One tends to imagine that the Highway Code is a standard document with only the minutest of variation from country to country. However, if one considers the different legal obligations (such as when one can turn right at a red light in the USA) or more simply national or regional differences (does one slow down or accelerate when the green light turns amber?), one has to reconsider potential translations and bear in mind the necessity of making commentaries when translating. Legal obligations also necessarily affect such things as guarantees: a ninety-day guarantee in the USA will have no legal basis in France, where there is a one-year minimum. Copyrights are modified on what are sometimes reasons of historical recognition: again in the USA, it is not enough to mention the USSR, one must add the three Baltic countries (Lithuania, Estonia, and Latvia) whose annexation the USA has never recognized.

One final example shows the extent of modifications that sometimes have to be carried out. When a document on statistical research published in the USA was to be translated into French, it was decided that the examples – in this case, statistics on American cars – had to be transposed into the French context. This not only meant replacing American models with French ones and finding the relevant French statistics, but also changing the whole SR coding from m.p.g. into litres/100km.

The second category that interests us in the LC2 context goes under the heading of 'Translation-localization'. As we pointed out above, we use this term to describe geographical transpositions. These are justified when a geographical reference is made not just to the physical place in question, but to the *signification that the place will have in the culture*. It is therefore necessary to decode this signification in order to find a LC2 equivalent. In an American television series (*Alf*) which appeared in a subtitled version in Yugoslavia, 'Warm Springs' was translated as 'Opatija', i.e. taken to mean 'a town where one goes to get away from it all'. This was an interesting choice, because of the very strong LC1 context, given that the programme was subtitled and not dubbed. However, the TO rightly saw that the LC1 reference would be totally lost, and therefore localized it accordingly, choosing a famous seaside resort in Croatia. This example provides a useful transition with the final point we shall make under the heading of 'LC2 parameters', because the TO's choice was based on a judgement of the geographical/cultural knowledge of the *LC2 receivers*.

Our final point in this section is therefore that the identity of the final receivers of the text may prove to be the most important parameter, and this especially so if the receivers belong to a clearly identified group – we looked at an example of this pages 161–2 of this chapter. On a more general basis, the TO will have to take certain decisions based on a subjective and generalized notion of the LC2 public. Such decisions can be imitative or creative, to the extent that they will either mirror perceived LC2 reading and comprehension habits, or seek to create new links within the SR. As we have mentioned before, this corresponds to the influence that translations can have on the development of a LC2, which deserves a chapter in its own right. Translation can thus in part be assimilated to a type of creative writing within the LC. Indeed, examples of intralinguistic translation abound in all LCs, which themselves reflect the different ideological struggles and power lines which are always undergoing modifications. If one thinks of how 'social ownership' has come to replace 'nationalize' in current British Labour Party jargon, one can see how the choice of a term may have very important consequences, especially when one's receivers are made up of several million future voters.[16]

The influence of existing translations

We have here another parameter which Translation theory has, up to the present, completely ignored, but which the professional uses to a greater or lesser extent. Indeed, the first task of the professional when tackling a specialized field is (i) to find a maximum number of documents both in LC1 and LC2, together with all the specialized dictionaries available, and (ii) to discover how key terms and expressions *have already been translated*. At first sight this may appear to be little more than dictionary work,[17] but in reality the TO may discover that for a certain field, there is a certain translating practice which has been established going beyond mere lexical equivalents, and which therefore he can choose to follow if the translation situation in general and the Translation order in particular justify this choice. Some examples should help to illustrate this point.

Perhaps the most obvious case is the translation of the title of works of fiction together with the characters' names, when they are already known in the Target Culture. A new translation of *Madame Bovary* would presumably be called by the same title, unless the TO could justify changing the name and hence taking the risk of the new name not being recognized.[18] In fact, any change of an accepted existing translation is made at great risk, or when the term originally chosen is felt to be inadequate. A fascinating study by Guy Leclercq[19] of the problems involved in translating *Alice in Wonderland* into French – where there are already very well known translations, with the characters' names firmly anchored in the culture – illustrates both the shortcomings of the existing texts, and the reasoning behind the proposed changes. By implication, one can see how the existing translations have come to be the accepted and, as it were, official terms to be used, permeating large areas of LC2 discourse and constituting the 'natural' choice of the TO.

Existing translations can constitute a 'style' which the TO may wish to imitate. The 'style' may consist of recurrent syntactic structures or the use of certain categories at levels which the LC2 reader would not normally expect when reading a document written directly in his own language. The translation of articles from *Le Monde* appearing in the *Guardian Weekly* is a case in point here. As we mentioned in Chapter 7, French newspaper discourse is saturated with anaphors used to introduce stylistic variation into the identification of important people and, in particular, politicians. Although one does find some anaphors of this type in the British press, they are (1) much rarer; (2) tend only to be used with very well known people; and (3) are much more limited in scope. When one reads the *Guardian Weekly* however, one becomes aware of a high use of these anaphors which seem to have become a style peculiar to this publication, but presumably one which the TO can emulate if he so chooses.

Existing translations can also constitute a TI-restricted norm. Computer terminology is a good example of this. The American 'drive' will be translated into French according to the translations already done for the particular make. For one company, 'unité de disquette' will be the correct term, in another, it will be 'lecteur de disquette'. The existing translation in many cases will have become the accepted LC2 term, and thus will have found a 'position' within the SR. It can also happen that a translated term can have such an influence that it will begin to find its way back into the original language as a replacement for the LC1 term. This is starting to be the case with the French translation of 'computer science' and 'data processing', both covered by 'informatique'. The French term is starting to appear in American texts as 'informatics',[20] which indeed shows the intercultural influence of translation.

To conclude our section on 'choosing the TT', we can now give an indication of weighting value to the different levels of influence that we have mentioned. Professional translators are particularly attentive to all the problems of LC2 influences, which very often distinguish them as professionals, as opposed to amateurs attempting to write in the LC2. For many professionals, then, these are felt to be the primary set of parameters to be taken into account. From our point of view, they are to be seen as important, but as part of the whole equation that each Translation situation will require. As we have tried to point out, each situation is unique, and will be weighted accordingly. It should not be forgotten that LC1 influences might be chosen as the most important, or indeed any of the other parameters we have identified.

ARTICULATION OF THE VARIATIONAL MODEL

Before moving to the next chapter, in which we look at the application of the Variational model to various fields, we should make some final comments about the articulation of the two 'halves' of our model. Our model is not so much a description of 'what happens' when one translates, but a proposition for a more dynamic approach to translating. The two complementary procedures of generation and selection are extremely productive, and can help the translator to break away from the somewhat mechanical notion of one-to-one equivalents which some people tend to work with. We summarize our model in Figure 8.4. The separation between the two halves of the model appears rigid in this figure, but given the speed of operations carried out, it is likely that there may be a to-and-fro movement within the model, as options are generated, selected, and then submitted to a regeneration process as certain parameters start to take precedence.

Socio-cultural parameters and norms 183

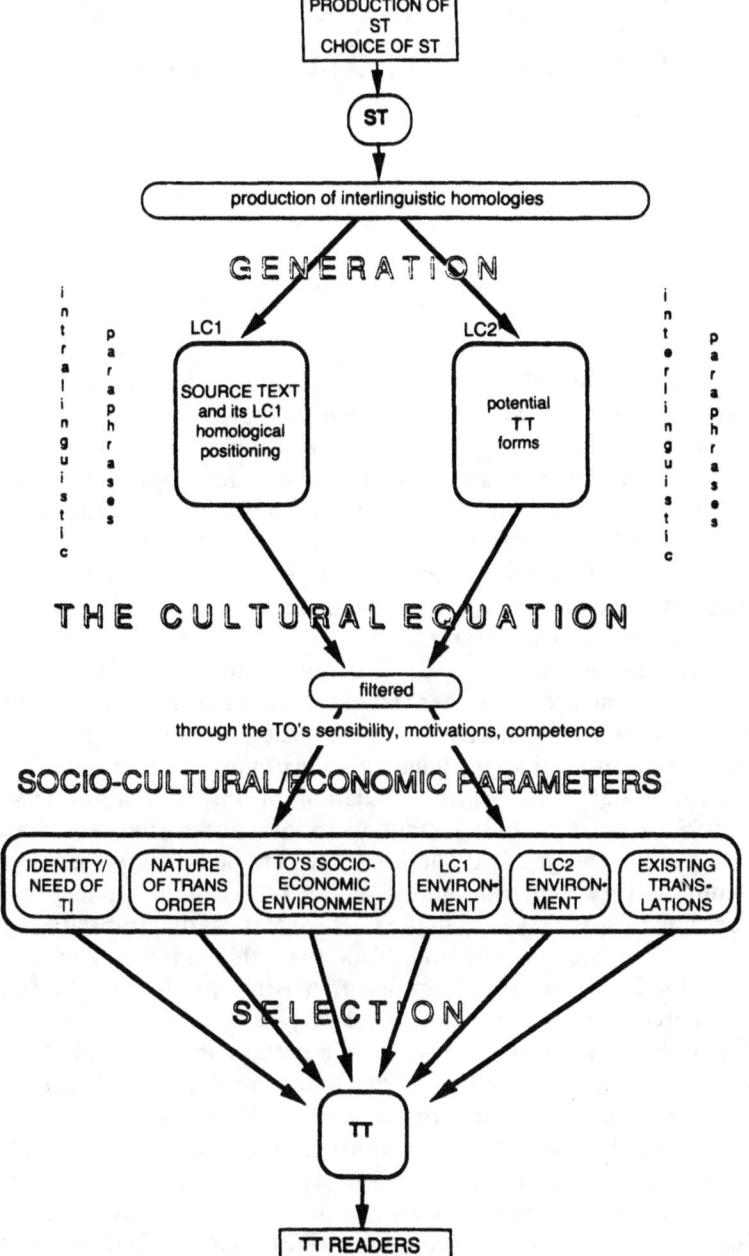

Figure 8.4 The articulation of the Variational approach

9 Applications of the Variational model to translations in various fields

Our aim all along in this book has been to rethink the theoretical basis of Translation Studies while at the same time producing a Translation model which can be applied by translators working in very diverse fields and with very different aims. The purpose of this chapter is to study different applications of the Variational model to texts coming from different fields. We have chosen to concentrate on a small number of passages taken from our Appendix, which we looked at in some detail in Chapters 4 and 5 – we will assume that the reader is familiar with the different analyses given above.

It must now be clear that the production of an individual text in some form of equivalence to another text in a different language is difficult to account for in its singularity. It is, nevertheless, possible to give a good approximation of the *conditions of its variations*. The homologizing process in our hypothetical simulation of the translation process produces a range of LC1 semantic variables and at the same time a corresponding range of LC2 options. The parameterizing stage fixes the conditions in which translations of the LC1 can be made possible according to specific norms in the LC2 context. Actual translations are variously situated at the intersection of this double network of determinations. Any specific translation is the product of the translator's predetermined but, in the final analysis, unpredictable choice.

It is the conditions of this act of selection that we will thus be investigating a little further in the following pages. Again, and in accordance with the general orientation of the Variational approach, the stress will not be laid on the justification of any particular translation choice but on the conditions under which this decision can be reached. It is our belief that absolute freedom of choice in translation is either an illusion or an excuse for irresponsibility. We rather tend to think that the 'creative' choice is situated within a set of identifiable translation strategies.

Up to now, we have considered the translation choice as a series of qualified decisions in the paradigm of possible options placed on a growing scale of complexity. For each translation unit decisions had to be taken at lexical, syntactic, and textual levels which, according to Jiri Levy (1967), constitute the semiotic dimension of translation. The semiotic factor underlines the specific nature of this choice: it describes the fixation of values abstracted and at the same time connected to a system of reference. The Variational concept corresponds to this double movement in so far as it is based on an exploration of the translation options and a description of the conditions of their applicability.

But there is another dimension to the production of translations that Levy has called the *pragmatic* dimension. He bases his argumentation on a theory of games. There are continuous and discontinuous games. In discontinuous games such as card games or lotteries, the situation of the players is reoriented each time the dice is thrown or the cards are dealt. Up to now, we have probably given the impression that translation could be compared to this type of game. The TO has appeared to be free at every stage to make decisions within the paradigm of options that could be produced by the Variation method for each translation unit. And it is true that the greater part of the semantic content of the translation product is defined at this level. But the translation operation has also to be assimilated to the second type of game. The continuous games such as chess are characterized by ordered sequences of strategic choices. Instead of being confronted with a new situation at every turn in the game, the players have to take into account their own strategic objectives: 'every move is influenced by the knowledge of previous decisions and by the decision which resulted from them' (Levy, 1967: 1172), but also their opponents' attempts at thwarting them in order to further their own interests.

Similarly the translation choice is a sequential and cumulative series of decisions for which Levy has given a simplified but extremely revealing diagram. The choices are defined as both selection and exclusion, which clearly shows that at every step in the translation process, the translator's decision is influenced by the orientation he or she has adopted from the beginning and by the alternatives that are left open to him or her at every move (see Figure 9.1). This double dimension could represent the homological process. Levy's diagram nevertheless has the disadvantage of giving the impression that the translator's decision – however complex – is perfectly free beyond the selecting stage. We should supplement Levy's diagram by adding on the opponent's counterstrategy. By this we mean, of course, the socio-cultural parameters which contribute to qualify and influence the translator's

186 Redefining Translation

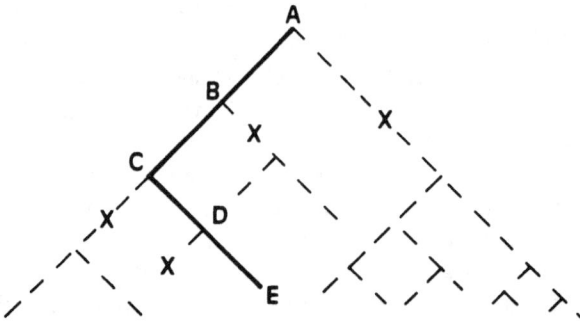

Figure 9.1 Translation choice diagram

sequence of choices so that the final product of his or her activity is at the same time a selection and referencing process.

In order to study this process, we have given priority to four texts which place the translator in front of major strategic choices and we have tried to reproduce as much as possible the progressive reorientations and describe alternative translation paths.

In the Albee text (Appendix 4), the problem of translating appears in various degrees as an anticipation of the theatrical context in which the play is to be performed. The Delisle text (Appendix 3) (1) places the translator under the necessity of determining the several planes of specific language characterizing this referential text and particularly the differences that must be observed between them; and (2) can be used to illustrate some of the 'liberties' the translator may take when translating for a specific medium such as a magazine or newspaper. In Kiwi (Appendix 6), the translator will have to assess, according to his target audience, to what extent and in what form his readership is prepared to recreate the degrees of ambiguity present in the ST. Finally, in our translation of Lawrence (Appendix 5) we first follow through the sequencing of correlated choices which have to be determined in order to simulate the systematic nature of this aesthetic text, and then consider other criteria which might take precedence when dealing with 'literary' language such as this.

Particular attention has been given in our choice of the four texts to the textual strategies they represent: Delisle is logical and Albee mainly analogical, Lawrence is aesthetic, and Kiwi ambiguous (see Chapter 5, pp. 96ff.). We feel, besides, that this concluding development is the logical extension and completion of our mainly analytical approach of the translation process in the preceding chapters.

Applications of the Variational model 187

The particular consideration attending the translation of Albee concerns the adaptation in translation of this fragment of dramatic text to the conditions of dramatic performance.

A dramatic text is by nature incomplete. It is limited to the strict linguistic content of the characters' expressions. The totality of the surrounding content is left unreferenced or rather given over to the actualizing function of the staging team – actor and director prominent among them The play's text is sometimes accompanied by 'stage directions' providing hints as to contextualization, but the rest of the text is usually left in various degrees of decontextualization. The difficulty facing the translator consists, according to the specific convention of the play's performance, in determining the respective values of text (written text and stage directions) and performance. Certain effects will be more linguistically enforced according to LC2 conventions or on the contrary will call for specific types of acting and explanatory stage directions. Besides, the translator must make the characters' expressions compatible with speech patterns, inflections, and idiomatic idiosyncrasies more or less identifiable in keeping with potential audiences.

In order to conduct our analysis of the sequence of options, we have deliberately confined ourselves to the comparison of two widely contrasted translation texts which will give rise to some incidental considerations referenced in alphabetical order. Our first version tries to reproduce as faithfully as possible the linguistic determination of our ST; the second takes into account the staging conditions of the play. Conventionally, whenever there is not any meaningful difference according to these criteria, the translation will be <u>underlined</u> and the text will be in **bold** characters in the opposite case.

(a) Martha's introductory exclamation, '**SCREW YOU!**' is a case in point since it demands enormous emphasis from the 'sub-human monster yowling ... from inside' as a final crushing retort likely to freeze everybody in a moment's confused silence when the guests appear at Martha and George's door. So, if the first solution is sufficiently strong to shock the arriving guests, the second adds the embarrassing (for Honey and Nick) dimension of revealing the relationship between the couple:

Va te faire foutre!   **Pauvre con!**

<u>[A ces mots, George ouvre brusquement la porte d'entrée, révélant la présence de Honey et Nick sur le palier. Après un bref instant de silence ...]</u>

G: [Apparemment enchanté de retrouver Honey et Nick, mais en réalité, ravi que les excès de langage de Martha ne passent pas inaperçus.]

Ahhhh!	**Tiens! Quel bon vent!**

(b) It seems obligatory in French to expand George's exclamation of welcome into a more voluble and socially clichéd formula. Thus the TO would normally be looking at LC2 reception parameters, and here at ways of 'greeting guests at the door'. These tend to be richer than the English equivalents, especially as greetings in general are more explicit. It is also possible to incorporate the stage direction into the body of the text by underlining George's pleasure at seeing the couple, with, for example, **Vous tombez bien!** The TO may, however, choose simply to simulate the Anglo-Saxon greetings context and thus produce a somewhat bare LC2 text (i.e. the first solution above).

M: [Haussant le ton pour couvrir la voix de G.]

Ah! Vous voilà!	**Salut, vous autres!**
	Entrez, entrez donc!

(c) Martha's initial 'HI!' both covers George's very marked greeting and corresponds to the enthusiastic – and long-drawn-out – American welcome which can be taken to signify either genuine delight at seeing the guests, or exaggerated social convention. This could be simulated in French by repetition several times of the initial **Salut**. It should also be noted that the idiolectal differences in the right-hand text highlight Martha's (apparent) breezy hospitality.

Honey et Nick [Improvisant librement.]: Bonjour. C'est nous. Comment allez-vous?

G: [Sur un ton parfaitement neutre.]

Mais ce doit être nos petits invités.	**On dirait que ce sont nos petits invités.**

(d) The simple change in modality type from probability to appearance will be enough to underline George's irony and dissimulation, which in the ST remains ambiguous until actually pronounced on stage ('must' either indicating a deduction – 'we are expecting guests and it must be you' – or an exhortation – 'please come in and watch my wife making a fool of herself' – which could then be made explicit in: **Ah! Voilà nos petits invités!'**).

M: [Partant d'un gros éclat de rire ironique.]

(e) Note the transformation of a character's expression into a stage direction - the irony in the original being indicated by a marker of intonation ('Ha, ha ha, **HA!**') which simply cannot be transposed into the second language. It therefore must be left to the actor to find the appropriate laugh.

Ne faites pas attention à M. Bougon. Entrez-donc les enfants! Et donnez vos affaires à M. Bougon.	**N'écoutez pas ce casse-pied. Entrez-donc et refilez vos affaires au casse-pied.**

(f) The problem posed here is one of socio-linguistic register. 'Sourpuss' is a very tame word for Martha to use, and has connotations of children's vocabulary (and thus also characterizes Martha and George's relationship). The change of register is a comic one, but also comes across as a compromise in front of the guests. The left-hand solution plays on this comic register and also adds an extra element (the tradition of 'M. Bougon' in French classical theatre), whereas the right-hand solution reproduces the slang register one may expect Martha to employ in French and maintains the tension produced by Martha's aggressive treatment of George.

N: [D'un ton neutre.]

Eh bien, je crois que nous n'aurions pas dû venir.	**Je crois vraiment que nous aurions mieux fait de ne pas venir.**

(g) Increased emphasis on formal politeness is normally necessary in order to express in French the character's embarrassment. The introductory 'Well, now' is therefore displaced in the translation, with the whole sentence becoming more voluble. This decision would be based on the assumption that LC2 norms of politeness should be adhered to, i.e. that in the French context, one would 'automatically' use a polite form of speech. The problem with the left-hand translation is that the initial 'Eh bien' can sound dismissive or supercilious, particularly as the formula used is very dry. Thus if the LC1-influenced (left-hand) text is chosen, it is necessary to underline the stage direction 'without expression'.

H: Oui, il est vraiment tard.   C'est vrai, surtout qu'il se
                                 fait tard.

(h) In addition to formality of address, the French adaptation will over-emphasize assertions, again to cover the character's embarrassment.

M: Tard? Mais vous plaisantez!   Tard? Mais vous voulez rire?
Mettez vos affaires   Laissez tomber tout ça
n'importe où et entrez donc!   et entrez donc!

Cf. (c) – the right-hand translation simulates Martha's breezy and casual hospitality.

G: [D'un air vague tout en s'éloignant.]

N'importe où ... sur les meubles,   N'importe où ... sur les
par terre ... aucune importance   meubles, par terre ....
dans cette maison.   Ici rien n'a d'importance.

Cf. (d) – same attitude expressed by change in modulation.

N: [S'adressant a H.]

Je t'avais dit que nous   Je te l'avais bien dit.
n'aurions pas dû venir.   Nous aurions mieux fait
                           de ne pas venir.

(i) Cf. (g) – Note the break-up of the ST into shorter units for greater emphasis.

M: [D'une voix de stentor.]

Je vous ai dit d'entrer.   Ne restez pas plantés là.
Entrez donc.   Entrez-donc.
                            Combien de fois faut-il
                            vous le répéter?

(j) (Cf. also (i)). Martha uses a slang register in the ST, together with a certain aggressivity. These two elements have been brought out in the right-hand translation, with the familiar 'plantés', and the increased emphasis by of 'Combien de fois faut-il vous le répéter?' replacing what in the original would be brought out by intonation.

[H et N entrent.]

H: [Avec un rire nerveux] Oh! **[Avec un rire nerveux] Vous**
Mon Dieu! **êtes trop aimable!**

(k) (Cf.(g)). Obviously literal translation cannot be contemplated here. Our two translations are again based on certain LC2 behavioural norms: the first emphasizes the embarrassment felt by Honey, whereas the second is the ready-made expression which people will come out with on such occasions.

G: [Imite le rire de Honey.]
M: [Se tournant vers G.]

Ecoute, espèce de mal **Dis-moi, mon salaud, tu**
embouché. Arrête ça! **vas la fermer?**

(l) Increased vulgarity will at the same time characterize Martha's style of address to George and stand in vivid contrast with her attempts at friendliness with the young couple.

G: [Feignant l'innocence et l'indignation.]

Martha! **Martha, voyons, tout de**
 même!

(m) As above ((e) and (j)) what in the ST is expressed by intonation becomes a periphrase reproducing predictable social intercourse.

[S'adressant à H et N.]

Martha ne fait vraiment pas **Martha a de ces**
attention à ce qu'elle dit, je **expressions!**
vous jure.

(n) Again an attempt to capture expressivity and emotional charge at the expense of literal exactitude.

M: Allez les enfants, asseyez-vous!

Allez, mes tout petits, asseyez-vous!

H: [S'asseyant.]

N'est-ce pas merveilleux?

Tout est divin! Tu ne trouves pas?

Cf. (k).

N: [D'un air détaché]:

Oui, en effet, c'est très bien

Oui, pas mal . . . très bien même.

Cf.(h).

M: Merci.

Je suis ravie de voir que cela vous plaise.

(o) It seems again here perfectly impossible for questions of social phraseology to have a character express a simple 'Merci' without being brusque.

**N: [Montrant un tableau abstrait]:
Et c'est qui l'auteur de . . .?**

G: Un Grec à moustaches que Martha s'est payé un de ces soirs.

Un Grec moustachu que Martha a entrepris un soir.

Cf. (i).

H: [Pour sauver la situation]:

Oh, oh!

**Eh bien, eh bien!
Voyez-moi ça.
Tiens, tiens!**

Cf. Comment p. 93.

N: Ce tableau est d'une . . .

Il y a dans ce tableau comme une . . .

G: Sobre intensité.
N: Pas précisément...

G: Oh! (Un temps) ou alors, une tapageuse nonchalance?

Voyez-vous ça! (Un temps) Ne serait-ce pas plutôt une tapageuse nonchalance?

N: [S'apercoit du manège mais continue imperturbablement sur le même ton de politesse glaciale.]

Non. Ce que je voulais dire...

Ce n'est pas ce que je voulais dire.

(p) A reorganization of propositional content exactly opposite to (i).

G: Que diriez-vous d'une intensité nonchalante sobrement tapageuse?

H: Ecoute, chéri! On est en train de se moquer de toi

Mon pauvre chéri! Je crois qu'on est en train de te charrier.

Cf. (g).

N: [D'un ton glacial.]:

Je m'en suis aperçu.

Ça m'en a tout l'air.

[Bref silence embarrassé.]

G: [Avec sincérité]

Je suis vraiment navré.

Je vous prie de bien vouloir m'excuser.

[N, condescendant, lui fait comprendre d'un hochement de tête qu'il ne lui en veut pas.]

G: Ce que c'est, en réalité, c'est une représentation graphique de l'état mental de Martha.

Pour tout vous dire, il s'agit d'une représentation de ce qui se passe dans la tête de Martha

(q) A certain expansion of LC1 semantic material in order to combine emphasis, idiomaticity and explicitness.

M: [Partant d'un gros rire]

Cf. Comment p. 92.

<u>George, offre donc quelque chose à boire à ces enfants. Qu'est-ce que vous prendrez? Qu'est-ce que vous voulez boire?</u>

<u>N: Honey, qu'est-ce que tu prends?</u>

H: Je ne sais pas, chéri. Un peu de cognac. Jamais ne mélangez et bien vous porterez!	Attends un peu, mon chéri, un doigt de cognac, peut-être. Jamais de mélanges!

(r) The greater conciseness in the second translation is justified by the necessity to find the right social stereotypes adapted to the situation.

G: Cognac? Rien que du cognac? Sans rien d'autre?	Un cognac? Un simple cognac? Tout simplement? On a des goûts simples! (On fait dans la simplicité!)

(s) The ST can be acted in different ways. 'Just brandy' can mean 'brandy and nothing else' or can be taken to point to the actual ('upmarket') drink requested. 'Simple; simple' can be an ironic comment on Honey's expensive taste, or indeed a veiled attack on her for being simply . . . simple. The left-hand text underplays this reading whereas the right-hand one brings out George's aggressive stance.

[Se dirigeant vers le bar]
<u>Et pour vous?</u>

<u>N: Un bourbon avec des glaçons.</u>

Si vous le voulez bien.	Si ce n'est pas trop vous demander.

G: [Tout en préparant les verres.]

Si je veux bien, bien sûr que oui.	Trop me demander? On ne m'en demande jamais trop.

(t) Here the reflectiveness and the double entendre of G's remark can be explicated.

Et pour toi, Martha, de l'embrocation?	**Et pour toi, Martha, de l'alcool à brûler, comme d'habitude?**

(u) As in (a), it seems that exactitude in content reformulation will have to be sacrificed in order to give more punch to this line.

When the two versions of this dramatic text are examined side by side they appear markedly different, although fairly consistent with their general objectives: the right-hand version takes greater consideration of the overall reception constraints that redefine a great deal of the translation options normally associated with the LC1 text as reproduced in the left-hand text.

It must by now be clear that the two tentative versions of the play presented above only cover the most predictable types of translations we may expect to find. The moment one begins to apply more varied sociocultural norms – at whatever level it may be – one either focuses more sharply on the LC1 text, or one simulates the LC2-receiving situation. According to the options defined in the Cultural Equation, the TO might find himself applying modifications to the original which go far beyond the scope of predictable forms – which is probably why so many translations of plays are in fact presented as 'adaptations' rather than 'translations'. The concentration on LC2 reception norms is a case in point. The nature of social intercourse in France being radically different from predictable forms in the USA, the TO will feel the need to expand certain exchanges to bring out indications of embarrassment, etc., as we have pointed out. But it may be felt that the LC1 context itself constitutes a norm which the cultivated LC2 audience will recognize, thus encouraging the TO to produce what would otherwise be felt to be a rather sparse French translation.

In the *Time* article studied by Delisle (Appendix 3), the initial problem we consider is one of *consistency* in the rendering of the clearly separated levels of specific language that can be distinguished in this text. Before the introduction of technical language from the second paragraph onwards, we find a neutral narration of the facts of Mrs Dawson's case. This journalistic account must be contrasted with the patient's own version and complementary comment on the situation. And as a transition, the journalist from time to time uses a form of indirect speech to report some of Mrs Dawson's feelings or reactions. We will respectively bring out each of these different forms of referential texts in ordinary type for objective narration, <u>underlined</u> text for Mrs Dawson's own speech, and **bold** type for the indirect speech.

Rebuilding the breast

After the removal of her left breast because of cancer in 1970, Mrs Joan Dawson, 54, of New York City, spent the next three years **battling depression and a sense of loss. Then she decided to do something about it.** Most women in the same situation turn to a psychiatrist. Mrs Dawson (not her real name) went to her doctor and asked him to rebuild her missing breast. '<u>I did not want to be made into a sensational beauty</u>', she explained, '<u>I just wanted to be restored.</u>' Her surgeon was able to do just that. In two separate operations, he implanted a silicone-filled sac under the skin where the breast had been removed, then reduced the size of the other breast to make it more nearly resemble the new one. The result is not a duplication of Mrs Dawson's pre-1970 figure, but **she is delighted nevertheless.** Says she: '<u>I can finally look at myself in the mirror without wincing.</u>'

Le Sein peut être refait.

Après avoir été opérée du sein gauche atteint d'un cancer, une Newyorkaise de 54 ans, Mme Dawson (nous avons voulu conserver l'anonymat) a passé les trois années qui ont suivi à lutter contre **la dépression et un sentiment de perte.** C'est alors qu'elle a **décidé de faire quelque chose**. Dans un cas semblable, la plupart des femmes se tournent vers un psychiatre. Mme Dawson est allée consulter son médecin pour lui demander de lui refaire un sein. '<u>Je ne voulais pas devenir une beauté</u>', a-t-elle expliqué, '<u>je voulais simplement être remise en état.</u>' C'est ce que fit le chirurgien. En deux interventions successives, tout d'abord, il implanta sous la peau à l'endroit de l'opération antérieure un sac rempli de silicone, puis, dans un second temps, il réduisit la taille de l'autre sein pour le rendre à peu près semblable au sein artificiel. L'opération n'a pas rendu à Mme Dawson sa silhouette d'avant mais elle s'est néanmoins déclarée **entièrement satisfaite**: '<u>Je peux enfin me regarder dans la glace sans avoir à fermer les yeux.</u>'

Our aim here is thus one of consistency between ST forms and TT forms. A comparison with the translation proposed by Delisle should make this quite clear: Delisle translates 'a sense of loss' by 'le traumatisme de la mutilation' – the indirect speech which is clear in the ST has been transformed into the journalist's (or in fact the translator's) comment, addressed, incidentally, to a fairly specialized public. There is obviously no obligation in French to transform the text in this fashion, and the TO will thus choose among TT alternatives accordingly.

It is interesting, however, to reconsider the TT in the light of LC2 reception norms, as medical discourse appearing in different press organs tends to take on fairly predictable characteristics. In fact, depending on the medium in question, either the medical discourse itself will tend to dominate, or the stylistic traits of the newspaper or magazine will attenuate the specialized content of the original. In other words, the rewriting and editing process set in motion in LC2 will follow a different set of criteria from those used in this instance by *Time* magazine, and in some cases, such an article may be taken in order to produce a different overall message. If the TO has been instructed to produce a 'normalized' translation, it may go well beyond the bounds of what one normally considers to be 'translation'. Thus what might be considered to be the 'limits' of the ST may be transgressed by, say, introducing a more specialized level of vocabulary in the very general introduction quoted above, or conversely by imposing certain syntactic forms or lexical choices that would not necessarily suggest themselves during the initial Translation operation.[1]

Given the variety of conceivable variations on this text, it is not the place (and hardly possible anyway) here to produce an exhaustive list of possible variants. What interests us is the possible applications of the Variational approach used to generate appropriate LC2 forms. The following examples should therefore be taken as indicative of some of the possible variations.

1 *The title of the article*. It goes without saying that titles are variously exploited by different magazines and newspapers for many different purposes. In more specialized magazines concentrating more on the medical aspects of this case, one might well find the nominalized (and more impersonal) form proposed by Delisle – 'La Reconstitution des seins'. But the story may well be given a much more 'human' treatment – in certain women's magazines, say – where the title would carry a message of hope.[2] This could be produced by using the catch-all (Fr.) 'on' form which might be reinforced with 'oui': 'Oui, on peut refaire un/les sein(s)'. Other syntactic variations are obviously conceivable ('Refaire le

sein, c'est possible/un espoir!', etc.). Finally, norms governing the titles of articles may impose certain additions such as subtitles, etc., which would be added by the TO or magazine editor.³

2 *Focusing the information.* Certain magazines will choose to focus the information in the article differently. If the 'human interest' element is to be brought out, there may be a total restructuring of the opening sentence to bring out first of all the problems encountered by Mrs Dawson – 'La dépression, un sentiment de perte, voici la lutte menée par une Newyorkaise . . .'. The same principle of restructuring can be applied throughout the text, by, for example, focusing on the end-result: ' "Je peux enfin me regarder dans la glace sans avoir à fermer les yeux," a déclaré une Newyorkaise . . .'.

3 *Syntax.* Certain French magazines use stylistic devices in order for their articles to be recognized as originating from the magazine itself (whatever the actual origin). Readers of *Libération* or *Le Nouvel Observateur* will have been struck by such devices, which may be liberally applied by the TO. One might cite for *Le Nouvel Observateur* the preponderance of questions asked and the tendency to drop main verbs. A typical form in this text would thus be: 'Que font la plupart des femmes dans un cas pareil? Elles se tournent vers . . .'; or combining the two forms: 'Vers qui se tournent la plupart des femmes dans un cas pareil? Leur psychiatre. . .'

4 *Lexis.* Enough has already been said about different levels of specialization in such texts to make much additional comment superfluous. We should stress, however, the productiveness of the Variational approach which, through the homologizing process, enables the TO to choose from a wide variety of parasynonyms and thus to match LC2 expectations as exactly as possible where this is felt to be necessary. The tendency in French medical discourse to slip into specialized jargon – even in the simplest of articles – can thus easily be emulated.

5 *Other semiotic codes.* Our final point in this section goes beyond the limited context of the article in question but should be considered by the TO as a potential part of the Translation situation. Magazine policy may be to modify the other semiotic codes used to convey a message – photographs, cartoons, statistical tables, etc. The TO will have to take into account such modifications when weighing up the overall impact of the text he or she is translating, as the modification of such codes may lead to a radical restructuring of the message perceived by LC2 readers. French magazine readers, for example, delight in opinion polls, statistics, visual representations, etc., that can be added in different

places in an article. Thus a compensatory strategy may be necessary in order to maintain the 'balance' of information of the ST.[4]

The Kiwi text (Appendix 6) is, as we have already shown, a text based on the textual exploitation of a fairly banal ambiguous situation characteristic of the modern world. This ambiguous relation can be formulated with more or less vigour according to the translator's individual perception and his anticipation of his readership's receptivity.

It is this variable that we intend to bring out through the definition of two and at times three degrees of ambiguity illustrated in the three columns below: the left-hand column expressing a moderate degree of ambiguity, the right-hand one an exaggerated degree and the middle one an intermediary degree of ambiguity.

Le Kiwi est à l'honneur	Le Kiwi est aux premières loges	Le Kiwi est comme un coq en pâte.

Quand les routes

étaient à la fleur de l'âge	avaient encore tout l'éclat de leur bitume	n'avaient pas perdu de leur vêprée

le citoyen américain qui ne désirait (ou ne savait) pas conduire

était considéré comme un	se voyait taxer de	se voyait stigmatiser du nom de

parasite ou de

simple d'esprit	demeuré	crétin
et condamné le reste de sa vie	et condamné à vie	et condamné le reste de son âge
à dépendre des	à être tributaire des	à s'en remettre corps et biens aux
voitures	bagnoles	tires
d'autrui	de son prochain	de Monsieur-tout-le-Monde

et, très probablement au célibat. Le non-conducteur était une espèce de 'rara avis'

| dont il ne partageait que le nom | de nom seulement mais pas pour les services | |

apparenté au Kiwi, oiseau qui ne vole pas. Dans un pays qui fait appel aussi massivement à l'automobile

| pour gagner son pain quotidien et faire la majeure partie de son beurre | pour faire son beurre et les épinards qui vont avec | |

il était considéré comme une espèce

| d'invalide volontaire | de condamné volontaire a l'invalidité | |

A présent cependant, à une époque ou la consommation excessive de carburant

| fait injure à nos narines, | blesse profondément notre odorat, | constitue une atteinte irréparable à notre odorat, |

(à) notre portefeuille et (à) notre orgueil national, l'abstinence automobile est devenue une vertu. Le Kiwi est comme un coq en pâte. Celui ou celle qui se rend au travail à bicyclette ou pedibus

| traîne derrière lui des nuées | porte sur sa tête une aura | |

de bonne conscience aussi palpable que les nuages de CO_2

| qu'il a abjurés. | dont il a fait vœu de se défaire. | |

Refus d'accepter une voiture au tarif actuel ou plus simplement refus ou incapacité de prendre le volant, on peut dire

| qu'il a tenu compte | qu'il s'est plié | qu'il a obtempéré |

Applications of the Variational model 201

aux recommendations officielles demandant de partager les transports individuels (bien que ce soit quelqu'un d'autre qui assume le partage). Même les voisins ou amis qui acceptent de lui faire ses courses, de retirer son linge à la blanchisserie et de lui acheter le journal du dimanche, risquent de se voir accusés, eux aussi,

| de servir les intêrets de | de faire le jeu de | de servir de courroie de transmission pour/de 'rouler pour' |

ces infames pays membres de l'OPEC.

The TO's final choice will be guided by *overall* considerations both of the style of the original and of LC2 reception norms. If it has been decided that the humorous and ambiguous elements should be brought out, the TO will look for the type of text put forward in the third column. It should be noted that the humorous elements are rarely in a one-to-one relationship between ST and TT, but are reproduced by means of a more general compensatory strategy. Such is, for example, the case with 'has become offensive to nostril ...', where the comic 'nostril' has been translated by the more neutral 'narines', but with a comic transposition for the neutral 'has become offensive' (translated as 'constitue une atteinte irréparable'). The same goes for 'obtempéré', which adds a humorous element to the original by diverging suddenly into administrative/police language. In this perspective, the TO would be seeking to reproduce an overall ST 'flavour' by using all the LC2 rhetorical devices available, at whatever level they happened to occur.

Our last example of pragmatically correlated choices does not concern the degree of variations in the ambiguous paradigm, as in the Kiwi text, but the syntagmatic construction characteristic of the aesthetic strategy. This particular type of textual strategy is, of course, based on ambivalence, just as the ambiguous text is. But in this case, it is not textually presented in order to be 'recognized' at the reception side but as an ambivalence introduced into the cultural system and made plausible by the persuasive nature of the text's own development. The text's aesthetic quality is tantamount to the plausibility it imparts to some specific ambivalence in the SR.

In 'Moony' (see Lawrence, Appendix 5) the different patterns of opposition between light and darkness and between conflict and growth are simply the outward manifestation of a sustained underlying confrontation between opposite concepts such as fragmentation and cohesion which the SR normally presents as contradictory. The moon, and what it represents for the young people standing on either side of the pool, is capable of transcending fragmentation and redeeming it into renewed cohesion; more precisely, the more it is destroyed the more cohesive power it can muster within itself in order to be reborn. Hence certain interferences with the phoenix myth or with the themes of Jesus and Mary ('reassumption') among others.

What we vaguely termed the text's development provides the necessary cohesive force in order for that ambivalence to be validated if not in the SR at large, at least within the confines of the novel. Instead of the sequences based on culturally established and widely accepted links that we find in logical texts, we discover a different text connection patterned not on concatenation but on its analogue, flux based on progressive evolution in continuity that we also called the *metamorphic* logic of that text. The general semantic structure could be represented as in Figure 9.2. The concepts bracketed together describe dualities; the vertical axis indicates flux; and the horizontal axis local, as opposed to syntagmatic, resolution.

Perceiving the structuring principle of the text not only confronts the translator with the usual responsibility of recreating local and strategic determinations but also of simulating the metamorphic quality of the linguistic designations, their sometimes wide-ranging affinities, and their cumulative build-up towards a semantic structure whose general contribution exceeds the sum of its constituent parts.

Each of the nodes in Figure 9.2 represented in bold characters does not exist as such but only for the purpose of schematic visualization. In textual reality, the value it represents is dispersed on a multiplicity of related lexical facets which put together might constitute a conceptual whole. Thus, the initial 'explosion' is refracted in a series of reflections of the same reality in expressions such as '*burst* of sound and a *burst* of brilliant light'; at least three aspects can be isolated – fragmentation, particles of light (sparks), and particles of sound – which must be rendered in translation with the same degree of complexity. The problem is less a question of choice between conflicting options as we already examined in cases of highly connotative texts than the necessity of abstaining from choosing and thus conciliating all the options. In this particular case, we found that 'éclat' would adequately satisfy this requirement.

A different aspect of the metamorphic logic is the different facets of one evolutive concept, as in the double progression (temporal and conceptual) in 'not quite destroyed' – 'not even now broken open' – 'not

Applications of the Variational model

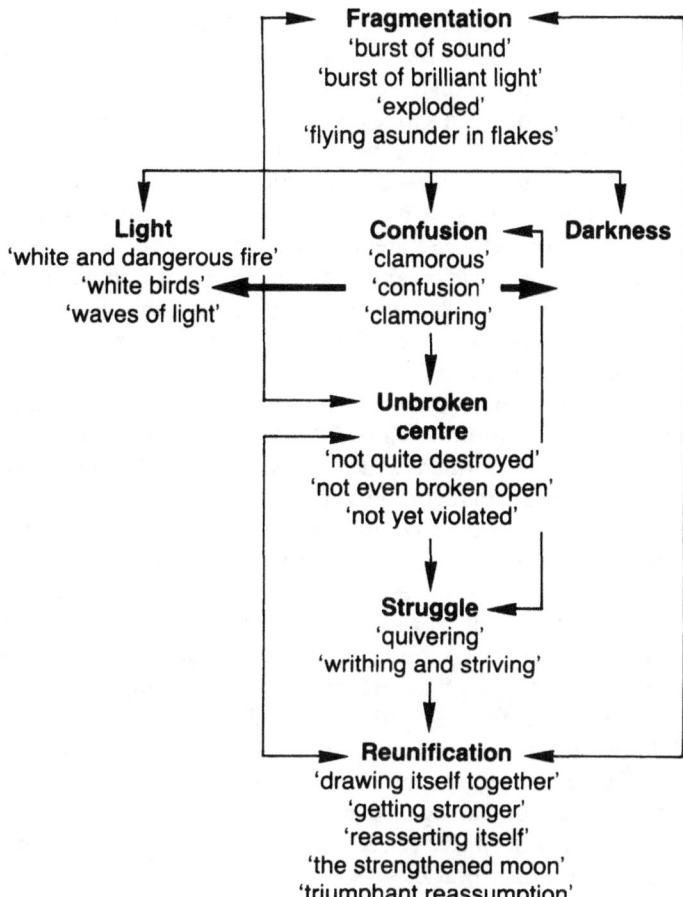

Figure 9.2 The semantic structure of the 'Moony' text

yet violated'; or between 'quivering' – 'writhing and striving' – 'violent pangs' – 'blind effort' – 'shook upon the water', recreating a climaxing then relapsing curve; or the evolutive sequence relating 'drawing itself together' – 'getting stronger' – 'reasserting itself' – 'strengthened moon'. It is clear, as we have tried to achieve in our translation, that the logic of these metamorphoses – sometimes reinforced by syntactic (not quite/not even/not yet) or alliterative (quivering/writhing/striving) elements – should guide the translator's choice and have precedence over the lexical content of individual words.

Opposed in their principles but nevertheless related to the overall purpose of the text are the near-repetitions ('clamorous/clamouring'), parallelisms in contradiction ('waves of light/dark waves/waves of darkness'), or variations on a single lexical root such as 'flying', 'flock', 'fleeing', or repetitions of a single pivotal word 'came *in* heavily, forcing their way *in*, hastening *in* in thin lines', with the curious grammatical redoubling of that highly charged thematic value. In these instances, as in the case of associative or oppositive links connecting the semantic poles of the text such as the references to 'brilliant light" – 'the white and dangerous fire' – 'the vivid incandescent quivering of a white moon' – 'a white body of fire', or to the 'waves of light', the translator's task is to construct and correlate rather than to proceed hierarchically from micro- to macro-structures.

Particular attention should be devoted to the concluding concept, 'in triumphant reassumption', which at the same time subsumes and epitomizes all the ambivalences developed in the text. The translation should try to recreate that combination of polysemy (inner complexity) and multireference (outer complexity, including intertextual reference), since that concept regroups the various meanings attached to 'assumption' and those accreting in the text's development such as references to self-integrity, privacy, virginity, individuality. Among the translated equivalents that might be thought of, such as 'régéneration', 'reconstitution', 'réunification', 'reconfirmation', 'réaffirmation', we will give preference to that which lends itself to a greater variety of associations rather than to an expanded translation, such as 'dans la gloire de son integrité retrouvée', (or 'réaffirmée'), which would produce the opposite effect of closing or overdefining the concept.

In the following proposed rendering our complementary remarks are placed between square brackets.

Puis, il y eut de nouveau des éclats de bruit et des éclats de lumière étincelante, la lune venait d'exploser à la surface de l'eau et volait en éclats d'un feu blanc et menaçant. Très vite, comme des oiseaux blancs, les flammèches éparpillées s'élevèrent à la surface de l'eau et s'échappèrent dans une mêlée emplie de clameurs, se heurtant au vol de vagues sombres qui se frayaient un passage vers l'intérieur. [The erotic reference apparently lost in 'forced' can be found compensated for in 'passage'.] Les vagues de lumière les plus éloignées qui cherchaient à s'échapper, semblaient assaillir les berges de leurs clameurs [this verbalization of a preposition is further justified by the consonant reference to 'warfare'] pour s'échapper, et les vagues d'ombre revenaient en force, regagnant [again, the reference to movement is enriched by association to warfare] le centre par en dessous. Mais au centre, au cœur de l'ensemble, une palpitation intense et incandescente de lune blanche, non entièrement détruite, une masse de feu blanc [obviously, this is an unsatisfactory equivalent for 'body (of fire)' but the equivalent should refer to a corporeal entity, and be compatible with fire and feminine] travaillée de spasmes et d'élancements [the gestative connotation homogenizes the three words], et pas même en cet instant fracturée, non encore violée. Elle semblait se reformer en d'étranges et violentes contractions [preferred to 'convulsions' denoting suffering rather than childbirth], avec une obstination aveugle. Elle se renforçait, elle se réaffirmait en tant que lune inviolable. Et les rayons revenaient à la hâte rejoindre la lune renforcée qui palpitait à la surface de l'eau dans la gloire de sa reconfirmation.

The translation we have given of the Lawrence text brings together a large number of the different elements developed particularly in Chapter 5. In this way, it represents what for us is the optimum translation of this highly intricate aesthetic text, given a LC2 readership capable of entering into the subtleties of the language used. In fact, translation at this level is tantamount to an extended reading or commentary of the ST, and thus becomes part of the overall interpretation of a work of art. The 'ideal' reader would be the bilingual student who would enter into the whole range of possible choices, thus recreating for himself or herself the Translation operation. However, the Variational approach is intended to introduce maximum flexibility into TT choices and thus to call on parameters which may be overlooked or played down by the TO aiming to produce a primarily aesthetic text. If these parameters are brought back into the Cultural Equation, the focus on the text necessarily changes, and the final choices made by the TO may turn out to be radically different. It is important to note that these parameters may operate at any level, from the most direct influences discussed in the last chapter, such as the requirements of the TI or the nature of the LC2 public, to the most esoteric. Rather than look at the former, which we have developed previously at some length, we shall briefly consider some of the latter in the following paragraphs.

One of the most delicate decisions for the TO to make concerns the act of literary creation itself, with the attendant notions of beauty, euphony, etc. Literary translators are more or less consciously concerned with 'writing well', which probably means imitating prevalent LC2 literary forms. If the TO puts the 'literary effect' very high on his list of priorities, this may mean taking a certain number of decisions at levels which would otherwise be passed over. Such decisions are, of course, based on

206 *Redefining Translation*

the TO's perception of the two cultures in question as independent and evolving entities which are both temporarily frozen, as it were, for the purposes of translation. The act of translation continuously links cultures together and, as we have discussed in Chapter 6, contributes to their separate development.

The TO may thus be faced with several different types of decision. The first concerns his diachronical perception of language. If his ST belongs to a distant period, choices will be generated within a *double perspective for each language*. In other words, lexis and syntax will initially be focused from within the LC1 – how far the forms used deviate from or stand in contrast to present-day ones – and then from the LC2 perspective, which will both consider equivalent 'old' forms and moderns forms. Schematically, one might represent this as in Figure 9.3. The 'present-day LC1 perspective on ST' implies the rewriting and expansion of the ST as in the homological processes described in Chapter 4, which are added to the alternative 'historical' forms

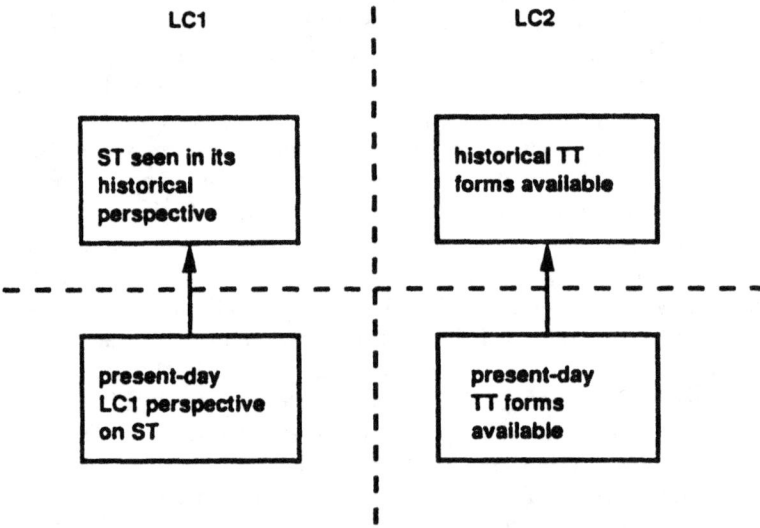

Figure 9.3 Translating a 'historical' text

available. Choices might thus arise as to the very vehicle chosen to convey the message. Should *La Chanson de Roland* be translated in verse form or prose? To what extent should an archaic element be preserved in the second LC? Should maximum accessibility be the prime criterion, or should the LC2 reader be invited to discover LC1 forms? Should the 'older' LC2 forms be used, or would they simply recreate a cultural entity which is quite distinct from the LC1 context?

When the TO begins to consider the notions of 'beauty' and 'literariness' with which he operates, he may come up against a highly restricted number of LC2 forms available. Certain choices can be made at these levels which will overrule many of the options previously considered and thus, using Levy's game analogy developed in the opening pages of this chapter, condition the final outcome: the TT. From our point of view, it is important to underline not just the necessary subjectivity of the TO, but the developments and changes that are always at work within a culture and which, of course, require works of literature to be retranslated at fairly regular intervals. In other words, the concept of Variation is again a fundamental one, and necessary to break out of the ideological position often adopted, either that beauty is the sole property of one LC, or that it is eternal (and the eternal property of a particular text or author).

If we apply such considerations to the translation of Lawrence proposed above, certain strategic choices might be made which will take precedence over the argumentation leading to the choice of such key words as 'éclat'. From one point of view, the triple repetition of 'éclat' goes some way to compensating for the alliterative effects which have not been rendered in the proposed TT. But it may be felt that verbal forms ('éclater' for the first 'burst', 'jaillir' for the second) produce a more apposite 'literary' effect (ridding the text of 'il y eut'), and that the ST form 'asunder' (itself restricted to literary discourse, and dated in relation to modern novels) should in some way be marked with a similar 'stamp', such as 'se disjoignant en éclats d'un feu'. Similarly, the TO may wish to give precedence to language effects: if, for example, his TT is to be read aloud. Thus his choices of terms to translate key words in the centre of the passage, with its preponderance of repeated consonant clusters ('h', 'wh', 'l', 'fl', 'cl', and 'w' in particular) may given precedence to pure language effects over exactitude of meaning. More radically, he may come out of the 'aesthetic' framework altogether and produce a different type of text, suitable for a different public with different needs – in order to emphasize narrative continuity for example.

The applications we have illustrated in this chapter are, of course, by no means exhaustive. The Variational approach is clearly a very productive one, but one which is tailored to meet the specific needs of most translation situations. Thus the illustrations we have given should be taken as indicative of the types of application the TO can envisage, by bringing in all the relevant variables for each text. Our concern here has been to show the wide range of potential applications, which we hope that the reader will subsequently develop. We now turn our attention to related fields of interest.

10 Related fields of interest

So far we have tried to generalize Translation in order to produce a working model corresponding to the phenomena under consideration and to bring about tangible improvements in the empiric practice of translators. Accordingly, a methodology has been developed in order to implement this body of concepts. Inevitably, if our conceptualization has been correctly oriented, the 'reality' of translation is bound to be altered. Or, to put it in a different way, we have placed ourselves in a position to conceive it in a different manner. Inevitably also, some of the distinctive features characterizing – some will even argue defining – that same reality have had to be eliminated.

It is time to reintroduce some of these previously excluded factors and to see how they can be systematically integrated within the general model. This ultimate stage that we call *application* is not to be seen as a devaluation or denaturing of the model, much less as a confirmation, but as the necessary extension of formal representation, its opening onto reality. As a matter of fact, theory leads nowhere and is locked in paralogic circles if it does not lead on to a rediscovery of the facts it is supposed to account for. Indeed, in the semiotic conception that has guided this research, and for those who are prepared to accept its postulates, it *creates* reality.

Already in Chapter 8, we caught a first glimpse of the complexity of phenomena when we discovered that Translation had to be presented as a series of *strategic* choices. The objective was no longer to explore the respective merits of abstractly envisaged options but to observe the consequences of oriented choices. Yet at that stage, the orientation was still hypothetical or secondary in our preoccupations in so far as the options were only compared between themselves and in sequences but never explicitly connected to the consequences they determined in context.

We intend now to envisage two concrete situations in which Translation can be considered as a determining factor: the Teaching of Translation and Translation Criticism.

Before reconsidering the teaching of translation in the perspective of the Variational approach, it is important to note that we have arbitrarily selected and privileged one of the options envisaged earlier. We chose to promote in our research the interactional relationship over the other two. It is necessary in practice to remind learners that our orientation not only coexists but is indirectly determined and frequently displaced by the other two. Something will have to be said in the translation class for the non-conventional procedures (acclimatization/reduction and insertion) that may be explored concurrently with the more traditional ones.

We do not intend to go through a full-scale criticism of previous practices in translation didactics. We refer the reader to well-documented and convincing studies such as Ballard (1987), Pergnier (1978) and Ladmiral (1979). In fact, these studies mark a turning-point in the perception of translation didactic practices, at least within the context of French education. Each author equally insists on the counterproductivity of current teaching practices, some of them dating back to the previous centuries and curiously preserved into this age of general reconsideration of linguistic practices. What we would like to underline is already perceptible in these earlier studies: the confusion of the objectives assigned to translation didactics. At least three of the most commonly practised orientations seem difficult to justify:

1 For some, the teaching of translation is geared to the production of the translation *object*, determined by a specific *expertise* corresponding to a *profession*, that of translator. The communicational approach emanating from the Paris ESIT school has concentrated on developing strategies to further this project together with the accompanying theoretical background.

We notice in the writings of both practitioners and theoreticians that the emphasis is on the Translation situation and on the decisions to be taken in keeping with the requirements of an immediate communicative task. The translator's main objective is to establish, maintain and facilitate the pragmatic exchange of information. He seems less concerned with what takes place in the relationship between the two cultural worlds brought together by the act of translation. Much of the communicationalists' teaching is validated by the results it brings about, by the practical and topical relevance of its solutions rather than by the intrinsic reliability of the techniques it brings to bear on the task. In short, the procedures that are being taught are pragmatically based and thus difficult to generalize and replicate. We feel, however, that the objective that we finally assign to translation teaching is not incompatible with this practical approach but that it is the natural extension of more general skills to be previously acquired by the translator learner.

2 The teaching of translation has been considered for a long time as the only reliable means to help students acquire a second language. More recently, it appears, the expectations have been noticeably lowered and translation is only envisaged as a reliable means of testing second-language acquisition.

The more or less clearly formulated idea at the back of this conception is that the foreign language could be seen as an extraneous but not unrelated appendage to the mother tongue. They both refer to the same things and are based on the same system. Acquiring foreign languages merely consists in adapting the native tongue in order to express oneself differently but basically along the same lines. Translation in that perspective is the main exercise facilitating conversions into the mother tongue and highlighting the foreign language in terms of resemblances and differences.

More recently, the swing of the pendulum has been completely pushed to the other extreme in an attempt to correct the obvious limitations of the previous approach. It is nowadays a well-established fact that second-language acquisition, although not unrelated to the mother tongue, constitutes a self-contained and organic process. In the wake of such orientations, translation was strictly banished from the language classroom and the emphasis was placed on 'total immersion' or, concurrently, in conceptually inspired didactic strategies, on inculcating the basic concepts of the linguistic system in order to master language production.

We feel that both approaches are equally misguided in their excessive exclusion of, or reliance on, translation. Translation needs neither to be banned from, nor overemphasized in, the language class. Indeed, even in the total immersion approaches it has never been totally excluded, only marginalized and left untaught in the learners' training. Our recommendation will be to associate acquisition strategies destined to promote proficiency in a foreign language and comparative skills, the objective being to acquire mastery of a second linguistic system and at the same time to take into account the situation thus created: two languages coexisting need to be positioned and converted.

3 Finally, another group of teachers of translation tend to consider this practice as an extension or application of the linguistic system they

have previously inculcated in the learner audience. Correct translation practice would thus be a projection of the linguistic concepts discovered in each separate language.

This conception has been carried one step further in the research of Guillemin-Flescher (1981) and Chuquet and Paillard (1987) through the definition of linguistically defined 'tendencies' or sets of structures contrastively privileged in certain languages. Translation would not only consist in matching concretizations of concepts in different languages as in the applicative approach but conversion should also reflect the 'idiomatic' predilections of each language for such and such a combination of linguistic features.

The problem with this approach is that whereas it is perfectly justifiable to identify linguistic items in different languages in keeping with linguistic concepts, it is far from proven that the correlation thus established guarantees convertibility from one language into another. To put it differently, any two texts in different languages that refer to the same linguistic description cannot be considered *automatically* as potential translations. Besides, the 'tendencies' generated by the statistical observation of corpora of translated texts are most probably only the reflection of translation *practices* rather than significant translation *regularities*. If this suspicion was confirmed then this type of approach would merely consist in the reproduction of a certain conception of translation practice rather than in an objective description.

Our practice will not disregard the importance of linguistics on the one side or the reality of linguistically based translation regularities on the other but consider them as options whose relative applicability has to be identified through socio-cultural determinants rather than recommended as translation patterns.

For us, the correct objective to be assigned to translation teaching is more fundamental and essential. Before translation can be adapted to the communicative situation, it has to be developed according to specific procedures which then place the TO in a favourable position to make the final choices in keeping with the relevant situation. As soon as two linguistic systems are positioned concurrently, the problem of their respective conversion must be envisaged. Linguistic information should not precede or subsume the acquisition of translation skills, it is a basis on which this particular aptitude can be founded.

The main objective to be aimed at is Dissimilative Competence (DC), that is the ability to compare and convert linguistic and cultural systems. This specific competence is adapted to the Cultural Operator's specific function between different systems of values. This situation could even be extended to the act of expression itself. Communication implies resorting to a common semiotic system and, so doing, appropriating and thus distancing it. Consequently, all forms of expression entail a certain amount of conversion or translation, the translation between foreign languages being nothing but a particular case of that very general necessity. In the course of their linguistic development, individuals progressively build up a specific aptitude that helps them negotiate messages with their interlocutors in accordance with their strategic aims. That aptitude we call Dissimilative Competence. Since it corresponds to the double development of the Variational approach, it comprises a generative and a normative aspect concurring to the production of expressions or texts across different systems or languages.

From this general definition of DC, we deduce a certain number of fundamental postulates that will found our didactic approach:

1 Since expression is inevitably bound up with translation, each individual acquires in the process of his or her development a double faculty: expression and conversion. Thus within his own language and, more episodically in his dealings with foreign languages, the potential learner already has a first-hand experience of conversion procedures. This entails a number of consequences:

the learner is not virgin ground which has got to be enriched with knowledge;
he or she has to be instructed into discovering, controlling and organizing a previously acquired competence;
the teaching of translation is based on the handling of interlingual paraphrases and more generally on adaptative procedures to unfamiliar situations, skills which the potential learner daily practises in his own language.

2 We should next observe – as Ballard has repeatedly indicated (1984, 1987) – that DC is exerted from the mother language or source system onto the target system. Our didactic aim will then be in opposition to our theoretical approach describing a *system* of cross-linguistic relationships and not an oriented *practice*. It should also be seen as markedly different from the definition of translation drills in terms of 'prose' or 'unseen' (or translation from or into the mother language) in which instructor-induced orientation rather than realistic motivation for translation tends to by-pass or downplay cultural insertion, thus justifying un-motivated back-and-forth conversions such as back-translations.

By contrast, our teaching strategy recognizes the priority of the ST system or teaching basis on which the DC is to be constructed. As a consequence, (a) the DC will develop from exploration of LC1 converting resources onto the practice of cross-linguistic conversions; and (b) a priority will be given to the LC1 given – as Ballard has observed – one of the systems involved in conversion has to be selected as metalinguistic basis.

3 Since in expression and communication the individual is automatically faced with the incommensurability of systems and their mutual tensions, the translation learner should never be viewed as immune from cultural conflicts but rather as positioned in a problematic but privileged place between them. He is always a focal point in cultural dynamics. This function should be clearly explained to the learner and his position marked out as that of a Cultural Operator not just a vector in communication.

4 Finally, and in accordance with the cultural function of translation, we should orient our students away from a conception of translation methodology as involving skills and techniques connected with practical expertise and towards the conception of DC as comparison and assessment of various conversion strategies; that is, more generally, away from an *instrumental* and toward an *adaptative* conception of DC.

Once the postulates have been firmly established both in our didactic concepts and in the learners' minds, a practical teaching strategy should be devised in order to inculcate that specific competence. We give below a number of indications of the strategies that can be followed; we intend to develop these suggestions more fully in a further publication.

1 The choice of a conception of learning which will be based on either of the following didactic options: the *empiric* practice of learning by trial or error; the *cognitive* acquisition of learning; or the systematic *conditioning* of translation skills. It seems that in this respect the Variational approach does not lend itself readily or exclusively to one or the other of these conceptions. At the level of translation learners – as opposed to the theoretician – the production of translations is both a practice and a reflection on that practice combined in what Ladmiral (1979: 189) describes as 'praxéologie'. Consequently, in order to correspond to this double aspect and reflect the recent research on second-language acquisition (Purdue and Porquier 1980), we would advocate *ad hoc* combinations of the three above-mentioned approaches in stages and degrees adapted to the learner audience.

2 As to the practical implementation of the Variational approach, its adaptation to objectives, conditions of learning and learner audiences, little will be said, pending further enquiry. Whatever the strategies selected for the specialists, a special effort should be devoted to two very special types of public: (a) the non-specialists at large, who should be made aware of the little-known conversion processes that regulate communication; and (b) the highly specialized translators who have a tendency to ignore theory. The objective in this latter case would not be to instruct those who already know but to help them relativize their practice and optimize their results.

3 Finally, a last option should concern the level of proficiency we intend to promote in the learners and the means of assessing their aptitudes. The Variational approach – based as it is on variability and relativity – excludes traditional normative conceptions which pose 'translation problems' issuing from systematic analysis of 'translation errors' which in turn lead to various 'tests' aiming at error-free productions according to 'translation models'. On the contrary, we advocate all forms of testing materials that would verify the learner's acquired competence in *generative*, *referencing*, and *discriminative* skills concerning the range of homological texts he is able to produce for any given ST.

Our main contribution for the time being will be a few guidelines which should preside over the definition of more finalized learning strategies. Three general orientations would have to be envisaged in sequence, alternation or combination:

1 *Theoretical sensitization*, based on acquired practice made conscious in various degrees of conceptual explicitness according to audiences' preparedness. This general introduction to translation processes would normally involve:

(a) a criticism of previous conceptions, practices, and experiences of translation-teaching situations;
(b) the discovery of the function and workings of intuitive conversion practices: paraphrases and judgements on paraphrases, semiotic conversion, and interlinguistic translation;
(c) all this in order finally to help the learner conceptualize for himself a systematic representation of translation phenomena that fits his intuitive perception of his practice and ideally approximates as closely as possible the Variational approach.

2 The second stage will be to train the translation learner into discovering the methodology of translation. This will comprise:

(a) the systematic handling of the *instruments* of homology production with the Variational approach: discovery of the possibilities of intra-linguistic paraphrases; discovery of homologies and homologizing processes; practice of the complementarity between paraphrases and homologies;
(b) an introduction to the *complementary subjects* necessary for the production of translations: linguistics and discourse analysis; semiotics; sociolinguistics;
(c) a critical examination of the various *aids* available to translators such as mono- or bilingual dictionaries, thesauruses, lexicons; to define their role and the limits of their contribution to DC.

3 The third stage concerns the actual practice of translation in the Variational approach perspective along the lines defined by Wilss (1982: 159):

(a) *retrospective* practice: translation comparison and criticism; work on corpora of translations in specific types of discourses or multiple translations for the same text; parametering of various translation styles;
(b) *prospective* practice: production of texts in keeping with varying TC norms; production of socio-culturally identified alternatives to the same ST; simulation of the process of translation in its actual development.

In spite of the tentativeness and generality of our guidelines, didactics inspired by the Variational approach leads the translation instructor into completely revised methodological ways, involving a general reversal of educational principles. They can be summed up in a series of contrasted concepts: generativity v. normativity, adaptability v. application, and interaction v. reproduction.

We finally come to look at Translation Criticism. This, as Wilss has pointed out (1982: 217), is a 'forbiddingly complex subject-matter', hence the relative lack of space devoted to it by theorists, and the 'mixed-bag' impression one has when reading criticisms. Wilss has identified some of the key problems of Translation Criticism to date:

> In view of the lack of a suitable methodological frame or reference, practical T[ranslation] C[riticism] has until recently confined itself either to the discussion of phenomena which are lexically or syntactically clear failures ... or it has practised an encyclopedic

approach, trying more or less plausibly to integrate a host of observations partly of linguistic, partly of extralinguistic nature, into a frame of reference which creates the impression of being rather haphazard and therefore lacks persuasive power. (1982: 217)

Indeed, one is tempted to think that Translation Criticism is often nothing more than a catalogue of failures, where perceptive critics point out all the shortcomings of different translators' works, and then suggest how they could have done better. But the very grounds for the different value judgements made are often barely explored at all, and one is often justified in wondering if the new TT constitutes an improvement in any way on the TT being criticized. Our aim is therefore (1) to try to explore the type of frame of reference which can be used in order to give Translation Criticism a more scientific basis; (2) to look at the different procedures which can be used; and thus (3) to go beyond what in the final analysis is a rather simple sport – 'proving' one translates better than one's predecessors.[1]

Let it be said at the outset that in our view it is vital to question both what it is one is trying to judge, and just what the 'position' of that person passing judgement may be. A TT is a curiously vulnerable text which leaves itself open to many different types of judgements. The translation critic is not just any reader of the text and, as Larose has said,[2] it is necessary to compare the aims of the original sender with those of the TO, but not to compare the TO's aims with those of the translation critic himself. In other words, the translation critic has to build himself or herself into the model used to evaluate TTs, taking into account the particular aims he has in comparing ST and TT. Such a step would probably allow one to 'tone down' many of the extremely virulent criticisms one finds of existing translations.[3] We shall be looking at the 'position' and possible aims of the translation critic once we have defined the successive stages that make up Translation Criticism.

THE STAGES OF TRANSLATION CRITICISM

Translation Criticism is clearly a very specialized sort of exercise which falls outside the more traditional applications of Translation Studies. It involves making a series of judgements in order to be able to compare two perceived messages – in the ST and TT. But, as we have suggested in early chapters, and particularly in Chapter 6, the Translation situation is never a simple question of a TO producing a TT, but a complex set of circumstances which has to be analysed in depth for each translation undertaken. It is thus necessary briefly to go back over some of the ground already covered in the above-mentioned chapter.

The Translation critic is sometimes assimilated to the Translation Operator, as the basis for his evaluation is usually the 'rival' TTs he produces.[4] But it should be pointed out that the translation critic has a very special status, where, at best, he is a TO operating *in a new set of circumstances*. In other words, he does not start off from the same point of departure, which, as we have discussed, is the translation order produced by the TI (see Chapter 6). All he can do at best is to try to *simulate* the translation order and the likely role played by the TI. Indeed, one of the shortcomings of Translation Criticism as it is normally practised is precisely that the role of the TI is never taken into consideration, and in cases where this is a preponderant role, the translation critic is operating without the key piece of information he needs. As we shall see below, this lack of information regarding the TI can be compensated for to a certain extent when the socio-cultural positioning of the ST and TT (and their channels of communication) are taken into consideration.

The Translation critic, then, is not confronted with a text to translate, but with *two completed communication situations*, and it is he or she who, paradoxically enough, is the receiver of both ST and TT. As any TT can only be one of many possible variations in a vast paraphrastic set, there is nothing easier than to highlight 'differences' and to propose 'improvements'. But in our view it is important that the translation critic analyses each of the completed communication situations separately and fully, before attempting to compare ST and TT, in order to have as wide a vision as possible of the different parameters to be taken into account. Thus it is not a *direct* comparison of two texts which is carried out, but a relativized overview of two complete situations. Part of the reason for this is that a TT – especially a literary one[5] – has a life of its own as it finds its place in the second LC. In other words, it starts to function as a text in its own right within the LC2, independently of the ST. This must be taken into account by the Translation critic. However, this does not mean that evaluation is impossible. But it does imply carrying out a *parallel* analysis starting from a *common* source (i.e. the sender of the ST, who is indirectly the sender of the TT[6]). This parallel analysis involves (1) identifying where possible the potential or actual readership both in LC1 and LC2; and (2) analysing the diverse facets which go towards making up the 'message' of the ST and TT. Following the basic precepts of the Variational approach, the textual analyses will be based on the homological positioning of the ST and TT, but, as will be seen below, using a wider frame of reference. Two examples will serve to illustrate these points (see Figure 10.1).

218 *Redefining Translation*

How to call home from the UK

[Photograph of Bob Hope holding a red telephone]

For visitors from USA and Canada

British TELECOM

When you're away from home, there's always someone who would like to hear from you. Phoning home from the UK is easy and economical and British Telecom has a range of services to suit your needs.

Ways of calling
Home Direct Operator
No cash required, paid at home.
By dialling a unique number you can speak to a familiar operator back home and either charge the call to your calling card or place a Collect call. You won't need to worry about having coins on you, and if you're calling from a private

Comment téléphoner chez vous depuis le Royaume-Uni

[Photograph of Michel Drucker holding a red telephone]

Guide édité à l'intention des visiteurs belges, français et suisses

British TELECOM

Vous vous trouvez au Royaume-Uni. Vous pensez à ceux que vous aimez. Et vous avez envie de les entendre au téléphone. British Telecom vous propose toute une gamme de services téléphoniques, économiques et simples.

Vous pouvez téléphoner dans votre pays:
France Direct
sans pièces – appel facturé chez vous
Composez le 0800 89 0033. Vous obtenez un Agent des Télécommunications en France. Vous pouvez appeler en PCV ou utiliser une Carte Pastel Internationale.

phone, you won't have the awkwardness of charging the call to your host. This International Cashless Calling service is available from most British Telecom phones in the UK.⁷	Pas besoin de pièces. Et si vous appelez de chez quelqu'un, vous ne commettrez pas l'indélicatesse de mettre cet appel sur son compte. France Direct s'obtient à partir de la plupart des postes téléphoniques de British Telecom au Royaume-Uni.⁸

Figure 10.1 How to call home from the UK

This is an extract from the first two pages of a leaflet published by British Telecom and readily available (in several languages) in Britain for overseas visitors. As with the French translation of Forsyth's *The Day of the Jackal* (see Chapter 8, pp. 158–60), one is tempted first of all to ask whether this could be called a 'translation' at all. It would be easy to show how this is a 'bad' translation, 'deviating' far from the original in every possible way. And indeed, such a translation – which is, after all, fairly representative of many of the texts of this type that one does find – is certainly a test for Translation Criticism. It is also an interesting case to consider, as the TT belongs to the class of texts which is, in fact, not available in the LC2 country, and is thus never absorbed into the second Language Culture. The most common document of this type is the tourist brochure, and any type of text aimed at the 'foreigner'.

Let us apply, then, the analyses suggested above. The common *sender* is British Telecom, whose first aim appears to be to facilitate telephoning abroad for foreign visitors. Clearly there is another aim hidden behind all the helpful information provided: to increase the number of international calls, and thus the profits of the company. Interestingly enough, the *receivers* of both texts are not LC1 receivers (taking British culture alone to make up LC1), therefore one can say that a degree of adaptation (and indeed translation, as discussed in Chapter 4) is present from the outset.

The left-hand text clearly plays on that very emotive idea – particularly in American culture – of 'home' (mentioned five times in the passage quoted and reinforced by the picture of Bob Hope). The American or Canadian tourist is not just being reminded of his or her nearest and dearest, but is also being told how easy – and cheap – it is to phone them. 'Phoning home' is something of a stereotype, and British Telecom is obviously hoping not only to play on this, but also to stir feelings of duty and/or guilt ('there's *always* someone who would like to hear from you'). What is more, 'home' plays on the idea of everything that is most familiar; even the telephone operator is 'a familiar operator back home', thus taking away the worry of communicating with the (supposedly) less familiar British operators. In fact, there are no worries to be had whatsoever, though just what is meant by 'economical' is a good question, given the relatively high price of calling the American continent from the United Kingdom, but clearly the appeal is aiming to transcend baser considerations such as money (and, after all, you can pay 'at home' – in what today is still considered as a strong currency).

The right-hand text is an interesting document for the native French speaker[9] to come across. The picture of Michel Drucker – a very well-known television MC – immediately calls up a certain idea of France. The highlighted and large title – 'Vous pouvez téléphoner dans votre pays' – informs the reader of the possibility of phoning France (Belgium and Switzerland), which is then subdivided into three paragraphs. The text in small print reads very much like a piece of French advertising discourse, drawing heavily on preconstructed notions (e.g. 'British Telecom vous *propose toute une gamme* de services téléphoniques'). The document is given an 'official' flavour with the mention of the 'Agent des Télécommunications en France', together with 'trendy' LC2 concepts such as 'PCV' and 'Carte Pastel Internationale'. The document is thus seen as both informative and useful, fulfilling its role of facilitating phone calls to France.

How, then, is it possible to compare these two texts and to evaluate the translation? What we are trying to avoid is the sort of argument which would either say that the TT 'Vous vous trouvez au Royaume-Uni' is (simply) a 'bad' translation of 'When you're away from home', or that would try to explain away the change of vision by a Vinay/Darbelnet-type judgement about 'national character', 'way of seeing', 'ways of cutting up the universe', etc. As this is a pragmatic text with a clear aim ('inform' + 'sell'), it should be judged primarily according to whether the aim of the sender is respected in both languages, given the particular nature of the receivers in both LCs and the cultural expectations surrounding a text of this type. Therefore a judgement should be made, for example, about the likely effect of the transformation quoted above whereby 'When you're away from home, there's always someone who would like to hear from you' becomes 'Vous vous trouvez au Royaume-Uni. Vous pensez à ceux que vous aimez. Et vous avez envie de les entendre au téléphone.' And indeed, if one puts the texts in their *socio-economic* context, the change of vision from the American being urged to phone home by 'someone' to the Frenchman in the active role thinking of his loved ones and wishing to hear their voices can be seen to be a very reasonable selling ploy, given the difference in cost of making such a call. In other words, the image cultivated of the American standing in

Related fields of interest 221

London reading the leaflet is that phoning home is something of a problem, being difficult (how does one use English phones?) and expensive. He is being assured that it is easy, 'economical', and expected of him anyway. The Frenchman can allow himself this luxury anyway, as phoning France is not very expensive, thus the desire can come from him.

If such an argument appears rather specious, it is helpful to consider at this stage some of the different forms available in both LC1 and LC2. In a text such as this one, these are not strictly based on the homological construction of the type used by the TO (Chapter 4), but aim at generating a homologically related effect by using diverse linguistic (and semiotic) forms that are predictable within the discourse family in question. In British advertising discourse, very many different linguistic strategies are used, including, for example, direct questions, or the posing of some form of enigma for the reader to solve (the answer often being the product). The use of interrogative forms would, of course, transform the overall effect being produced, and in particular the type of public being aimed at. None the less, considering such forms as 'Away from home? Isn't there someone waiting to hear from you?'/'Isn't it time you called home?' does enable one to situate more accurately what is, after all, a fairly downbeat and conservative text undoubtedly reflecting the choice of Bob Hope on the first page.[10]

As for the LC2, there clearly is nothing stopping the TO from producing an 'equivalent' sentence in French based on the ST which will tell people that someone in France is waiting to hear from them.[11] For example, 'Outre-mer (sur le continent) il y a toujours quelqu'un qui aimerait vous entendre' simulates French advertising discourse fairly accurately. The same holds true for the beginning of the second sentence, which can be based on the same structure as the ST: 'Téléphoner chez soi depuis la Grande Bretagne est facile et économique.' Clearly the variations in both languages can be multiplied almost endlessly.

It is only when one has first considered both ST and TT in their contexts of communication, and *only then* produced other potential LC2 forms that one can begin to evaluate the actual TT in question. The Translation critic is always faced with weighing up different choices and coming to a conclusion about the appositeness of the form chosen. In this particular instance he will be struck by the decision not to maintain certain ST forms, such as 'there's always someone who would like to hear from you', by a certain rewriting or normalizing which the TO has chosen to introduce – 'Guide édité à l'intention de' – and the combination of 'official' LC2 terms and an advertising style (for example, 'You won't need to worry about having coins on you' becomes the very effective 'Pas besoin de pièces'). Given the fairly obvious aims of the sender, and the limits imposed by the type of discourse, it is possible to say that the overall result is quite successful,[12] despite the rather unfavourable impression the bilingual reader receives on first comparing ST and TT. A judgement of this kind should also, finally, encompass the likely role of the Translation Initiator. In such instances, where large economic units are producing messages on which substantial sums of money are dependent, it is reasonable to expect that the role of the TI goes beyond simply ordering a translation. The Translation order would be to produce a very definite effect on an identified target audience. Market studies are frequently carried out for advertising campaigns, including tests on psychological motivations, questions on the impact of different forms, the clarity of the message, and so on. Without having access to such data, the Translation critic is rather limited in the extent of the judgements he can make. It should nevertheless be stressed that at this level, the production of a TT belongs to a very vast network of socio-cultural relations, whose constitutive elements may be given a very uneven weight when the choice of the final message is made. And it is only by opening out to such possibilities that Translation Criticism can begin to come into its own.

Our second example comes from the field of journalism – not the 'instantaneous' news article reporting what has just happened in the world, but the more measured and distanced tone of the leading article. In this case, the ST – ' "Scénario cubain" au Nicaragua?' – comes from *Le Monde*, and the TT – 'Nicaragua: remake of Cuban scenario' – from the *Guardian Weekly* (Appendix 10). It is important once again to bear in mind the communication circuit in which both texts function: on the one hand as an expression of opinion by *Le Monde* to its readers, and on the other as a direct translation in the name of *Le Monde*[13] to the readers of the *Guardian Weekly*. If the sender of both texts is specifically identified as being the same, this is not the case for the readership, apart from the more obvious differences between the two, and in particular the expatriate status of the typical *Guardian Weekly* reader, one might note the somewhat 'up-market' pretensions of the latter.[14] The difference in readership therefore somewhat colours the message being given, moving from the (authoritative) voice of *Le Monde* both in France and seen from France to the expression of what a *foreign* newspaper thinks about a particular (foreign[15]) problem.

The ST is made up of a series of comments on the different measures taken by the Reagan administration and on the fate of Nicaragua and the Nicaraguans. The former is criticized, whereas the latter is given, in

Related fields of interest   223

general, a sympathetic treatment. The article is an attempt to answer the question hinted in the title: whether the effect of American policy will be to forge lasting links between Managua and Moscow, as was the case with Cuba. One is struck by the extensive use both of military vocabulary ('*avertissement, contraindre, essuyer un revers, revenir à la charge, trahir, économie de guerre, mobiliser, dénoncer, fronts de lutte, militaire, embargo, formation militaire, rétorsion, alliés*', etc.) and the reinforcing of the opposition between strength and weakness ('*fléchir, pression, vulnérable, fragile, fatigué, épuisement, au bord de la rupture*'). The choice of such vocabulary both adds to the aggressive image the reader receives of the Reagan administration and heightens one's sympathies for the victims of such a policy.

The first impression received when reading the TT is that the newspaper is not being particularly tender either with the Reagan administration or with the Nicaraguan government. But we begin to see that the relatively clear image presented by *Le Monde* has not just been blurred, but at times blatantly altered, as if the TT were being made to conform to a different vision of world politics, or to fit into another ideological mould. As we shall see below, this is not a constant difference, but a series of patchwork impressions *built up from the translation choices made by the TO*.

The Translation critic cannot help but be struck immediately by two major discrepancies between ST and TT: the title has been radically altered and the fifth paragraph of the ST has not been translated. The title of *Le Monde* article is a question and in fact sets the tone for the whole article, which is seeking to judge both the actions of the Reagan administration and their validity, given their effect on Nicaragua. In the TT, the title has become a statement, thus putting forward an opinion that history is in fact repeating itself. What is more, the TO has chosen – by the addition of 'remake' – to reinforce the idea of 'cinema'. Now this is, of course, one of the connotations produced by the word 'scénario', but such an addition also completely neutralizes the other connotations of the word – which belongs to French economic and political discourse where the 'cinema' connotation has been nearly completely lost.[16] Now this is not in itself a 'bad' translation, but it does go towards forming the overall impression received by the reader which is subsequently reinforced by the choices made further down. We give a small number of examples of some of the more surprising choices (the paragraph numbers refer to the ST):

1 'L'adage' has become 'the old saw', beginning the article with what is generally felt to be a highly negative connotation, absent in the ST.
   The first sentence of the TT ('The old saw about history never

repeating itself, but only stammering, is well known') is surprising anyway on two counts: (a) this proverb is not known at all, let alone 'well known' in a British LC2 environment,[17] and (b) proverbs are not normally introduced at the beginning of an article in the British press.

The addition of 'performance' in the TT reinforces the 'cinema' connotation of the TT title, once again reducing the serious nature of the subject-matter.

'Fléchir la volonté' is translated as 'force ... to cry Uncle': this purely American expression often perplexes British readers, and when they can decode it, they see a negative connotation made up of the combination of a war image and a child's (frivolous) game; the negative and childish connotation replaces the very strong military image which adds to the overall critical vision given of the Reagan administration.

2 'Très important' becomes 'fairly drastic' (adding an element of melodrama).

'De multiples interventions' is translated as 'several (successful) approaches': there is a change of meaning, and the critical stance adopted by the ST is watered down.

3 ' "Tout faire" ' loses its inverted commas, weakening the effect made by the quotation from the government.

'Get back at' is again a very watered down version of the military image used in 'revient à la charge'.

5 This paragraph is the one in which we learn most about the terrible problems and sufferings which are being imposed on the Nicaraguan people because of the war, and by implication because of the attitude of the American administration. We learn of the fatigue of the population who both cannot see the end of their sufferings and who are the victims of corruption among officials; there is, moreover, implied criticism of the Nicaraguan government as well with the ' "jeunes classes" ' carefully put between inverted commas, thus creating a distance between the sender of the article and the label used by the government.

6 'Avec des charges financières et humaines excessives pour sa défense' becomes 'with the heavy drain in money and manpower its defence is imposing': the viewpoint is radically changed, with the negative criticism implied in 'gaspillage' being turned round so that the reader of the TT thinks that defence should not impose such a 'drain'. 'Manpower' is a simple repetition of the same word used in paragraph 4, without the wider denotation and richer connotations of 'humain'.

When one tries to weigh up the different impact of ST and TT, it is tempting to see the work of an ideologically motivated TO, or the imprint of a TI who wants to produce a certain image. This would be closer to the pro-American stance prevalent in Conservative circles in Britain in 1986, rather than the 'North–South' perspective in favour in Paris. But in our view, such a judgement would go beyond the limits which should be set for Translation Criticism, and would turn criticism into something of a parody, where, at worst, the particular obsessions of the critic would take precedence over the objective evidence presented by the TT. In this particular instance, it would be all too easy to overlook some of the biases going in the *opposite* direction – where, for example, the French negative term 'régime' (paragraph 1) is translated by a neutral term ('government'). It is thus essential always to weigh up the total number of factors present in any Translation Situation – and here there are 'external' factors which undoubtedly had their role to play. The *Guardian Weekly* only makes a small amount of space available for its translations from *Le Monde*; it may well be that the 'censoring' of paragraph 5 corresponds to a necessity to cut down the size of the article. Second, the translations are produced relatively rapidly after the publication of the originals, which may affect the overall quality of some of the texts. However, the translation critic would have to point to what is here an *accumulation* of details which undoubtedly do go towards creating a different overall impact on the reader of the TT; his job, in the final analysis, is to give an objective account as possible of the range of choices facing the TO and the image (or images) resulting from the choices made.

The problem faced by the Translation critic in such instances, then, is to come to some general conclusions from what may well prove to be a mosaic of individual details. Although there undoubtedly are some cases of ideological distortion, censorship, manipulation, etc., one is often confined to cataloguing the alternative forms available, and the impact that such forms would have on the TT. When certain distinctive patterns begin to appear, it is often helpful to consider what the role of the Translation Initiator might have been in the particular translation under consideration. 'Marked' translations often belong to particular communication circuits, of whatever kind they may happen to be. But in all types of texts, it must be remembered that certain very strong external constraints[18] may have exercised an excessive influence on the work of the TO, and thus on the final TT produced.

THE 'POSITION' OF THE TRANSLATION CRITIC

We said above that the Translation critic should build himself or herself into the model used for evaluating TTs. One of the main characteristics of Translation Criticism to date has been the apparent omniscience of the translation critic standing 'above' the TT he or she is evaluating. The position we adopt, as will by now be clear, is to take into account the socio-cultural positioning of the critic as one of the factors present in the exercise of Translation Criticism. The advantage of this stance is to bring out the critic's expectations, in order to be able to compare them with the more general criteria of any one communication situation. So, on the one hand we have the particular position of the socio-culturally defined individual, and on the other, the norms governing the discourse family in question, modulated by the particular circumstances to which the text belongs.

If one considers literary texts in general, one can see some of the advantages of our approach. We spoke in some detail about the 'ambivalent' strategies that tend to characterize the literary text (Chapter 5, p. 97). Such strategies explicitly contradict cultural values, and thus produce a permanent tension both within the SR, and, of course, in the reading practices of the receiver, whose 'appropriation' of the SR is being both tested and remodelled. Needless to say, there cannot be one 'correct' interpretation of such a text, let alone a 'correct' translation. But both the TO and the Translation critic can explicate the particular textual functions which they see fit to highlight. Very often an optimum translation will reflect the most recent critical work done on an author, and will bring out the 'discoveries' – or readings – which the critic has brought to people's attention. A new 'reading' of a text can completely modify an approach, calling for a radically new translation. If the Translation critic is particularly concerned with the interpretation of a novel, he or she will clearly be checking whether the TT enables a comparable reading to be made. This may seem to be obvious to the extent that people believe that this is the main role of the Translation critic. But it should be said that evaluation is carried out for many different reasons, and if 'readability' is selected as the main criterion, literary effects will be deemed to be secondary, and, if necessary, to be dispensed with. In other words, the critic may – consciously or unconsciously – situate himself or herself somewhere on the continuum linking LC1- and LC2-biased translations (Chapter 6, p. 128), and thus be, as it were, programmed to applaud certain types of TT and reject others.

Our final example to illustrate the above points is therefore a literary one: we return to Kafka's *Die Verwandlung* (1915) which we referred to in Chapter 6, with some of the published translations.[19] The opening is as follows (the German original on the left, Vialatte's French translation on the right; the English text underneath with the translation in Croat):

Als Gregor Samsa eines Morgens aus unruhigen Träumen erwachte, fand er sich in seinem Bett zu einem ungeheuren Ungeziefer verwandelt.

Un matin, au sortir d'un rêve agité, Grégoire Samsa s'éveilla transformé dans son lit en une véritable vermine.

As Gregor Samsa awoke one morning from uneasy dreams he found himself transformed in his bed into a gigantic insect.

Kad se Gregor Samsa jednog jutra probudio iz nemirnih snova, našao se u svom krevetu pretvoren u golema kukca.

Let us briefly consider some of the different viewpoints the critic might adopt.

1 If euphony and readability are the criteria selected by the critic, he or she will be looking at the necessity of transforming the syntax of the ST, together with certain language effects such as the alliteration and assonance in '*unge*heuren *Unge*ziefer'. The French translation may be thought of as particularly successful, with the transformation of the first clause of the ST into the simpler 'au sortir d'un rêve agité', the normalization of the hero's first name, and the euphonic effect produced by '*véritable vermine*'. The other two TTs follow the ST more closely and read less well – 'gigantic insect' and 'golema kukca' lose the language effect, though each have a minimal element of alliteration.

2 Some critics emphasize the need either to maintain a maximum number of LC1 elements, or, on the contrary, to normalize a text as much as possible. For the former, the change of first name would cancel all the positive LC1 effects of the 'strange'-sounding name and immediately situate the action in a more accessible universe. The English and Croat texts may be judged as good compromises between the strictures of the ST structures and the possibilities offered by the two LCs. Both TTs follow the initial structure ('Als' + 'Gregor Samsa')[20] and place the time adverbial straight after the verb in second position. Needless to say, this is the result of a *choice* by the TO, as in both languages it is possible to restructure the order of the different elements: for example, 'One morning when Gregor Samsa awoke from'; 'Kad se jednog jutra Gregor Samsa probudio'. But if such variations are to be taken into account, the critic would have also to weigh up the different focalizing effects of syntax, which are obviously not the same as one passes from one language to another.[21]

3 If the critic is more concerned about possible interpretations of the text, he will note (a) that 'fand er sich' disappears in French, and the

richness of 'Ungeziefer'[22] is lost in all three TTs. Now the shape of potential criticisms will depend, in the final analysis, on the type of reading he or she gives to the text. If, with Luke (1964), he or she is convinced of the importance of the question whether the hero is objectively transformed into an 'Ungeziefer', or whether it all takes place in his head, then clearly the verb 'fand er sich' must be maintained to give the possibility of the double reading, and, if possible, the multiple possibilities of 'Ungeziefer' at least partially reproduced. With such a reading, the poetic effect produced by 'véritable vermine' – not to mention the distanciation and the element of moral judgement – would be considered totally wrong, as it reinforces the idea of an 'objective' transformation.

This selection of comments gives some idea of the changes of vision that naturally come about with the variations in the positioning of the Translation critic. Once the critic is built into the Translation Criticism model on a systematic basis, the evaluations gain a degree of objectivity otherwise absent.

The three examples taken for the purposes of discussing Translation Criticism were deliberately chosen for their diversity. Translation Criticism can, in our view, be practised at any level and on any type of text. By applying the Variational approach, it is possible both to see the range of possibilities which any ST offers, and to see the conditions in which one TT might take precedence over another. Thus Translation Criticism becomes a motivated judgement which tries to encompass as many different factors as possible to explain both the actual impact of a TT, and to compare this with the aims of the ST and the possibilities present in the LC2 system. As Wilss (1982) has suggested, Translation Criticism needs to become a field of application its own right, and our own aim is to devote considerably further space to it in a further publication.

11 Conclusion

Coming to the end of a research project of this kind, one is always struck by the vast quantity of material that has been left unsaid. Translation Studies is a particularly vast field, being placed, as it is, at the intersection between many different disciplines. Indeed, the translator has to be something of a virtuoso, passing in one day through fields as different as medicine, nuclear physics, agronomy, etc. Small wonder, then, that the theorist has some difficulties in encompassing such wide possibilities into one study.

However, we do feel that we have contributed to the impressive amount of literature already available on the subject. The Variational approach does, we believe, constitute both a new way of thinking about Translation Studies, and a practical way of translating which can benefit students and professionals alike. It is, perhaps, in the practice of translating that a final judgement will be made on this book. One is struck only too often either by the impractical nature of theories of translation, which can never really be applied to 'real' Translation situations, and by the unreliability of 'methods' advocating certain fixed rules for passing from one LC to another. Our aim, of course, has been to bridge the 'gap' between theory and practice in order to produce both a theory which is intellectually as satisfying as possible and in line with the latest research in the field, and a series of identifiable practices which do not constitute 'rules', but a whole approach to translation. It is our belief that the practice of the Variational approach will prove to be most rewarding, especially as it is based on the first comprehensive theoretical approach bringing together both the generation and selection phases in the Translation operation.

As a final word, it should be said that no research project is really ever over. As we have indicated in several places, we are pursuing various aspects of our research, and in particular with relation to the teaching of translation and Translation Criticism. Our hope is to be able to build on the foundation that we have laid, in order to contribute further to the advance of Translation Studies.

Appendix

1 SILLITOE

The following extract concerns two characters, called Frank and John.

Many people in the country had twentieth-century brains and energy but were held under by the eternal sub-strata of hierarchical soil-souled England. They didn't even know how to pull themselves up by their own bootlaces, because they were made of silk and gold-tipped and might snap if yanked too hard. The soul of indoctrinated England was sprayed at the people every night like deadly insecticide, spew created by intellectual semi-demi-masterminds in the form of advertisements and songs of yesteryear, and those were the days, and these you have loved, and scrapbook for this and that, and as you were, and this is how you are as other see us, and O'Grady says, as you were then exactly and nothing more, and you'll never be any different because that is how God made this right-little-tight-little offshore island and you should be proud of its past greatness.

(A. Sillitoe, *A Tree on Fire*. London: Macmillan, 1967, pp. 415–16)

2 ZOLA

Alors, íls se mirent tous les trois à pêcher. De leurs filets étroits, ils fouillaient les trous. Estelle y apportait une passion de femme. Ce fut elle qui prit les premières crevettes, trois grosses crevettes rouges, qui sautaient violemment au fond du filet. Avec de grands cris, elle appela Hector pour qu'il l'aidât, car ces bêtes si vives l'inquiétaient; mais, quand elle vit qu'elles ne bougeaient plus, dès qu'on les tenait par la tête, elle s'aguerrit, les glissa très bien elle-même dans le petit panier qu'elle portait en bandoulière. Parfois, elle amenait tout un paquet d'herbes, et il lui fallait fouiller là-dedans, lorsqu'un bruit sec, un petit bruit d'ailes, l'avertissait qu'il y avait des crevettes au fond. Elle triait les herbes délicatement, les rejetant par minces pincées, peu rassurée devant cet enchevêtrement d'étranges feuilles, gluantes et molles comme des poissons morts. De temps à autre, elle regardait dans son panier, impatiente de le voir se remplir.

'C'est particulier, répétait M. Chabre, je n'en pêche pas une.'
(E. Zola, 'Les Coquillages de M. Chabre', Paris: Gallimard-Pléiade, 1976, p. 884)

3 DELISLE

Rebuilding the Breast

La Reconstitution des seins

After the removal of her left breast because of cancer in 1970, Mrs. Joan Dawson, 54, of New York City, spent the next three years battling depression and a sense of loss. Then she decided to do something about it. Most women in the same situation turn to a psychiatrist. Mrs. Dawson (not her real name) went to her doctor and asked him to rebuild her missing breast. 'I didn't want to be made into a sensational beauty', she explained. 'I just wanted to be restored.' Her surgeon was able to do just that. In two separate operations, he implanted a silicone-filled sac under the skin where the breast had been removed, then reduced the size of the other breast to make it more nearly resemble the new one. The result is not a duplication of Mrs. Dawson's pre-1970 figure, but she is delighted nevertheless. Says she: 'I can finally look at myself in the mirror without wincing.'
(*Time*, 14 April 1975, pp. 71–2)

Une Newyorkaise de 54 ans, Mme Joan Dawson* subit en 1970 l'ablation du sein gauche atteint de cancer et passa les trois années suivantes à lutter contre la dépression et le traumatisme de la mutilation. Un beau jour, elle décide d'agir. La plupart des femmes, en pareil cas, vont s'en remettre à un psychiatre, mais Mme Dawson, elle, retourne chez son médecin pour qu'il lui refasse un sein. 'Je ne voulais pas qu'il me transforme en une beauté sensationelle, a-t-elle expliqué par la suite, mais simplement qu'il élimine les traces de l'amputation'. Elle avait frappé à la bonne porte. Le chirurgien inséra sous la peau un sac de silicone en remplacement de la glande mammaire et, par une seconde intervention, il réduisit les proportions de l'autre sein pour le rendre à peu près de la même grosseur que le sein artificiel. Mme Dawson n'a pas retrouvé sa silhouette d'avant 1970, mais elle est enchantée du résultat. 'Je peux enfin me regarder dans un miroir sans grimacer', a-t-elle confié.

*Ce nom est fictif.

(J. Delisle, *L'Analyse du discours comme méthode de traduction*, University of Ottawa Press, 1984, p. 99. Delisle works on an English text extracted from *Time*, 14 April 1975, given here. We in our turn reconsider that translation in the light of the original English text.)

4 ALBEE

MARTHA: SCREW YOU!
[*Simultaneously with* MARTHA'S *last remark,* GEORGE *flings open the front door.* HONEY *and* NICK *are framed in the entrance. There is a brief silence, then* . . .]

GEORGE: [*ostensibly a pleased recognition of* HONEY *and* NICK, *but really satisfaction at having* MARTHA'S *explosion overheard*]: Ahhhhhhhhh!

MARTHA: [*a little too loud . . . to cover*]: Hi! Hi, there . . . c'mon in!

HONEY and NICK [*ad lib*]: Hello, here we are . . . hi . . . [*etc.*]

GEORGE [*very matter-of-factly*]: You must be our little guests.

MARTHA: Ha, ha, ha, HA: Just ignore old sour-puss over there. C'mon in, kids . . . give your coats and stuff to sour-puss.

NICK [*without expression*]: Well, now perhaps we shouldn't have come . . .

HONEY: Yes . . . it *is* late, and . . .

MARTHA: Late! Are you kidding? Throw your stuff down anywhere and c'mon in.

GEORGE [*vaguely . . . walking away*]: Anywhere . . . furniture, floor . . . doesn't make any difference around this place.

NICK [*to* HONEY]: I told you we shouldn't have come.

MARTHA [*stentorian*]: I said c'mon in! Now c'mon!

HONEY [*giggling a little as she and* NICK *advance*]: Hee, hee, hee, hee.

GEORGE [*imitating* HONEY *giggle*]: Hee, hee, hee, hee.

MARTHA [*swinging on* GEORGE]: Look, muckmouth . . . you can cut that out!

GEORGE [*innocent and hurt*]: Martha! [*To* HONEY *and* NICK] Martha's a devil with language; she really is.

MARTHA: Hey, kids . . . sit down.

HONEY [*as she sits*]: Oh, isn't this lovely!

NICK [*perfunctorily*]: Yes indeed . . . very handsome.

MARTHA: Well, thanks.

NICK [*indicating the abstract painting*]: Who . . . who did the . . .

MARTHA: Oh, that's by . . .
GEORGE: . . . some Greek with a moustache Martha attacked one night in . . .
HONEY [*to save the situation*]: Oh, ho, ho, ho, HO.
NICK: It's got a . . . a . . .
GEORGE: A quiet intensity?
NICK: Well, no . . . a . . .
GEORGE: Oh. [*Pause*] Well, then, a certain noisy relaxed quality, maybe?
NICK [*knows what GEORGE is doing, but stays grimly, coolly polite*]: No. What I meant was . . .
GEORGE: How about . . . uh . . . a quietly noisy relaxed intensity.
HONEY: Dear! You're being joshed.
NICK [*cold*]: I'm aware of that.
[*A brief, awkward silence.*]
GEORGE [*truly*]: I *am* sorry.

[*NICK nods condescending forgiveness.*]

GEORGE: What it is, actually is, it's a pictorial representation of the order of Martha's mind.
MARTHA: Ha, ha, ha, HA! Make the kids a drink, George. What do you want kids? What do you want to drink, huh?
NICK: Honey? What would you like?
HONEY: I don't know, dear . . . . A little brandy, maybe. 'Never mix – never worry'. [*She giggles.*]
GEORGE: Brandy? Just brandy? Simple; simple. [*Moves to the portable bar.*] What about you . . . uh . . . .
NICK: Bourbon on the rocks, if you don't mind.
GEORGE [*as he makes the drinks*]: Mind? No, I don't mind. I don't think I mind. Martha? Rubbing alcohol for you?
MARTHA: Sure. Never mix – never worry.
(E. Albee, *Who's Afraid of Virginia Woolf?* Harmondsworth: Penguin Books, 1965, pp. 19–21)

5 LAWRENCE

And his shadow on the border of the pond was watching for a few moments, then he stooped and groped on the ground. Then again there was a burst of sound, and a burst of brilliant light, the moon had exploded on the water, and was flying asunder in flakes of white and dangerous fire. Rapidly, like white birds, the fires all broken rose across the pond, fleeing in clamorous confusion, battling with the flock of dark waves that were forcing their way in. The furthest waves of light, fleeing out, seemed to be clamouring against the shore for escape, the waves of darkness came in heavily, running under towards the centre. But at the centre, the heart of all, was still a vivid, incandescent quivering of a white moon not quite destroyed, a white body of fire writhing and striving and not even now broken open, not yet violated. It seemed to be drawing itself together with strange, violent pangs, in blind effort. It was getting stronger, it was reasserting itself, the inviolable moon. And the rays were hastening in thin lines of light, to return to the strengthened moon, that shook upon the water in triumphant reassumption.

(D. H. Lawrence, *Women in Love*, p. 278)

6 KIWI

Kiwi in the Catbird Seat

In the era of OPEC, non-drivers come into their own
When the bloom was on the roads, the American who would not – or could not – drive a car was dismissed as a sponger or a dimwit, doomed to a life of dependence on alien wheels and, quite likely, celibacy. The non-driver was a *rara Avis* (though he could not rent one), akin to the kiwi, a bird that cannot fly. In a country that relies so heavily on the auto for its bread and butter and most of its honey, he was seen and often scorned as a kind of self-decreed cripple.

Now, however, in an era when excessive gasoline consumption has become offensive to nostril, pocketbook and national pride, automotive abstinence has become a virtue. The kiwi is in the catbird seat. The man or woman who gets to work by bicycle or shanks' mare trails clouds of self-esteem as palpable as the carbon dioxide fumes he has forsworn. Whether he refuses to buy a car at today's prices or simply will not or cannot take the wheel, he can be said to have heeded official pleas to share the ride (though it is someone else who does the actual sharing). Even friends and neighbors, who consent to pick up his groceries, cleaning and the Sunday paper, can be made to feel that they too are camshafting egregious OPEC.

(*Time*, 26 January 1981)

7 LUFTHANSA

We just can't say "cheese!".

Lufthansa

8 BAILLARGUES

'Baillargues devient une véritable ville périphérique, le contraire d'une ville-dortoir.' André Noy, Conseiller Municipal délégué aux affaires économiques est aussi représentant de Baillargues au District. Avec l'équipe municipale, il s'appuie sur un développement harmonieux de la ville. Un travail constant basé sur des paramètres solides: équipements structurants, activités socio-culturelles, sportives. Bien que très forte, la croissance est savamment maîtrisée. En dix ans, le nombre d'habitants a plus que doublé, pour frôler maintenant les 4.000. La démographie témoigne du phénomène d'attraction que joue la ville. Baillargues reste un village, un espace de vie sans cesse alimenté par de nouvelles réalisations: le moderne et l'ancien réconciliés, pour utiliser l'espace au mieux de ses potentialités. Sur le terrain, cette volonté se traduit par une alliance harmonieuse de bâtiments neufs et anciens. L'église, classée, affiche sereinement neuf siècles d'existence. Le centre est une épine dorsale dans le plus pur style patrimoine vivant. Les façades ravalées se dressent au-dessus d'une ruelle rêveuse menant vers une antique porte de pierre (la 'Vieille Porte'). Les voisins se parlent de fenêtre à fenêtre. Quelques jets de boules plus loin, la vie active reprend ses droits. Avec délicatesse. Les arbres ouvrent des parenthèses sur des résidences typiques, égrenées au détour de placettes. La commune se préoccupe aussi de la construction d'une résidence 3e âge. 'Les Pins Bessons', seront équipés d'une soixantaine de lits, et d'un secteur médicalisé. Première pierre dans un avenir tout proche. Les bancs, symboles d'une vivante humanité, accueillent des brochettes d'hommes en casquette et d'enfants joueurs. Un tiers de la population a moins de 20 ans.

(*Puissance* 15, District de Montpellier)

9 *GUARDIAN*

Mystery dash of Ivan the Terrified
by Philip Jordan

A man who scrambled out of the window of a Soviet-owned house in central London and then ran screaming along balconies in front of adjoining houses yelling 'They are trying to kill me. Help me. I have information, get the police!' was believed to be inside the Soviet Embassy later.

The man is understood to be Dr Guennadij Petrov, a linguist studying at the Institute of Linguistics, at University College, London. He had been in Britain since last September, one of about 30 Soviet students involved in a British Council exchange scheme. He is about 35 and married, with two daughters.

The man burst out of the first floor window of 10 Earls Terrace in Kensington High Street at 9.15 on Thursday morning, on to a wrought-iron balcony.

Residents in the terrace threw open doors and windows as the man screamed dementedly 'Help me! Help me! They are trying to kill me!' and watched as he began to scramble from balcony to balcony along the fronts of the houses towards a wall at the end.

At one point, as startled residents looked on, he smashed a pane of glass in a window, and with blood over both hands, moved on, still shouting at the top of his voice.

Down below, four or five other men emerged from the Russian-owned house – one of three in the terrace used by junior embassy staff – and began shouting in Russian to the man to come down.

But, said Mr Michael Spencer North, a resident who saw the whole incident, the man reached the end of the terrace shouting 'The Soviet ambassador will get me,' or, possibly 'The Soviet ambassador is out to get me,' jumped on to a 12-foot wall and then into a side street.

From there he ran out in to Kensington High Street and ran off in the direction of the Soviet Embassy in Kensington Palace Gardens over a mile away. Mr Spencer North said the man was pursued for part of the way by some of the Russians.

Scotland Yard said later that the man had actually reached the Soviet Embassy. But the police were in no way involved in the incident, the spokesman said. 'As far as we are concerned it was a case of a Russian student who was unwell and went voluntarily to his embassy for help.'

Mr Spencer North said the Russians who had been pursuing the man questioned him closely about what he had told the police. 'But I said it was none of their business. They kept telling me that he was mad or that he was drunk. They were anxious to play down the whole operation.' He added: 'He was hysterical and distraught but he was not drunk.'

Earls Terrace is a period terrace of about 20 houses subdivided into flats, many of them let off to actors and actresses. The last house in the row, where the man jumped into the street, is occupied by actor Rowland Davies, who said: 'The man jumped from balcony to balcony, a gap of about 12ins between each, and then down on to the wall and into the street. The man in the street said he was mad and demented.'

A woman neighbour said: 'The man in the street was very well dressed, and so I thought, well, there can't be anything really wrong. The man on the balcony shouted "I am going to jump" and the man below shouted

"You are mad, you are crazy" then he disappeared. The woman newspaper seller outside the Odeon Cinema told me she saw him running past with blood on his hands.'

(*Guardian*, 24 April 1977)

10 *LE MONDE/GUARDIAN WEEKLY*

'Scénario cubain' au Nicaragua?

L'histoire ne se répète jamais, elle bégaie, l'adage est bien connu. A un quart de siècle de distance, il semble pourtant que le 'scénario cubain' soit sur le point de se renouveler au Nicaragua. L'embargo commercial total décrété le mercredi 1er mai par le gouvernement Reagan contre le régime de Managua n'est sans doute pas la première mesure de rétorsion économique adoptée par les Etats-Unis pour tenter de fléchir la volonté des dirigeants sandinistes. Mais c'est la plus spectaculaire.

La 'pression' économique américaine a commencé en 1983 avec une très importante réduction du quota d'importation de sucre nicaraguayen. Elle s'est poursuivie avec de multiples interventions de Washington auprès des différents organismes de financement internationaux, en particulier la Banque interaméricaine de développement, pour bloquer, avec succès, des demandes de crédits présentées par Managua. Mais bien qu'ils aient décru avec régularité depuis quatre ans, les échanges commerciaux entre les Etats-Unis et le Nicaragua sont restés importants. L'Amérique du Nord demeure malgré tout, et en dépit de la guerre 'non déclarée', entre les deux pays, le premier client et le premier fournisseur du Nicaragua sandiniste.

L'embargo commercial a d'abord valeur d'avertissement. Il illustre la très ferme volonté de l'administration Reagan de 'tout faire' pour contraindre les sandinistes à revenir sur la 'ligne de départ' de 1979 et à respecter réellement des principes qu'ils affirment de leur côté ne pas avoir trahis: économie mixte, pluralisme politique, non-alignement. M. Reagan, qui a essuyé un revers au Congrès en n'obtenant pas les 14 millions de dollars destinés à aider les organisations antisandinistes armées, revient à la charge sur un terrain où les dirigeants de Managua sont particulièrement vulnérables.

Les actions de la Contra ont obligé le Nicaragua à adopter une économie 'de guerre'. La défense absorbe officiellement plus du quart du budget et mobilise des énergies, des moyens et des hommes qui seraient plus utiles au développement d'une petite nation fragile sous-développée, sans véritables ressources et frappée comme ses voisins par la récession mondiale.

Le gouvernement de Managua a dû décréter à la fin de mars de très importantes hausses de prix des produits de première nécessité, aggravant ainsi la grogne croissante d'une population fatiguée qui ne voit pas le bout du tunnel, dénonce la corruption de certains dirigeants et résiste, plus ou moins passivement, aux sévères mesures de mobilisation des 'jeunes classes' envoyées sur les fronts de lutte contre la Contra sans une formation militaire suffisante.

Avec des charges financières et humaines excessives pour sa défense, une dette extérieure de l'ordre de 4 milliards de dollars, des difficultés accrues pour son approvisionnement en pétrole en raison des réticences du Mexique, l'épuisement de ses réserves de devises, l'économie nicaraguayenne, au bord de la rupture, va devoir se tourner plus encore vers les pays de l'Est pour tenter de trouver une issue.

La décision de Etats-Unis intervient au lendemain du troisième voyage à Moscou de M. Daniel Ortega, président du Nicaragua. L'URSS a promis une assistance 'économique et diplomatique' importante à Managua, sans cependant s'engager dans le domaine militaire. Dans les années 60, les mesures de rétorsion économique à l'égard de Cuba ont sans doute contribué à pousser La Havane dans les bras de Moscou. Mêmes causes, mêmes effets? Les conseillers de M. Reagan ont déjà répondu. Ils estiment que, de toute manière, les sandinistes sont déjà des alliés des Soviétiques.

(*Le Monde*, 24 April 1986)

Nicaragua: remake of Cuban scenario

The old saw about history never repeating itself, but only stammering, is well known. Yet, a quarter of a century later, the 'Cuban scenario' seems set for a repeat performance in Nicaragua. The total trade embargo imposed on May 1 by the Reagan administration on the Managua government is certainly not the first measure of economic retaliation taken by the United States in a bid to force the Sandinista leaders to cry Uncle. But it is the most spectacular.

The economic pressure began in 1983 with fairly drastic reduction of US imports of Nicaraguan sugar. It was followed up by several successful approaches by the US to various international financing bodies, in particular the Interamerican Development Bank, to reject Nicaraguan requests for credits. Though US–Nicaraguan trade has been declining regularly for the past four years, it has nevertheless remained substantial. Despite the 'undeclared war' between the two countries, North America is still Nicaragua's first client and first supplier.

The trade embargo is primarily meant as a warning. It shows the Reagan administration's very firm determination to do everything possible to force the Sandinistas to go back to the 1979 'starting point' and genuinely abide by the priniciples they for their part claim they have never repudiated – a mixed economy, political plurality, non-alignment. President Reagan, who suffered a defeat when the Congress refused to give him the $14 million he sought for helping armed anti-Sandinista organisations, has got back at Nicaragua in an area where its leaders are especially vulnerable.

The Contras' activities have forced Nicaragua to adopt a war economy. Officially, defence is using up more than a quarter of the budget and mobilising energies, resources and manpower that would be more useful for development in a fragile, underdeveloped nation without any real natural wealth and, like its neighbours, hit by the world recession.

With the heavy drain in money and manpower its defence is imposing, a foreign debt in the neighbourhood of $4 billion, increasing problems in obtaining oil supplies because of Mexican reluctance and exhausted foreign currency reserves, the Nicaraguan economy is on the point of collapse. The country will now have to rely increasingly on East European countries to try to find a way out of its predicament.

The United States' decision came on the heels of the third visit to Moscow made by the Nicaraguan President, Daniel Ortega. The USSR has promised substantial 'economic and diplomatic' aid to Managua, but has said nothing about any military commitment. The measures of economic retaliation taken in the '60s against Cuba no doubt helped to push that country into Moscow's arms. Will the same causes have the same effects? Reagan's advisers have already answered. They consider that in any case, the Sandinistas are already the Soviet Union's allies.

(*Guardian Weekly*, 3 May 1986)

Notes

1 Introduction

1 Robert Larose's book, *Théories contemporaines de la traduction* (1987), is a mine of information and comments concerning the more recent developments in TS.
2 'On ne peut, certes, pas douter de l'existence de la traduction. Mais ce qui est plus douteux, c'est son existence comme domaine défini d'avance et susceptible de recevoir un traitement scientifique unique. Plus probable est que cet objet mal défini relève de plusieurs approches scientifiques à la fois' (Pergnier, 1978: 4–5).
3 One could quote as representative of this style of approach among the articles collected in R. A. Brower, *On Translation* (1966) Dudley Fitts, 'The Poetic Nuance' and Renato Poggioli, 'The Added Artificer'.
4 'qu'on le veuille ou non, toute traduction ... est déjà une "pensée" consciente ou inconsciente sur la traduction et s'inscrit dans une option existante, quand elle n'inaugure pas l'option qu'elle met en place' (Oseki-Dépré, 1985: 72).
5 A very loose designation referring to professors sharing the theoretical conceptions underpinning the teaching at the École Supérieure d'Interprétariat et de Traduction of Paris: M. Lederer, D. Séleskovitch, F. Herbulot, but also M. Delisle and M. Pergnier.
6 'Le linguiste ne peut réfléchir que sur la façon dont on traduit, autrement dit sur le produit fini.... Or les textes traduits font apparaître des récurrences qui ne peuvent être arbitraires' (Guillemin-Flescher, 1986: 59).
7 'des tendances assez nettes se dégagent: une faible détermination en français, les marques de repérage étant souvent floues et mêmes absentes; une forte détermination en anglais, grâce à un réseau de repérage très serré' (Guillemin-Flescher, 1981: 153).
8 Il ne s'agit donc pas de simples variantes stylistiques mais, plus fondamentalement, de la stratégie propre à chaque langue dans l'orientation de l'énoncé dans son ensemble. C'est le respect des schémas dominants à ce niveau, avant même le détail des choix lexicaux ou grammaticaux, qui donne à une traduction un caractère authentique dans la langue d'arrivée' (H. Chuquet and M. Paillard, 1987: 135).
9 Une traduction qui se veut uniquement linguistique est une traduction culturelle que se méconnaît comme telle' (Meschonnic, 1972: 52).

2 The nature of translation

1 More about this fundamental concept and about the reasons for delaying its introduction later in this chapter. For the immediate purpose of our discussion, this term will be understood to refer to the set of spontaneous ideas associated by most people with the basic facts of their experience.
2 The necessity of translation can also correspond in the case of the Amazons and the Scythians in Herodotus' 'Histories' to a difference between the genders and the preconceived roles associated with them. (We owe this interesting sidelight to Nancy Blake.)
3 More information on the subject can be found in Norton (1984), and in Kelly (1979), for a historical overview.
4 Quoted in Cary (1963: 51).
5 Poggioli, 'The Added Artificer', in Brower (1966: 137–47).
6 Pêcheux and Fuchs (1975: 20).
7 The word 'appropriation' refers simultaneously to a reconfirmation of the SR and its utilization for specific purposes.
8 The concept 'Language Culture' is adapted from one of the dualist notions like 'forme/sens' or 'lecture/écriture' introduced by Meschonnic (1973: 349) as 'langue–culture–histoire'.
9 'Il y aurait quelque idéalisme à penser que la traduction puisse se tenir en équilibre à la limite des systèmes socio-culturels, dans un espace neutre miraculeusement libéré par le double reflux des irréductibles spécificités. Sans doute se constitue-t-elle au contraire à partir de la disjonction de ces systèmes, exhibant, plutôt que des identités, le travail profond de la différence' (Nemer, 1975: 213–14).
10 'notre rapport au sens passe par l'altérité . . . . Ou bien nous signifions avec les autres, ou bien ce n'est pas du sens que nous produisons' (F. Jacques, 1985: 585).
11 'Le caractère préconscient de l'activité paraphrastique serait en oeuvre dans tout processus énonciatif, c'est-à-dire dans tout processus de production et de reconnaissance de séquences linguistiques par des énonciateurs. Nous pensons en effet que pour produire une séquence, l'énonciateur se réfère doublement à la dimension paradigmatique métalinguistique: d'abord pour sélectionner un domaine sémantique (au niveau de l'énoncé entier . . . la sélection suppose l'élimination de tout ce qui est "autre" . . .) , puis sélectionner, à l'intérieur de ce domaine, un sous-domaine (ce qui suppose l'élimination de tout ce qui est "semblable" . . .). Inversement, pour reconnaître une séquence, le sujet remonte de cette séquence à la classe des possibles similaires exclus, et à la classe des possibles différents exclus' . . . (Fuchs, 1982: 172).
12 'Bien plus, la traduction est un cas remarquable de la communication, c'est une *méta-communication*, une communication au second degré qui, d'une langue à l'autre, porte sur la communication au premier degré qu'elle prend pour objet. C'est-à-dire que la traduction procède à une *objectivation* de la communication en langue-source, qu'elle globalise pour en faire le contenu du message qu'elle a à traduire en langue-cible' (Ladmiral, 1979: 144).

3 Building a theory of translation

1 '[On en vient à l'idée que] l'universalité est moins du côté des

noèmes . . . que dans les opérations qui permettent de les isoler' (R. Martin, 1983: 87). For the term *noème* see R. Martin's (1983: 84) 'primitif sémantique' (undefined semantic root).
2 The development of the Peircian theory of signs would take us too far away from our main objective. Two very helpful shortcuts could be recommended: C. S. Peirce's 'Letters to Lady Welby' (1966: VIII, Ch. 8) and Gérard Deledalle, *Théorie et pratique du signe* (1979).
3 'La signification n'est donc que cette transposition d'un niveau de langage dans un autre, d'un langage dans un langage différent et le sens n'est que cette possibilité de transcodage' (Greimas cited by Fuchs, 1982: p. 77).

4 Interlinguistic homologies

1 The passages reproduced in the Appendix will be referred to by using either the author's name or the title of the text: i.e. Zola, Sillitoe, Lawrence, Kiwi, Albee, Delisle, and Lufthansa. Most of the illustrative material used in Chapters 4 and 5 are extracted from these texts. It is hoped that the inconvenience caused by dispersed referencing will be compensated for by the cumulativeness of our definition of translation options building up from chapter to chapter into fully documented translated texts.
2 'Our ordinary notion of sameness of meaning is such that rival teams of linguists, applying this notion to a given pair of languages but deliberately disregarding all constraints of simplicity and practicality, could produce rival manuals of sentence translation which fitted all the physically statable evidence (or facts) yet were mutually incompatible' (Quine, 1977: 193).
3 See J. Martin (1985a: 4).
4 We will adopt for the purpose of this concluding example the convention of using **bold type** for the English ST and underlined characters for the French suggested renderings.

5 Extrapropositional relationships in homologon definition

1 We make a distinction between *referentiation* (see Chapter 4, p. 75) which deals with the linguistic markers indicating the predication's relationship with the Situation of Communication, and *referencing* which describes the semiotic relationship of a text to outside determinants: co-textual, situational, and intertextual.
2 To cite a few among the most influential: de Beaugrande and Dressler (1981); Maingueneau (1984); Vignaux (1976); Van Dijk (1972).
3 The following development is to be considered as a condensed version adapted to translation problems of a more extended study of textual strategies published by J. Martin (1985: 217–47).

6 The Cultural Equation

1 The terminology is used by Ladmiral (1979).
2 Our approach invalidates the rather gross distinctions between translator-artists and mercenary translators – aesthetic and pecuniary considerations are just two of very many conditions which we explore below.
3 The most stressing one is often the short time available to do the work.

4 This point will be developed in some detail in Chapter 8.
5 See, for example, Chuquet and Paillard (1987: 67–70).
6 There is evidence that younger people in France are no longer aware of the cultural event referred to, and that the prime connotation for them is simply 'something positive', without them being able to say what. The utterance is undoubtedly doomed to disappearance as memory of the virtually dead cultural reality fades.
7 'Ovaj tjedan klat će svinju.'
8 Where one parent speaks each language, the associations developed with the mother tongue are different from those developed with the father tongue; when the home language is different from the school language, the child grows up in two parallel linguistic universes which in many fields do not touch (thus there will be one language for doing mathematical calculations, etc.).
9 Working on the assumption that most translators prefer going towards their mother tongues (which in certain technical fields is not necessarily the case).
10 Norms are a good case in point. In France, they are controlled by an official body (the AFNOR) which lays down the terminology that must be used in certain fields. In computing, a VDU is, curiously enough, 'la visu' – a norm most translators ignore unless, precisely, translating for an official government organization.
11 See Chapter 2, p. 23.
12 See p. 96.
13 This is one of the arguments advanced by Meschonnic – see page 128, below.
14 See the translators' postface to the new French translation of *Die Verwandlung*, cited below, page 245, note 33.
15 That is not to say that simply because a certain strategy is widely used in one language, the translator will necessarily opt for that strategy; but it will undoubtedly be an important factor to be weighed up when deciding between the different paraphrastic texts he or she produces.
16 The problem for the TO is to produce an advertisement which corresponds to the most recent 'style' used by advertisers – advertisements in France tend to follow Anglo-Saxon models, and thus ambivalent strategies are now becoming more and more common.
17 For example, an advertisement for the Nationwide Building Society catches the eye with a very prominent picture (taking up about 80 per cent of the page) of a young woman wearing underwear, making herself up and about to put on an expensive dress, who is quoted saying 'I'm Virgo ... I suppose I'm a perfectionist.' A very complex series of codes are being played, delaying the eye which will eventually come down to the bottom of the page to discover the Nationwide name and slogan ('It pays to decide Nationwide'). On the left is a long text 'spoken' by the young woman explaining what a perfectionist she is, and why she has chosen this particular building society. The whole point of the advertisement is that there is no apparent identification possible between the dominant semiotic code – the beautiful woman – and the building society. The value is put forward as primordial, leading the reader finally to make the inference: if perfectionists choose Nationwide, it is the best building society.

18 Our thanks to Tony Weymouth for his research here.
19 This analysis does not take into account strategies based on implication as in 'Sainsbury's price' – i.e. a good price:quality ratio (relying, of course, on the image nurtured by long advertising campaigns).
20 Though it is often considered as if it was, as in the case of literature studied *in translation* at university level, as Susan Bassnett-McGuire (1980) has pointed out.
21 People have considered Sanskrit texts to be untranslatable (or only translatable when accompanied by a commentary) because the very vibration of the word corresponds to the vibration or essence of the object in extralinguistic reality. See, for example Lama Anagarika Govinda, (1960); C. G. Jung's preface to Evans-Wentz (1954); the preface to the *Śiva Sutras* (Jaideva Singh 1979).
22 One is accustomed always to thinking in terms of loss – this is again an ideologically biased argument which hides the fact that TTs are often based on terms which are equally 'rich', but with different denotations and/or connotations. So the 'loss' is compensated for by a 'gain' in the richness of the particular word in LC2.
23 The problem here is to define the knowledge of the readership – one common response to this translation is the identification of such connotations as 'fee-paying' and 'elitist', which tends to prove that such a TT would work quite well for the more educated public.
24 One should question the widely spread assumption that notes = translator's failure – see Nida (1964: 165).
25 Generalization is impossible here, as all examples can be balanced by counterexamples – if political systems in Western Europe can be described as 'democratic', the structures used to implement 'democracy' are radically different, as are the significations of the labels designating political parties ('liberal' is not the same as 'libéral'), etc.
26 See Titone, (1974: pp. 266ff.) for a discussion of linguistic and cultural problems in Yugoslavia; for a description of the political and economic systems and the social structure, see McFarlane, (1988).
27 See, for example, Bassnet-McGuire's illuminating remarks on 'butter' (1980: 18f.).
28 One might expect a series of modalities in English ('May I first of all say ..' ('Ecoutez'), 'We simply *cannot* let them get away with it' ('Il faut prendre ...')).
29 See Newmark (1981: 22, 38f.); the terminology, however, is by no means standard – Meschonnic (1973) speaks of 'annexing' in relation to TL-influenced texts.
30 See Wilss (1982: 48).
31 See on this point Berman (1984: 17f.).
32 French translation by A. Vialatte, *La Métamorphose*, Gallimard, Paris, 1955.
33 A comparison with the most recent translation by Brigitte Vergne-Cain and Gérard Rudent (1989) shows this quite clearly – the passages highlighted above are translated as follows: 'ils avaient à cette heure tant à faire avec les soucis du moment qu'ils en avaient perdu toute faculté de penser à la suite. Mais Gregor, lui, en était capable.' 'Si seulement la sœur avait été là! Elle était avisée, elle avait déjà versé des larmes quand Gregor gisait immobile sur le dos.' '. . . c'était à Gregor lui-même d'agir.'

34 See our section on Translation Criticism (Chapter 10, pp. 216–28).
35 Readers are probably aware of the endless debate in France on this subject, where the 'threat' to the 'purity' of the French language is continually evoked.
36 Although one does not normally translate geographical names, the problem has to be posed when (in this case) the street names chosen have echoes within the play (i.e. Bolsover Street, p. 62)
37 See page 18. The fact that Spooner vigorously and periphrastically denies 'resting (his) peep on sexual conjugations' makes one believe just the opposite.
38 If we take this description at face value.
39 The last meeting between Hirst and Spooner was – according to Hirst in Act 2, and if we are to believe him – in the pavilion at Lord's during a Test Match. More importantly, we should note that the four characters are named after famous cricketers, and that cricket is part of the upper-middle- or upper-class elitist atmosphere evoked during the second act, with the recollection of their student days at Oxford.
40 One of our criticisms of the texts published in French and Serbo-Croat is that they are not consistent in their translation strategies.
41 For the latter language, it was necessary to find a sport practised by the aristocracy before Tito came to power, which also 'works' in a British context. In both cases, it would be possible to assimilate the woman to the horse being ridden, with a choice of more obvious sexual images, or more subtle ambiguities, which are, in our view, more appropriate for Pinter's text ('google', for example can be assimilated to deceive/betray).
42 This point is developed in some detail in Chapter 8, under the title of 'Existing translations'.
43 Which one does not find in the *Grand Larousse*, for example.
44 Plays constitute a particularly rich material for the translator, as one can envisage using all the different codes that a play calls on (see, for example, Elam, 1980).
45 Translated by Eric Kahane, Paris: Gallimard, 1979.
46 Translated by Antun Soljan, Belgrade, Nolit, 1982.
47 In English: 'How pretty she was, how svelte/easy-going/loose (unfaithful), how faithful/reliable. Tell me how handy she was to load (be stuffed), how smoothly she was cocked/fucked or loudly fired (came?), whether she was responsive to (under) the finger, how wonderful her front sights/whims were, how easy it was to tighten her trigger/how easily she turned you on, if she could be used in all weathers/any old how. In other words did she recoil/turn people on, did she get blown off course/seduce (become pregnant)?

7 The Translation Operator as a Cultural Operator

1 Few theorists, for obvious reasons, have undertaken extensive descriptions of the work of the TO; for a summary of some of the models proposed, see the excellent first chapters of Garnier (1985) and also the general remarks concerning the back-and-forth movement between cultures described by Pergnier (1978).
2 People questioned about 'what happens' when they read a foreign text tend to give rather hazy answers. Some claim to read without any (conscious)

translation, others to translate the difficult words and phrases, still others to translate everything immediately. There does, however, seem to be general agreement that the perspective of future translation radically alters the reading strategy and *immediately highlights the potential translation problems*.

3   This agrees with Bassnett-McGuire's view (1980: 33) when she says, commenting on Catford's discussion of the translation of 'democracy', 'The problem here is that the reader will have a concept of the term based on his or her own cultural context, and will apply that particularized view accordingly'. Also quoted by Larose (1987: 51ff.).

4   We are not seeking to imply here that there is just *one* reading strategy employed by all LC1 readers; but even if one argues that there are as many strategies as there are readers, the strategies are still normally culture-bound, which is the essential difference we are stressing here.

5   Our thanks to Heidi Rumble for her comments on LC2 readers.

6   It comes from a free newspaper distributed by the 'District' of Montpellier – i.e. depending on the town council, and thus aiming to produce a positive image of the different activities of the council. The people we questioned showed little interest in reading such articles.

7   These are analysed below.

8   It could, in fact, be assimilated to a type of propaganda, to the news-sheet of a political party, or more generally to advertising discourse and analogical strategies. Our choice of tourist discourse was motivated by the fact that one can identify a large number of shared characteristics, and notably that of bringing out the positive side of a place.

9   One recognizes here the problem of the use of animate/inanimate verbs in the two languages. Readers should consult Guillemin-Flescher (1981: 201ff.) for a detailed discussion of this point, added to which we would underline the necessity of considering the different characteristics of different discourse families.

10 That is, articles dealing with projects of construction or urban development for 'équipements structurants', general newspaper discourse for 'démographie', political discourse for 'la vie active'.

11 LC1 readers are far from unanimous about the meaning of certain expressions – 'la vie active' is a case in point, where some argue that it refers to professional activities, others that it is the whole context of village activities (the shops, cafés, children playing, etc.).

12 The word 'volonté' is a good example of the problem of frequency. In French it decorates and predominates in very many types of discourse, going from political via advertising to technical styles; English dictionary equivalents ('will', 'willpower') are, however, much more restricted.

13 The contrast is very noticeable as young people in France emerge from the secondary education system. Sport is thought to have such a positive image that in interviews for the (private) schools of commerce, candidates inevitably speak of their great interest and participation in sporting activities – so much so, that occasionally a crest-fallen and guilt-laden future student will confess: 'I'm sorry, but I don't practise [*sic*] sport'!

14 This very general statement is meant to exclude such 'professionals' as university lecturers, literary critics, etc.

15 Golding (1954: 211).

16 Translated by L. Tranec, *Sa Majesté des Mouches*, Paris: Gallimard, 1956, p. 233.
17 Ladmiral (1979, x). See also his most interesting discussion of the translations (into French) of the German *naturwüchsig* in the work of Habermas (Ladmiral 1979: 217ff.).
18 See J. Martin (1985b: 4).
19 See the very penetrating analyses of Mouillaud and Tétu (1989).
20 *Methods and Sources* (1979: 27ff.). The categories adopted by the authors have been used below.
21 See Mouillaud and Tétu (1989: 153ff.) for a development of this theme. One can also look at the way in which British newspapers present themselves ('The *Sun* brings you all the news').
22 *Her Majesty's Guide* (HMSO, 1988).
23 Our thanks to Philippe Maruéjol for this example and suggestions made.
24 None of the readers who were questioned noticed this detail, and replied to the question 'Where is Dr Petrov?' by 'In the Soviet Embassy.'
25 ' "Scénario cubain" au Nicaragua?'/'Nicaragua: remake of Cuban scenario'.
26 In their analysis of cables from press agencies, Mouillaud and Tétu conclude (1989: 41): 'in a completely systematic way, the "political" domain dominates overwhelmingly all the other types of information, and in particular economic information which only come in second position . . . . After political and economic news, there is "sensational" news (political violence, crimes and catastrophes) which make up between 20 and 25 per cent of all the news in all the wires. The rest is taken up by information of every sort, where sport however regularly has an important place.'
27 *Methods and Sources*, pp. 45–7.
28 See the leader published in *Le Monde* ('La "main tendue" de M. Gorbachev', April 20/1 1986), translated in the *Guardian Weekly* as 'Gorbachev's message for Europeans', with both a different page set-up, and more importantly, a caricature of (Mr) Gorbachev which was hardly flattering.
29 If these references sound a little absurd to English readers who are not very familiar with the French press, it should be pointed out that biographical details are often used in France to ring the changes in anaphorical reference. How many readers of the French press do not know that François Léotard had a vocation to be a monk, or that Jacques Delors is a Christian, and this through anaphoric reference?
30 A 'who clause' appears more natural in English than anaphorical reference, given the very high level of repetition of a person's name in a British newspaper article. The post is now (1991) held by Charles Million.
31 Unless a text is totally 'normalized', with all LC1 elements being changed.
32 This is as opposed to certain English slang words, such as '(old) banger', which denote a car of a certain age and in a certain state. 'Bagnole', on the other hand, can be used to designate a big new modern car, and there are certain people who use the word systematically.
33 The problem posed by names which have an understandable and relevant meaning for LC1 readers has to be treated separately.
34 Bassnet-McGuire (1980: 119) quotes Robert Adams (1973: 12) on this

problem: 'Paris cannot be London or New York, it must be Paris; our hero must be Pierre, not Peter; he must drink an aperitif, not a cocktail; smoke Gauloises, not Kents; and walk down the rue du Bac, not Back Street. On the other hand, when he is introduced to a lady, he'll sound silly if he says, "I am enchanted, Madame".'

35 British attitudes to 'Ities' or 'Wops' can hardly be compared to French attitudes to 'Ritals'.
36 The whole question of the use of slang, and 'proper' sentence structures is so complex that no attempt can be made here to go beyond very general statements. An interesting 'counterexample' appeared in the *Guardian Weekly* of 9 July 1989. In an article entitled 'Charles says written and spoken English "taught bloody badly" ', not only are people scandalized by the royal use of such a terrible swear-word, but the very syntax used by the prince comes under fire: ' "All the people I have in my office, they can't speak English properly, they can't write English properly," added the prince, his fervour clearly affecting his sentence structure.'
37 'Four-letter' language might well be predictable in a purely English context, but again this would force attention away from the original cultural context.

8 Socio-cultural parameters and norms

1 We use the word here in the most general sense possible, to include informal agreements regarding price, time limits, etc.
2 The importance and implications of the whole debate have become much clearer since the 'Spycatcher' affair.
3 Page 291 in the original, 375 in the translation.
4 Translated by Gerard Hopkins, Harmondsworth: Penguin Modern Classics, 1975.
5 In our view, Guillemin-Flescher's very interesting analysis of the phenomenon of inchoativeness should be modulated by taking into account socio-cultural criteria of the type we deal with in this chapter. It is also helpful to integrate some of the criteria of Translation Criticism into such analyses – otherwise certain phenomena tend to be emphasized at the expense of others. The first two passages quoted by Guillemin-Flescher (1981: 65) are cases in point, where inchoativeness has been introduced at the expense of other elements which are quite simply dropped.
6 'Sara', by Annie Leclerc, translated with a commentary by M. Van Ooïjen, (1987).
7 Collaboration of this type can be particularly fruitful when the TI has a very good knowledge of LC2. In our own experience, there has often been a radical rewriting of the ST when the limitations of the original text became clear because of the draft translations made.
8 This includes not just 'exotic' languages such as Japanese – translations of Mishima into French via English, for example – but also between (to us) common languages: the first French translation of *Die Verwandlung* was made from the English TT.
9 Research done by the ILSER centre in Montpellier has shown the comparative paucity of such texts accompanying medicine in Britain when compared to the 'notices pharmaceutiques' produced in France. The

250   *Redefining Translation*

10   In France, for example, one can have a text translated on one's 'Minitel' (a computer terminal in the home connected by a telephone line to centralized data banks). Although certain basic operations are carried out correctly, the TTs produced are best used for amusing one's friends rather than for any other purpose.
11   The text is written in Serbian rather than Croatian (cf. 'lično' vs. 'osobno'), with all that this means in the current climate of unrest.
12   Thus, if one asks for tourist brochures in Serbo-Croat, one is likely to be disappointed, especially when one considers the wealth of brochures written in a large number of other languages.
13   In reality, one would have to take into account the whole range of semiotic codes at play in such situations, which obviously vary considerably from culture to culture.
14   One would expect 'artificial colouring and preservatives' in English: the fact of finding a questionable translation illustrates well the gap between the launching of a product and the time it often takes for the accompanying text to conform not just to LC2 legal requirements, but to discourse family expectations.
15   The difference in legal structures can be seen not only with the presence or absence of identity cards, but also with the French notion of 'état-civil'. It should be added that the same questionnaire may well contain other questions in other countries – such as the notion of 'race' in the USA or colour in South Africa – and may be based on the whole problem of immigration status (cf. 'resident alien' in the USA).

(but the first item I see in the list starts with "differences can be induced by mere cultural habits, but can also be the result of different official instructions or legal requirements." – this appears before item 10)

16   The distinction between 'cohabitation' and 'co-existence' is a telling example in France between 1986 and 1988, where the French president refused the first term, which was the one normally used, and coined the second to point to his different vision of the 'same' situation.
17   It would be interesting to study the correlation (or lack of correlation) between dictionary translations and actual translations in designated fields.
18   The six current translations bear this name: see Guillemin-Flescher (1981).
19   To be published in *Encrages*, Université de Vincennes.
20   The same is true of 'bureautics'.

9 Applications of the Variational model to translations in various fields

1   This explains why some 'translations' hardly resemble the ST at all. The economic or ideological impact of the text (to name just two key factors) can be of such importance that the TI requires radical rewriting of the original.
2   If the magazines present such articles as 'messages of hope', the *economic* interest of the articles should not be underplayed (i.e. 'Buy our magazine regularly to have hope').
3   Articles in the *Guardian Weekly* are presented as 'translations' of articles from *Le Monde*. It should be noted that very significant modifications often intervene in the titles of the articles – they are often totally rewritten with a complete change of focus, or subheadings are introduced or left out, seriously altering the impact (and sometimes the content) of the message.

4 *Le Monde* articles in the *Guardian Weekly* are again a good example of this. The cartoons in the original are sometimes left out, or indeed another cartoon is substituted. The same goes for photos, which the *Guardian Weekly* tends to add to the original texts. Needless to say, the overall effect – for example of Plantu's acid sense of humour – can be radically changed, particularly when a cartoon is replaced by a photograph.

10 Related fields of interest

1 Apart from Wilss's book, readers should also consult Larose (1987), who devotes a whole chapter to textual evaluation of translations, and Newmark (1981) for a very concise presentation of the aims of TC and some of the methods that can be employed.
2 'Toute traduction doit être évaluée, en tant que traduction, en fonction de l'adéquation entre le but du traducteur et celui de l'auteur, et non entre le but du traducteur et celui de l'évaluateur' (1987: 223).
3 Garnier (1985: 62) cites the following example from Leyris (1971): 'M. Boutang n'a que sarcasmes pour les traducteurs qui l'ont précédé. Il rit à gorge déployée de Madeleine Cazamian, de Gide . . . . Si je disposais de quelques pages au lieu de quelques lignes, je montrerais que *Le Tigre* est à chaque vers affadi, gauchi, détruit.'
4 If, ideally, the Translation critic produces other TTs in order to form his or her judgement, one must not forget that many evaluations are made simply on the basis of how the TT 'sounds', with no reference whatsoever to the ST.
5 The same applies, in fact, to any text with a long life in the second LC, i.e. that has the time to find its own position and to enter into the culture.
6 The TO has traditionally been absent from the TT in its published form – or at best marginalized to a brief mention at the beginning. One of the positive aspects of the greatly increased interest in Translation Studies in recent years has been the appearance of the TO as a factor to be taken into account – hence the space devoted to his or her role in book reviews of translated novels.
7 There follow five paragraphs on the different ways of phoning.
8 There are two further paragraphs describing how to phone using the operator etc.
9 As often happens in the translation of such documents, the majority language – and in this case country – is thought to be sufficient for the purposes of the sender. Non-French speakers in Belgium and Switzerland obviously have to manage as best they can.
10 It should be added that such texts in fact reflect a certain tradition in British advertising strategies used for many years by the GPO (and therefore aimed at British receivers). This tradition in particular relies on the use of hoardings and posters reminding people both of the ease of phoning and of the expectation of the nearest and dearest that one will keep in touch.
11 Such advertising strategies have been used both on the radio and in magazines to encourage people to telephone by playing on the expectations of members of the family.
12 The problem of Translation Criticism is that one can engage in endless quibbles: 'France Direct' is a case in point, which does not seem a very happy turn of phrase, but which seems to have been officially adopted, and

has thus become an instance of the 'weight' of existing translations.
13 This will be a crucial point when we come to judge to overall impact and message of ST and TT, and it should thus be underlined that the *Le Monde* logo is reproduced at the beginning of the articles translated from this newspaper.
14 The classified advertisements give an interesting image of the typical *Guardian Weekly* reader: he or she would appear to enjoy a certain social and financial standing which sets him apart from the average *Guardian* reader (cf. the advertisements describing the merits of different off-shore bank accounts, unit trusts, etc.). The letters published also provide an interesting image, though one which has been 'filtered' through the editor.
15 It may be helpful to underline once again how the Variational approach encourages the Translation critic to take such elements into account. As we shall see below, our final judgement of the two texts will be influenced by the contrasting visions of the two Americas held in Great Britain and France, which would seem – at a certain level – to determine some of the elements making up the ST and TT.
16 Economists, for example, now envisage different 'scénarios' in French.
17 It is a relatively simple matter to make this proverb more understandable for the LC2 readership, given that the TT is printed as being a translation from *Le Monde*: for example, 'History never repeats itself; it merely stammers, says the French proverb'.
18 These will include space available, time available, money proposed and the way in which the work is paid (by the amount of text translated, the number of days spent etc.)
19 English translation by W. and E. Muir, 'Metamorphosis' in *Metamorphosis and Other Stories*, Harmondsworth: Penguin, 1961; Croat translation by I. Adum, *Preobražaj*, Zagreb: Epoha, 1954; the references for the German and French texts are given in Chapter 6, p. 126.
20 The position of 'se' is obligatory in Croat.
21 The changed word order tends to focalize more strongly on the time adverbial in Croat than in English.
22 The problem is, of course, to know just what this might be taken to denote among the several insect – and human – possibilities.

Bibliography

Adams, R. (1973) *Proteus his Lies, his Truth: Discussions on Literary Translation*, New York: W.H. Norton.
Althusser, L. (1976) *Positions*, Paris: Editions sociales.
Angenot, M. and Robin, R. (1985) 'L'Inscription du discours social dans le texte littéraire', *Sociocriticism* 1: 53–82 (Universities of Pittsburgh and Montpellier III).
Arrowsmith, W. and Shattuck, R. (eds) (1964) *The Craft and Context of Translation. A Symposium*, Austin: The University of Texas.
Ballard, M. (1980) *La Traduction de l'anglais*, Lille: Presses Universitaires de Lille.
Ballard, M. (ed.) (1984) *La Traduction. De la théorie à la didactique*, Lille: Presses Universitaires de Lille.
Ballard, M. (1986) 'Pour un enseignement de la traduction', *Franco-British Studies*, 1 (Spring), 27–40.
Ballard, M. (1987) *La Traduction: de l'anglais au français*, Paris: Nathan University.
Bassnett-McGuire, S. (1980) *Translation Studies*, London and New York: Methuen.
Beaugrande, R. de (1978) *Factors in a Theory of Poetic Translating*, Amsterdam: Van Gorcum Assen.
Beaugrande, R. and Dressler, W. (1981) *Introduction to Text Linguistics*, London and New York: Longman.
Benjamin, W. (1969) *Illuminations*, New York: Editions H. Arendt, Schocken Books.
Berman, A. (1984) *L'Epreuve de l'étranger. Culture et traduction dans l'Allemagne romantique*, Paris: Gallimard.
Brislin, R. (ed.) (1976) *Translation – Applications and Research*, New York: Gardner.
Brower, R. (ed.) (1966) *On Translation*, New York: Oxford University Press, Galaxy Books.
Brower, R. (1974) *Mirror on Mirror. Translation, Imitation, Parody*, Cambridge: Cambridge University Press.
Bruce, R. and Anderson, W. (1976) 'Perspective on the role of the interpreter', in R. Brislin (ed.), *Translation – Applications and Research*, New York: Gardner.
Cary, E. (1963) 'L'Indispensable débat', in E. Cary and R. W. Jumpelt (eds), *Quality in Translation*, Oxford, London, Paris: Pergamon.

Cary, E. (1985) 'Comment faut-il traduire?', Lille: Presses Universitaires de Lille.
Catford, J. C. (1965) *A Linguistic Theory of Translation*, London: Oxford University Press.
Cavanna, F. (1978) *Les Ritals*, Paris: Editions de la Seine.
Choul, J. C. (1980) 'Paraphrase et Traduction', *Sigma*, 5, 61–88.
Chuquet, H. and Paillard, M. (1987) *Approche linguistique de la traduction*, Gap: Ophrys.
Culioli, A. (1987) Interview, *Le Français dans le Monde*, (August/September).
Dagut, M. (1981) 'Semantic voids as a problem in the translation process', *Poetics Today*, 2–4 (Summer/Autumn), 61–71.
Deledalle, G. (1979) *Théorie et pratique du signe*, Paris: Payot.
Deledalle, G. (1987) *Charles S. Peirce, phénomenologue et sémioticien*, Amsterdam, Philadelphia: John Benjamins.
Delisle, J. (1984) *L'Analyse du discours comme méthode de traduction*, Ottawa: Editions de l'Université d'Ottawa.
Duff, A. (1981) *The Third Language, Recurrent Problems of Translation into English*, Oxford: Pergamon.
Eco, U. (1965) *L'Œuvre ouverte*, Paris: Seuil.
Eco, U. (1972) *La Structure absente*, Paris: Mercure de France.
Eco, U. (1976) *A Theory of Semiotics*, Bloomington: Indiana University Press.
Elam, K. (1980) *The Semiotics of Theatre and Drama*, London and New York: Methuen.
Evans-Wentz, W. Y. (1954) *The Tibetan Book of the Great Liberation*, London: Oxford University Press.
Flores, A. and Swander, H. (1964) *Franz Kafka Today*, Madison: The University of Wisconsin Press.
Forsyth, F. (1971) *The Day of the Jackal*, London: Corgi. French translation: *Chacal*, translated by H. Robillot (1971), Paris: Mercure de France, Collection Folio.
Foucault, M. (1969) *L'Archéologie du savoir*, Paris: NRF.
Foucault, M. (1971) *L'Ordre du discours*, Paris: Gallimard.
Frawley, W. (ed.) (1984a) *Translation*, Newark: University of Delaware Press.
Frawley, W. (1984b) 'Prolegomena to a theory of translation', in W. Frawley (ed.), *Translation*, Newark: University of Delaware Press.
Fuchs, C. (1982) *La Paraphrase*, Paris: PUF.
Fuchs, C. and Pêcheux, M. (1985) 'Mises au point et perspectives à propos de l'analyse automatique du discours', *Languages*, 37 (March), 7–80.
Gaddis Rose, M. (1981) *Translation Spectrum. Essays in Theory and Practice*, Albany: State University of New York Press.
Garnier, G. (1985) *Linguistique et traduction*, Caen: Paradigme.
Golding, W. (1954) *Lord of the Flies*, London: Faber. Translated by L. Tranec (1956) *Sa Majesté des mouches*, Paris: Gallimard.
Gouadec, D. (1974) *Comprendre et traduire, techniques de la version*, Paris: Bordas.
Govinda, Lama A. (1960) *Les Fondements de la mystique tibétaine*, Paris: Albin Michel.
Graham, J. (1985) *Difference in Translation*, Ithaca: Cornell University Press.
Grass, G. (1976) *From the Diary of a Snail*, Harmondsworth: Penguin.
Greimas, A. (1970) *Du Sens*, Paris: Seuil.

Grunig, B. N. and Grunig, R. (1985) *La Fuite de sens. La Construction du sens dans l'interlocution*, Paris: Hatier-CREDIF.
Guenthner, F. and Guenthner-Reutter, M. (1978) *Meaning and Translation. Philosophical and Linguistic Approaches*, New York: New York University Press.
Guillemin-Flescher, J. (1981) *Syntaxe comparée du français et de l'anglais*, Gap: Ophrys.
Guillemin-Flescher, J. (1986) 'Le Linguiste devant la traduction', *Fabula* 7, 59–68 (Presses Universitaires de Lille).
Hermans, T. (ed.) (1985) *The Manipulation of Literature. Studies in Literary Translation*, New York: St Martin's Press.
Holmes, J. (ed.) (1970) *The Nature of Translation. Essays on the Theory and Practice of Literary Translation*, The Hague: Mouton.
Ingerman, P. (1966) *A Syntax-Oriented Translation*, New York: Academic Press.
Jacobsen, E. (1958) *Translation. A Traditional Craft*, Gyldendalske Boghandel; Copenhagen: Nordisk Forlag.
Jacques, F. (1985) *Espace logique de l'interlocution*, Paris: PUF.
Jakobson, R. (1963) *Essais de linguistique générale*, Paris: Editions de Minuit, Collection Points.
Jakobson, R. (1966) 'On linguistic aspects of translation', in Reuben A. Brower (ed.), *On Translation*, New York/Oxford: Oxford University Press.
Kafka, F. (1952) 'Die Verwandlung', in *Gesammelte Werke*, Frankfurt: S. Fischer. Translated by A. Vialatte (1955) *La Métamorphose*, Paris: Gallimard.
Kelly, L. G. (1979) *The True Interpreter. A History of Translation Theory and Practice in the West*, New York: St Martin's Press.
Kirk, R. (1986) *Translation Determined*, Oxford: Clarendon Press.
Ladmiral, J. R. (1979) *Traduire: théorèmes pour la traduction*, Paris: Payot.
Lambert, J. and Van Gorp, H. (1985) 'On describing translation', in T. Hermans (ed.), *The Manipulation of Literature. Studies in Literary Translation*, New York: St Martin's Press.
Larose, R. (1987) *Théories contemporaines de la traduction*, Quebec: Presses Universitaires de l'Université du Québec.
Lefevère, A. (1977) *Translating Literature: the German Tradition*, Amsterdam: Van Gorcum Assen.
Levy, J. (1967) 'Translation as a decision process', in *To Honor Roman Jakobson*, The Hague: Mouton.
Leyris, M. (1971) 'A propos de W. Blake', *Le Monde*, 19 February.
Ljudskanov, A. (1969) *Traduction humaine et traduction automatique*, (Documents de Linguistique Quantitative, 2 and 4), Centre de Linguistique Quantitative de la Faculté des Sciences de Paris: (91) Saint Sulpice de Favières.
Luke, F. D. (1964) 'The Metamorphosis', in A. Flores and H. Swander (eds), *Franz Kafka Today*, Madison: The University of Wisconsin Press.
McDonald, C. (ed.) (1985) *The Ear of the Other, Otobiography, Transference, Translation*, New York: Schocken Books.
Macdonell, D. (1986) *Theories of Discourse*, Oxford: Blackwell.
McFarlane, B. (1988) *Yugoslavia*, London and New York: Pinter.
Maingueneau, D. (1976) *Initiation aux méthodes de l'analyse du discours*, Paris: Hachette.

Malone, J. (1968) *The Science of Linguistics in the Art of Translation*, Albany: State University of New York.
Martin, J. (1977) "The Prose and the Con": pour une typologie des configurations discursives', *Sigma*, 2, 105–27.
Martin, J. (1981) 'Traduction et interprétance', *Sigma*, 5, 89–113.
Martin, J. (1982) 'Le Concept de traduction', *Méta*, 27, 4, 357–74.
Martin, J. (1985a) 'Propositions pour l'analyse du discours: les configurations textuelles', *Sigma*, 9, 211–47.
Martin, J. (1985b) 'Essai de formalisation d'un type de discours specifique: les schémas d'objets et la constitution des objets dans le discours météorologique', *Cahiers de l'ILSER*, 4, 99–115.
Martin, J. (1987) 'La Recherche récente en traductologie', *Sigma*, 11, 50–80.
Martin, R. (1976) *Inférence, antonymie et paraphrase: éléments pour une théorie sémantique*, Paris, Strasbourg: Klincksieck.
Martin, R. (1983) *Pour une Logique de sens*, Paris: PUF.
Meschonnic, H. (1972) 'Propositions pour une poétique de la traduction', *Langages*, 28 (December), 49–54.
Meschonnic, H. (1973) *Pour la Poétique II*, Paris: Gallimard.
Methods and Sources: a Bilingual Guide to the Study of American or British Society and Culture (1979) Nancy: CRESAB.
Morrison, T. (1989) 'Unspeakable things unspoken: the Afro-American presence in American literature', *Michigan Quarterly*, 28 (Winter), 1–34.
Mouillaud, M. and Tétu, J. F. (1989) *Le Journal quotidien*, Lyon: Presses Universitaires de Lyon.
Mounin, G. (1963) *Les Problèmes théoriques de la traduction*, Paris: Gallimard.
Mounin, G. (1976) *Linguistique et traduction*, Brussels: Dessart et Madraga.
Newmark, P. (1981) *Approaches to Translation*, London: Pergamon Press.
Newmark, P. (1988) *A Textbook of Translation*, New York: Prentice Hall.
Nida, E. A. (1964) *Towards a Science of Translating*, Leiden: E.J. Brill.
Nida, E. (1975) *Language Structure and Translation*, essays by E. Nida, selected and introduced by Anwas Dil, Stanford: Stanford University Press.
Nida, E. (1976) 'A framework for the analysis and evaluation of theories of translation', in R. Brislin (ed.), *Translation – Applications and Research*, New York: Gardner.
Nida, E. A. and Taber, C. R. (1969) *The Theory and Practice of Translation*, Leiden: E.J. Brill.
Norton, G. (1984) *The Ideology and Language of Translation in Renaissance France and their Humanist Antecedents*, Geneva: Droz.
Oseki-Dépré, I. (1985) 'La Lettre de l'étrange. Remarques sur le concept de litteralité', *Actes des deuxième assises de la traduction littéraire*, Arles: Actes du Sud, Hubert Nissen Editeur.
Pêcheux, M. and Fuchs, C. (1975) 'Mise au point et perspectives à propos de l'analyse du discours', *Langages*, 37 (March), 19–20.
Peirce, C. (1966) *Collected Papers*, ed. Arthur Burks, 8 vols, Cambridge: The Belknap Press of Harvard University Press.
Pergnier, M. (1978) *Les Fondements socio-linguistiques de la traduction*, Lille: Champion.
Pinter, H. (1975) *No Man's Land*, London: Methuen. French adaptation by E. Kahane (1979), *No Man's Land*, Paris: Gallimard. Croat translation by Antun Šoljan, *Ničija Zemlja*, Belgrade: Nolit.

Purdue, C. and Porquier, R. (1980) 'Apprentissage et connaissance d'une langue étrangère, *Langages*, 57 (March).
Quine, W. (1960) *Word and Object*, Cambridge, Mass.: MIT Press.
Quine, W. (1977) 'Facts of the matter', in R. W. Shahan and K. R. Merrill (eds), *American Philosophy from Edwards to Quine*, Norman: University of Oklahoma.
Raffel, B. (1971) *The Forked Tongue*, The Hague: Mouton.
Roberts, R. P. and Pergnier, M. (1987) 'Equivalence en traduction', *Méta*, 32, 4, 392–402.
Robin, R. (1973) *Histoire et linguistique*, Paris: Armand Colin.
Rose, M. G. (ed.) (1977) *Translation in the Humanities*, Binghampton: State University of New York Press.
Rose, M. G. (ed.) (1981) *Translation Spectrum. Essays in Theory and Practice*, Albany: State University of New York Press.
Savory, T. (1968) *The Art of Translation*, London: Jonathan Cape, 1957, revised and enlarged.
Schogt, H. (1988) *Linguistics, Literary Analysis and Literary Translation*, Toronto: University of Toronto Press.
Sillitoe, A. (1967) *A Tree on Fire*, London: Macmillan.
Singh, J. (1979) *Śiva Sutras*, Delhi: Motil Banarsidass.
Steiner, G. (1975) *After Babel. Aspects of Language and Translation*, London: Oxford University Press.
Thomas, A. and Flamand, J. (1984) *La Traduction: l'universitaire et le praticien*, Congrès Université de Québec et Montréal (Cahiers de Traductologie, 5), Ottawa: Editions de l'Université d'Ottawa.
Titone, R. (1972) *Le Bilinguisme précoce*, Brussels: Dessart.
Toury, G. (1985) 'A rationale for descriptive translation science', in T. Hermans (ed.), *The Manipulation of Literature. Studies in Literary Translation*, New York: St Martin's Press.
Van Dijk, T. (1972) *Some Aspects of Text Grammar*, The Hague, Paris: Mouton.
Van Ooijen, M. (1987) 'Traduction commentée de "Sarah" in *Le Mal de Mère* d'Annie Leclerc', MA thesis, University of Montpellier III.
Vignaux, G. (1976) *L'Argumentation. Essai d'une logique discursive*, Geneva, Paris: Droz.
Vinay, J. P. and Darbelnet, J. (1958) *Stylistique comparée du français et de l'anglais*, Paris: Didier.
Wandruszka, M. (1969) *Sprachen: Vergleichbar und Unvergleichlichkeit*, Munich: R. Piper.
Weaver, W. (1965) 'Translation', in N. Locke and D. Booth, *Machine Translation of Languages*, London: Chapman and Hall.
Wilss, W. (1976) 'Perspectives and Limitations of a Didactic Framework for the Teaching of Translations', in R. Brislin (ed.), *Translation – Applications and Research*, New York: Gardner.
Wilss, W. (1982) *The Science of Translation*, Tübingen: Gunter Narr.

Index

advertising 115, 117, 119, 121; discourse 118, 119, 220–1
aesthetic 113, 158; text 166
allocutor 76
alternatives 54
Althusser, L. 144
ambiguity 89, 90, 127, 186, 199
ambiguous reference 70; text 97
ambivalence 99, 201, 202, 204
ambivalent strategy 119, 226
analogy 30
anaphoric reference 149, 180
Anderson, W. 43
Angenot, M. 144
annexing 127
anteposition 78–9
Antioch 18
application 131, 208
aspect 76
axiological system 24

back-reference 6
Bailly, C. 6
Ballard, M. 3, 209
basis: observation 59; working 59–61
Beaugrande, R. de 7
Benjamin, W. 30, 36
Berman, A. 127
bilingualism 52, 116
Brislin, R. 43
by-pass strategies 82

cartography 23–4
Cary, E. 5
Catford, J. C. 11
Cavanna, F. 153

censorship 158, 160, 225
chaining 87
Chanson de Roland, La 206
character 89
Choul, J. C. 43
Chuquet, H. 9–10, 211
cliché 76, 94, 95, 119, 149–50
code-switching 28
collocate 66
collocational 73
commentary 140
communicability 26
communication 12, 15, 16, 23, 26ff., 37–40, 117, 124, 164, 172, 177, 212; breakdown 113, 165; circuit 112, 113, 115, 169, 175, 222, 225–6; cross-cultural 22; intercultural 28; interlingual 29; intralingual 29; partial 26; situation 31, 125, 211, 217
communicational approach 8, 209
communicationalist 9–10
communicative strategies 29, 100
competence 52ff., 116, 135; bi-cultural 46; dissimilative 52, 211ff.; transferred 52; translation 52
complexification 162
complexity 122
componential analysis 66
compromise 36
concatenation 203
concept 111, 120, 123–4, 128, 131
conception 16, 131
conceptual definition 23; field 24; network 24; representation 23
connotation 115, 125, 128, 131, 153, 223–4

consistency 195
Constantinople 18
context 87, 114, 117–18, 124, 128; free 126
contextual(-ization) 32, 112, 115, 187; constraint 68; determination 42, 89ff.; discontinuity 80–3
contract 34ff., 157–8, 162–3
contraction 102
contrastive patterns 90
convention 71ff.; pragmatic 72; social 72
conversion 25ff., 51, 211ff.; function 15; interlinguistic 30–1; intralinguistic 32; procedures 30; sequence 29; strategies 7, 29, 30
convertibility 14, 20, 35, 55, 154, 211
co-significance 26ff., 174
co-signification 26
corpus 63
Culioli, A. 45, 50
cultural 114–15, 123–31, 144, 152–4, 213; equation 32, 51ff., 57, 111, 118–21, 131–2, 136, 158, 173, 195, 205; operator 111, 133ff., 173, 211, 213; relationships 38; system 15, 23
culture 115, 118, 121–4, 127–8, 133; gap 121; specific 123, 128

Dagut, M. 101
Darbelnet, J. 6, 7, 10, 22
David, King 17–18, 22
decentre (decentring) 128
decontextualization 114
Delisle, J. 8, 101, 125, 197
denominator: common 48–9
designation 16, 28
determination 10, 119
determiner 76
didactics 52, 209ff.
difference 46ff.; reformulative 46
differential 140
discourse 116–26; family 53, 111, 117–26, 138, 142, 150, 177, 221, 226
discursive: norms 53; production 54; situation 92; structures 54
distortion 87
Duff, A. 123

Eco, U. 23, 96, 118
economic 124, 145, 157ff., 173–5, 179, 222, 223
emphasis 78–9
enigma 17
enunciative linguistics 27
epistemological: clarification 23; definition 4, 56; receivability 55
equivalence 14, 21, 29, 35, 63, 112, 124, 150; semantic 65
exception 20
expansion 102
explicating 104ff.
extralinguistic; reality 124, 151
extra-propositional: determinations 81, 86ff.

faux-amis 124
feminity 18
field: operation 58
flux 201
foreignness 18
Forster, E. M. 123
Forsyth, F. 158–60, 219
Foucault, M. 119, 128, 144
Fuchs, C. 20, 27, 31, 43–5, 88
fuzzy: logics 56

game: continuous 185; discontinuous 185; theory of 185
gap 121, 127; LC 111–12, 115, 132; historical 118
Garnier, G. 11
generative: process 42–3; stage 105
global village 22
gloss(ing): expliciting 50; process 44
Golding, W. 142–3
Grass, G. 158
Greimas, A. 45
Grunig, B. N. and R. 65
Guillemin-Flescher, J. 9, 10, 50, 98, 161, 211

hermeneutic process 38; translation 9
hermeneutics 3
heuristic perspective 55
homological 214, 217, 221; generation viii; process 185; relationships 31; variation 54
homologon 49ff., 77, 86–7

homology 30, 43, 47ff., 101, 120, 214ff.; interlinguistic 13, 59ff.
Humboldt, W. von 37
humour 119, 201
hyperonym(ically) 68
hyponym(ically) 68

ideological(ly) 122, 126–7, 139, 144–7, 158, 160, 165, 180, 223, 225; bias 3, 20; delusion 36; image 3, 142; preconception 21; representation 14ff.
ideology 138
illusion 20
image 129–31, 140
implicating 104ff.
incommensurability 28, 30, 37, 56, 213
incommunicability 26
indeterminacy 56
information 123
insertion 11, 154
interaction 37
intercomprehension 16
interlocution 30
interpropositional level 88ff.
intertextual determination 93ff.

Jacques, F. 26
Jakobson, R. 30, 43, 47, 69
jargon 139
journalism 125, 222
journalistic discourse 118–19, 138, 144, 148

Kafka, F. 119, 126, 226

Ladmiral, J. R. 6, 29, 30, 125, 209, 213
Lambert, J. 12
language 23, 27, 114, 116, 118–19, 124–5, 128, 130; communicative aspect 126; second 111, 113, 115, 210; source 114, 121, 212; target 121, 212
Language Culture (LC) 25, 111, 133ff., 156ff., 173, 217; influences 123ff.; parameters 176ff.; perspective 136ff.; surroundings 173ff.

Larose, R. 10, 59, 216
Levy, J. 36, 87, 185, 207
legal system 178–9
level of description 60, 63
lexical: definition 65; item 65, 69, 124, 130; unit 24; variant 70
lexicalizing 69
lexicon 64ff.
lexis 65ff.; definition 68, 84, expansion 65ff.; formulation 68
linguistic 112, 114, 118, 122, 130, 210–11, 221
linguistics 3, 11, 45, 211; contrastive 50
literariness 206
literary 122, 126–7, 158, 176, 217, 226; discourse 118–21; effect 205, 226; language 186; references 95; translators 205
Ljudskanov, A. 11
localization 164, 176, 179
loopback effect 55
Luke, F. D. 228

Macdonell, D. 144
map 24
marginalization 154
Martin, R. 45, 47, 65, 67
material conditions 163
Mauriac, F. 161
meaning 115; contextual 9, core 44–5; definition 88ff.; linguistic 9; peripheral 44; production 23; textual 9
meaningfulness 27
mediation 51ff.
'médiatisation 10'
mediator 9, 33, 134
Meschonnic, H. 9, 11, 38, 127–8
metamorphic logic 202
metaphoric power 73
metaphoring 80ff.; inverted 81
meta-textual entities 89
modality 75
modifier 66
modulation 77ff., 107; ordering 78; substitutive 79–81
Morrison, T. 154
Mounin, G. 4, 19, 124
multi-formulation 28

myth 15

newspaper 118; discourse (see also journalistic) 144, 148
Nida, E. A. 3, 8, 11, 21
normalization 121, 126, 221, 227
normalized 126, 129
normative: process 42; stage 51ff., 105
norms 33, 56, 117, 127; behavioural; LC2 126; socio-cultural 156–83
nucleus 66

object of study 58, 61ff.
objectivity, illusion of 146
Oedipus 17, 22
operator: 112; cultural 111, 132
option 129
Oseki-Dépré, I. 6
overtranslation 103ff.

Paillard, M. 9–10, 211
parameters viii, 13, 39, 63, 114, 131, 162, 217; economic/LC1/LC2 175, 176ff.; socio-cultural 111, 121
paraphrase 29, 31, 43ff., 50, 60, 66, 120, 134, 150, 214; closed 46; definitional 50; discriminating 47; explanatory 29; interlinguistic 212; intralinguistic 118, 215; metalinguistic 44; normed 45; open 46; 'spot' 29; syntagmatic 47, 50
paraphrasing 15, 46, 120; selective 31
paraphrastic: determination 31; difference 67; expansion 69; option 33, 61; possibility 118, 120, 156, 161; reformulation 54, 63;
parasynonym(ically) 67
patterning 87
Pêcheux, M. 20, 88
Peirce, C. 46
Peircian semiosis 45
Pergnier, M. 5, 8, 57, 209
Pentecost 17
perception 16
peripheral 66; determination 44
periphrasis 65, 71
phraseology: social 95
Pinter, H. 125, 128
plane of definition 59ff., 63; prop-ositional 59; extra-propositional 60; strategic 60
Poggioli, R. 19
polemic: representation 18; stage 19
political 124, 141, 154, 158, 165, 179, 223
Porquier, R. R. 213
potentiality: text 31
practical: application 131; translation production 112
pragmatic 138, 220; dimension
preconstruction 72
preconception: cultural 110; social 75
predication 74ff.
predictable 40, 116, 118–19, 121, 123, 144, 168, 177
presupposition 73
procedure 58, 61, 111; transfer 69
production conditions 144ff., 147
proposition 59
Purdue, C. 213
Pythoness 16

quantifier 76
Queen of Sheba 17–18, 22
Quine, W. 62

reality (see extralinguistic) 151-2
receiver 112–14, 117, 120, 162, 168–71, 172ff., 219
recursivity 62
redundancy 70
reference, culture-specific 114, 122–3, 128; LC1 129; LC2 129
referencing 88ff., 96; process 51
referent 24
referential: structure 126; system 24
referentiation 75ff.
regularity 10
relativist 34, 41
representation: cultural 3; second degree 22
rhetorical: device 122; structure 125
riddle 17
Robin, R. 144

Sapir–Whorf hypothesis 25
Savory, T. 18
Séleskovitch, D. 8, 9
semiosis 45

semiotic 125, 214; codes 20, 198, chains 30
semiotics 3, 11, 47, 215
sender 113, 117, 168-9, 174-5, 219-22
shift: strategy 89; translation 100ff.
signification 15
situational determination 91ff.
slang 151-3
social 177; class 117, 123, 129; science 14
socio-cultural 111-17, 121, 154, 156ff., 174-5, 211, 217, 222, 226; factors 21, 98, 110, 185; identity 161; norms 52, 57, 87; parametering 88; parameters 156-83, 173
socio-economic 152, 220; basis 124
socio-linguistic norms 176
specification 71ff., 74
Sphinx 17, 22
stage direction 92, 104, 187
statement: objective 39ff.
Steiner, G. 9, 34, 37-9, 47
stereotype 73, 144, 219
strangeness 17, 18
strategy; advertising 110, 119-20; aesthetic 97-8, 186, 201; ambiguous 97; analogical 97, 99, 109; compensatory 199; interpreting 135ff., 142-3; logical 96, 99; reading 135ff., 142-3; textual 118-19; translation 128-9
synaptic 30
synonymy 67
syntax 72ff., 126, 198
system of representation (SR) 14, 20, 23, 88, 118-20, 123-4, 128, 137-9, 141, 144-5, 151-2, 174, 177-80, 226

Taber, C. R. 3
teaching of translation 13, 135, 163, 166, 209ff.
technical(ity) 72, 129, 166, 172, 177; language 124, 195; level 6, 72; terms 164
tendency 10, 50, 78, 211
tense 76
tension 29, 32, 118, 132, 137, 150, 154, 226
text: dramatic 92, 187ff.; grammar 91; pragmatic 100, 104; social 94; translated 31
textual: strategy 71, 91ff., 98
titles 197
Toledo 18
topology 47
Toury, G. 12
Tower of Babel 16
transcoding 36
transference 35, 36, 121; information 39
transgression 16
translatability: impossible 56; partial 56
translatable 112
translating 1, 2
translation 2; automatic 2; choice 185; criticism 13, 116, 161, 215ff.; cross-7; diachronical 206; existing 173, 180ff.; initiator 113-16, 122-3, 128-9, 131, 141, 146, 156ff., 217, 222, 225; intercultural 26; interlinear 29; interlinguistic 30, 214; intracultural 25; literal 115, 126; machine 8; methodology 58ff., 86-7, 215; model 185, 214; objective 3; operation 113, 134-5, 153, 156; option 63; order 113, 115, 123, 156ff., 165ff., 222; parallel 29; partial 28, 44; procedures 57; process 131; product 1; production 1, 112, 214; slanted 104; studies viii, 1, 4-5, 9, 11, 14, 41, 123, 144; technique 7, 20, 100; theoretician 11; theory 111-12, 116, 121, 131, 137, 156, 173, 176, 180; unit 59, 177; version 63
translator 27, 32, 36, 41-2, 49, 51ff., 57
translator's choices 184, 203; competence 6, 83
transparence 36

undertranslation 103ff.
universalist 34, 41
universality 20
universals 4, 26, 37, 39, 41, 48;

operational 45; semantic 45
untranslatability 14, 20, 122–3, 154
Ursprache 37

Van Gorp, H.12
variability 11
variant 115, 177
variation 31, 45, 49, 197; concept of 39–40, 207; option 40; range 11, 40–1, 51, 54, 101; reformulative 74

Variational: approach viii, 39, 41, 52, 56, 87, 105ff., 113, 136, 153, 173, 205, 209, 212ff.; concept 41; model 42, 54, 183–4; procedure 87
Vialatte, A. 126, 226
Vinay, J. P. 6, 7, 10, 22
voids 101

Weaver, W. 36
Wilss, W. 12, 215, 228

For Product Safety Concerns and Information please contact our EU representative GPSR@taylorandfrancis.com
Taylor & Francis Verlag GmbH, Kaufingerstraße 24, 80331 München, Germany

www.ingramcontent.com/pod-product-compliance
Lightning Source LLC
Chambersburg PA
CBHW071814300426
44116CB00009B/1308